Britain's Army in India

Books by the same author

The 30th Punjabis
The Battle of Vitoria
Wellington's Peninsula Army
Solah Punjab, A History of the 16th Punjab Regiment (ed.)
Clive, Proconsul of India

In conjunction with Brigadier Peter Young

Charge
Wellington's Masterpiece, The Battle and Campaign of
    Salamanca
A History of the British Army

Britain's Army in India

From its Origins to the Conquest of Bengal

James P. Lawford

London
GEORGE ALLEN & UNWIN
Boston   Sydney

First published in Great Britain in 1978

© Copyright George Allen & Unwin (Publishers) Ltd, 1978

ISBN 0 04 954020 3

Printed in Great Britain
in 11 on 12 pt Imprint
by the Alden Press, Oxford

Contents

Wandewash Fort surrenders 30 November. Lally moves to retake Wandewash. Battle of Wandewash, 22 January 1760.

Chapter 16. *The Second Siege of Pondicherry* 266

Coote isolates Pondicherry, 17 June 1760. Coote besieges Villanore Fort, 17 June. Lally's counterattack fails, 4 September. Monson breaks through Boundary Hedge, 10 September. Pondicherry surrenders, 16 January 1761.

Chapter 17. *The Rebellion in the South* 277

Reorganisation of Madras Army, 1759. Yusuf Khan appointed Governor of Madura and Tinnevelly. Rebels. First siege of Madura, 28 August–12 November 1763. Second siege of Madura, 9 March 1764. Storm fails, 26 June, and Madura blockaded. Madura surrenders and Yusuf Khan hanged, 11 October 1764.

Chapter 18. *Bombay; The Consolidation of British Power in Bengal; The Battle of Buxar* 291

Role of Bombay Presidency. Dutch defeated at Bedarra, 25 November 1759. Caillaud at Seerpore, 22 February 1760. Deposition of Mir Jafar, October 1760. Battle of Suan, 19 January 1761. Break with Mir Kassim, 17 July 1763. Action at Cutwa, 19 July. Battle of Sooty, 2 August. Attack on Oodanulla, 5 September. Monghyr captured and Mir Kassim executes his hostages, October. Patna falls, 6 November. Mutiny of Bengal Army, February 1764. Suja-ud-daula repulsed at Patna, 3 May. Mutiny of 9th Sepoy Battalion, September. Battle of Buxar, 23 October.

Appendices

Maps and Diagrams

Britain's Army in India

Chapter 1

Origins

'You may take it as a fact that it is the richest and most splendid province in the world.' So wrote Marco Polo of the Coromandel coast that extends down the eastern shore of the Indian Peninsula. He continued: 'You must not suppose that the diamonds of the first water come to our countries of Christendom. Actually they are exported to the kings and noblemen of these various regions and realms. For it is they who have the wealth to buy the costliest stones.'

When towards the end of the thirteenth century Marco Polo paid his visit, Southern India was still Hindu; but sixty years before the Normans set foot in England, the first wave of Muslim invaders thrust through the northwest passes into the Indian plains beyond. Over the next five centuries in successive waves, the followers of the prophet penetrated almost to Cape Comorin, the southern tip of the Indian peninsula. Unlike England, where after two centuries Norman and Anglo-Saxon merged to form one nation and one culture, in India Muslim and Hindu never lost their separate identities, so much more divisive is religion than race. This fundamental division between its peoples, still bloodily apparent nine centuries later, vitally affected the social structure of India and needs to be taken into account when considering the impact subsequently made by the Europeans.

The last major Muslim invasion, that of the Moghuls, occurred early in the sixteenth century, when Babur, a descendant of Tamerlane the Great, led an army on Delhi, overthrew the ruling Afghan dynasty in 1526 on the fateful battlefield of Panipat, captured the Imperial city, and swept onwards to conquer Hindustan. He had entered an India fragmented into

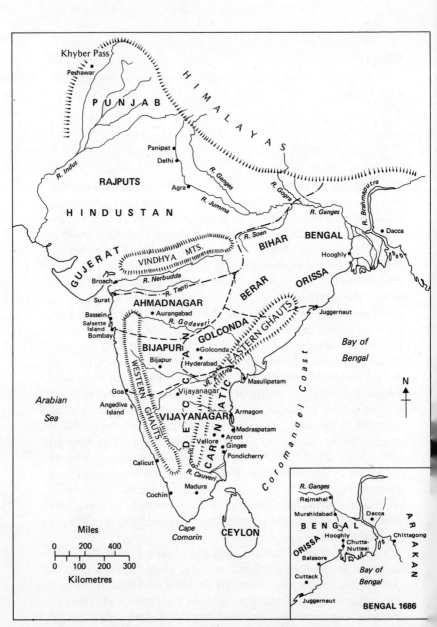

India in the sixteenth and seventeenth centuries

a number of independent kingdoms, most with Muslim Kings reigning over subjects who clung obstinately to their ancient Hindu beliefs. Only in Rajputana to the west and south of Delhi and in the south of the Deccan did Hindu princes still rule over independent realms. Before Babur died he had conquered the Kingdom of Delhi, the Hindu princes of Rajputana paid him tribute and all Hindustan proper, up to the borders of Bengal in the east, acknowledged his authority. Only in the Deccan, the mighty Peninsula of India that, bounded in the north by the Nerbudda river, juts out for a thousand miles into the Indian Ocean, did four great kingdoms remain unsubdued, the Muslim kingdoms of Ahmadnagar and Bijapur in the west, Golconda in the east, and the Hindu realm of Vijayanagar in the south.

At this time the social structure of India differed somewhat from that of sixteenth century Europe. The density of population in relation to arable land was low, most of the inhabitants lived in self-sufficient village communities under a village headman, disputes between villagers being settled by councils of five elders known as panchayats; so long as they paid their dues the villagers were to all intents and purposes free-holders of the lands they tilled. A number of these semi-independent villages would come under an individual variously entitled a *zemindar*, a *naik*, a *poligar*, or a *deshmukh*, depending largely on the district in which he lived.

The main function of this individual was to collect the taxes due to the monarch, keeping a reasonable amount to himself for his trouble; he was a man of substance and authority, but the revenues he collected were taxes rather than rent and he was not a landlord in the European sense. He might be subordinate to some great noble, or if his revenues were substantial he might rank as such himself. The governors of towns held similar titles with similar responsibilities and on occasion arrogated to themselves the title of raja.

The amount of money these nobles remitted to their monarch depended almost entirely on how capable he was·of enforcing his demands, and frequently he had to collect it sword in hand. If the central power was weak the nobles had no hesitation about ignoring it and despoiling their weaker neighbours, forcing them to pay tribute or yield villages. The villagers themselves were generally little troubled by such changes of allegiance, so long as their new masters demanded no more than their old.

When Babur died in 1530, the Empire he had won so quickly, started to disintegrate equally quickly. His eldest son, Humayun, facing the inevitable challenge to the succession from other members of the royal family – there was no automatic right of primogeniture – with difficulty retained his title and his life. At one period he ruled little more than the territory round Delhi and Agra, and at another thought it wise to seek sanctuary in Persia. It was his son Akbar who created the famous Moghul Empire that for more than a century was to be perhaps the most powerful in the world.

But even before Babur led his Moghul soldiers on Delhi, the first high-pooped, tall-masted European ships had cast anchor off the west coast of the Deccan. In 1498 Vasco da Gama circumnavigated Africa and sailing across the Indian Ocean came to the sea port of Calicut. The ruler of the Hindu province, known as the Zamorin, welcomed him at first, but the Arab traders already established in his realm, who feared the Portuguese might snatch a share of their trade, intrigued ceaselessly against the newcomers. His early friendliness turned into covert then open hostility, but Vasco da Gama, meeting duplicity with duplicity, extricated himself and his ships, sailed home to Portugal and revealed the rich harvest waiting to be garnered in the East. Soon fresh Portuguese fleets were sailing for the west coast of India.

At Calicut the Portuguese came to blows with the Zamorin, but the Raja of the neighbouring province of Cochin to the south, anxious to free himself from the authority of the Zamorin, his nominal superior, welcomed their assistance and the Portuguese sailors noted that the harbour of Cochin was better than that of Calicut. A profitable trade between Portugal and India began to spring up.

Hitherto the products of the East had been conveyed partly in Arab ships, partly overland by camel caravan, to the Mediterranean and thence in the galleys of Venice to the countries of Europe. Despite the hazards of the long ocean voyage, Vasco da Gama's expeditions showed that cargoes shipped from the shores of India direct to Portugal cost far less to transport than those brought through the eastern Mediterranean, with all the transhipments that involved. Venice, at the zenith of its power, heard the news with dismay, while the Portuguese with the energy of a young and ebullient nation zealously exploited the opportunities opening before them.

In 1507 they fitted out a fleet of twenty-two vessels, carrying 1,500 men, to sail for India under Don Francisco Almeida, giving their commander, perhaps a trifle prematurely, the grandiloquent title of Viceroy of India. The title illustrated their intentions. They sought conquest as much as trade. On arrival Almeida cemented the existing alliance with the Raja of Cochin and waged a vigorous war against the Zamorin. In the sixteenth century nations gave short shrift to their trade rivals. The leading merchants of Venice saw clearly enough that, if the Portuguese succeeded in their enterprise, their own days of prosperity were numbered. They helped the Sultan of Egypt, also an interested party, to fit out a fleet to aid the Zamorin and destroy the Portuguese. It was an attitude to competitors to be practised in turn by all the European nations; cutting throats was preferred to cutting prices.

The Portuguese under Almeida, after an initial reverse, inflicted a severe defeat on the Egyptian fleet, but Almeida's personal triumph was shortlived; owing to an intrigue in Portugal he was abruptly superseded by Don Alphonso Albuquerque, a man of outstanding ability. Under his command the Portuguese achieved complete supremacy at sea, a supremacy they consolidated by keeping a permanent naval presence in the Indian Ocean. He tried to seize Aden at the entrance to the Red Sea and Ormuz in the Persian Gulf to seal off the routes to the eastern Mediterranean from the Arab traders in India. He forced Ormuz to surrender and pay tribute to him, but Aden successfully defied him. Nevertheless, with unquestioned mastery of the sea he established trading posts round the coast of the Deccan and built forts to safeguard them. He captured Malacca in Malaya to furnish a staging post on the route to China and at the second attempt stormed Goa to make it the capital of Portuguese India. Comparing the limited manpower of Portugal with the vast numbers of India, he tried to breed a race of Portuguese Indians to support the new Empire he intended to create, and encouraged his men to take Indian wives, a policy they adopted with no little alacrity.

However, he fell victim to the strange law of the Orient that decreed that those achieving renown in India would almost certainly be disgraced in their native land. In 1515 a squadron of ships from Portugal that he confidently expected to bring him the title of Duke of Goa, instead carried peremptory instructions for him to hand over command and return home. Overcome with vexation at the ingratitude of his countrymen, it is said, he died before he could sail back to Portugal.

After his death, under a succession of incompetent governors and viceroys the initial impetus was lost and on occasion the Portuguese were hard put to retain what they had won; and indeed India, now coming under the influence of the Moghuls, was no Brazil to be conquered by a handful of conquistadores. One more major acquisition the Portuguese made. The Moghul Emperor, Humayun, in one of his more fortunate periods, sought to reimpose his rule over the kingdom of Gujerat. Its King, menaced by the Portuguese at sea and the Moghul armies on land, tried to buy off the Europeans, and in 1534 ceded them the island of Diu with the right to build a fort at Bassein. After they had taken possession of their new acquisitions the Portuguese rewarded the unfortunate monarch by contriving to drown him, the result, it was asserted, of an unfortunate misunderstanding; his death contributed to the eventual subjugation of Gujerat by the Moghul armies, driving in from the north.

For the remainder of the century Portuguese naval supremacy continued unchallenged and they spread their trading posts round the coast wherever suitable harbours existed. Anger at their aggressive acquisitiveness eventually united the princes of the Deccan against them, and only some notable feats of arms by the Portuguese infantry saved them from extinction. Then in 1580 Portugal lost her independence and under the paralysing hand of Spain much of her ancient vigour disappeared. Meanwhile the Dutch, who were in the process of casting off that paralysing hand, and Elizabethan England, intent on despoiling the Spanish, had begun to appear in eastern waters.

Spices furnished the most profitable cargoes and most could best be obtained from the islands of modern Indonesia, sometimes referred to at that period as the 'Spice Islands'. The Dutch established trading posts in Java, Sumatra and Amboyna. The English, looking for fresh fields to conquer after triumphing over the Spanish Armada, and urged on by their ageing but indomitable Queen, Elizabeth I, were not slow to follow.

On 31 December 1600, Elizabeth granted a charter to a company to which she gave the exclusive right to trade with the East. The constitution of the Company is of interest as it altered very little over the next two centuries. It was to have an executive body consisting of a governor and twenty-four directors; these were to be elected from those subscribing money to the Company, termed the proprietors, at their annual court to be held on every first of July or within six days of that date; a subscription of £500 entitled a proprietor to a vote.

Since the Company was intended only for trade, 'gentlemen' were expressly excluded from joining, on the grounds, presumably, that they would certainly pick a quarrel with someone. The worthy merchants, however, were to prove not lacking in pugnacity. The Queen further directed that the Company was not to give offence to any Christian power, already trading in India, which did not desire its presence, an injunction that was cheerfully disregarded almost from the outset. The ships of any English merchants not of the Company who were caught trading with the East were to be confiscated, together with their cargoes, and sold, the proceeds to be split equally between the Crown and the Company.

The first trips prospered, although the Queen complained irritably that there seemed an unconscionably long interval between them. Regrettably, despite the absence of gentlemen, some of the ships' masters found that it saved both time and tedious haggling to seize Portuguese ships already loaded with the produce of India. To the aggrieved Portuguese some of the English bore a striking resemblance to pirates. As trading prospered, the Company set up its first trading post, or factory as it was called, at Bantam on the northeast coast of the island of Java, to the intense annoyance of the Dutch, who already considered the Spice Islands to be their own particular preserve.

However in 1609 Captain Hawkins sailed over to the west coast of India and called in at the port of Surat in Gujerat, where the Portuguese were already well established. Hawkins found the prospects for trade alluring, loaded his ships and sent them home, while he himself remained with a small body of men to set up a trading post in the port. The Portuguese saw no merit in sharing their trade with the English and prevailed on the Governor of Surat, who held the Portuguese fleet in some reverence, to expel the intruders. Hawkins, in peril of his life, hastily set out for the Imperial Court, then at Agra, to seek redress and official permission to trade.

His arrival at Agra created something of a sensation and, according to his own account, the Moghul Emperor, Jehangir, the dissolute son of Akbar, showed him favour, even to the extent of offering to provide him with a wife. Such sentiments were noticeably absent from the Portuguese who contrived to thwart all his efforts to obtain Imperial sanction to open a trading post.

Obstacles, however, were not likely to deter the robust merchants of England, whatever the prohibitions against offending a fellow Christian power. In 1612 a trading fleet under Captain Thomas Best appeared off Surat. Portuguese ships engaged them on 29 November. Thomas Best, in his own words, 'played on the ship of the Portuguese Admiral with small and great shot that by an hour we had peppered him well'. Three or four Portuguese vessels ran aground and the remainder broke off the action. The Moghul governor of the port, delighted to see the arrogant Portuguese humbled, allowed the English to re-establish their factory.

In 1615 a British convoy decisively beat a large Portuguese fleet and Portuguese naval supremacy in Indian waters vanished forever, carrying with it much of their prestige. That year Thomas Roe, as a fully accredited ambassador from England, visited the Emperor Jehangir. He judged his journey something of a failure and he was not replaced, but English factories began to sprout wherever it seemed likely that a profit might be made. These factories consisted initially of one or two warehouses in charge of a factor, with under him a few English assistants and some local Indians recruited as storemen and guards. Their main function was to dispose of English goods brought out in the Company's ships and to buy stocks of muslins, silks and other produce, termed 'the investment', with which to load them for the journey back to England.

In a hot climate English broadcloth possessed only a limited appeal and part of the Company's purchases had to be financed by silver or gold. These factories, bringing trade and money into the country, were popular with the local governors, who could impose on them taxes, the proceeds of which often disappeared into their own personal treasuries.

However, despite an auspicious start, difficult times lay ahead for the servants of the Company. The Dutch harried them unmercifully at every opportunity and at home Charles I, ruling without that collection of fractious rascals, his Parliament, possessed an unfettered prerogative but a distressingly empty purse. Looking for means of raising money, he revoked the Company's monopoly by Proclamation and sold a charter conceding equal rights to a newly constituted company. Fortunately the new company was improvident and inefficient, but the Company's finances sank so low that, unlike the Portuguese and the Dutch, they were unable to find the money to fortify their warehouses adequately against the depredation of their competitors or the acquisitiveness of local officials.

When matters looked grave, however, the Company had a stroke of good fortune. A factory under an agent subordinate to the Council of Bantam had been set up at Masulipatam in the Kingdom of Golconda on the east coast of the Deccan. The Port authorities levied such extortionate duties that the Council of Bantam closed the factory down and moved it south to the port of Armagon. The move proved unsatisfactory, for suitable produce was hard to come by; meanwhile the avaricious Governor of Masulipatam, realising 'he had over-played his hand, offered good terms for their return. The factory at Masulipatam was reopened, but it was clear that a factory at an existing port was at the mercy of its governor. While the Council at Bantam reflected on this unpalatable if obvious fact, a local Naik made an interesting proposition. He ruled a stretch of coastline in the Carnatic, a province that formed part of the Kingdom of Vijayanagar, at that time steadily falling apart after a disastrous war with the Kingdoms of Golconda, Ahmadnagar and Bijapur in 1564–5; only the jealousies of the allied monarchs had allowed it to survive. The province extended for some 300 miles along the coastal plain, which was about 100 miles wide and separated from the high tableland of the Deccan by the steep and jagged hills of the Eastern Ghats – some Indian historians applied the name to the inland region as well, but the English generally limited the name of the province to the coastal strip stretching from the Kistna river in the north to the Cauveri in the south.

The Naik saw that he might turn the Company's difficulties to his personal advantage. He suggested to the Company's Agent at Masulipatam that he should set up a factory on a deserted stretch of coast near the village of Madraspatam where two streams, the Triplicane and Elambore, converged to flow into the Bay of Bengal, and offered also to build the Company a fort at his own expense.

The Council at Masulipatam wrote to their superiors at Bantam describing the Naik's offer, 'First he desires his country may flourish and grow rich, secondly he desires for his money good horses from Persia, thirdly that yearly upon our ships he may send a servant into the Bay of Bengal to buy him hawks, parrots, apes and suchlike baubles. And lastly, the fort being substantial and strong, may be able to defend his person on occasion against his insulting neighbours.'

The Portuguese established at St Thomé three miles south of Madraspatam did not relish the prospect of a rival, and with great apparent good nature, offered the Company accommodation there. The little Council at Masulipatam was not to be deceived by such apparent magnanimity; as the guests of the Portuguese they would be exchanging one irresponsible authority for another; they politely declined, and sent one of their number, Francis Day, to look into the Naik's proposition. Day reported that the proposed site suffered from certain drawbacks. The lagoon formed by the mouth of the two streams was separated from the sea by a bar that could only be crossed for a short period, after the rains; the sea broke in a heavy surf on an open beach and could only be negotiated by special flat-bottomed boats, called mussoolas; passengers and cargoes would be lucky to escape a drenching; ships would have to anchor in an open roadstead and, owing to the shallowness of the water, about a thousand yards from the shore; they would have no protection from storms or bad weather, and the roadstead would be unusable during the period of the monsoon from October until the end of December.

A less promising site for a port could not well be imagined; but inland there were some compensations: communications, taking into account the standards of the day, were reasonable and goods suitable for shipment to Europe would not be difficult to obtain. Above all, by developing so inhospitable a tract of coast the Company would be free from all interference by grasping local officials, a consideration that Francis Day, with considerable foresight, considered outweighed all else. The Council at Masulipatam agreed and while awaiting sanction from Bantam resolved 'speedily to send back the said Francis Day to Madraspatam with horses, sugar and cloves to keep a fair correspondence with that place . . . if the Naik shall earnestly persist therein the said Francis Day shall on occasion *pishcash* him [present him] with one of the horses'.

Their scheme worked admirably. Bantam sanctioned the move, the Directors in London countermanded it, but by then it was too late, and on 20 February 1640 Francis Day, accompanied by a fellow Councillor, Andrew Cogan, led a party to take possession of the strip of land running for about three miles along the seashore and one mile inland. He was probably accompanied by Lieutenant Jermin, Sergeant Jeffery Bradford and about twenty-five soldiers. On his arrival he traced out a fort roughly in the shape of a square with walls about one hundred yards long and with bastions at the corners; he began work on the first bastion immediately, but it was some fourteen years before the fort was completed. Day named it Fort St George for reasons that are now obscure. It was agreed that the British should collect the revenues from their territory and remit half to the Naik; his promise to build a fort at his own expense, however, appeared to slip his mind, and the Company thought it injudicious to remind him.

By now the Moghul Empire was on the march southwards. Much had happened since the Emperor, Humayun, first encountered the Portuguese. When his son Akbar, perhaps the greatest of the Moghul Emperors, succeeded him in 1556, he set himself methodically to rebuild the empire his father had so nearly lost. By 1594 all India north of the River Nerbudda accepted his authority and the more nervous of the Deccan monarchs were prepared to pay him tribute.

Akbar gave the Empire its form. He possessed a powerful mind; having little education himself, he respected learning but distrusted theory and dogma, particularly in matters of religion; seeking to knit together the great religious rift in his Empire, he opened high government appointments to Hindus. By the nature of its conquest his Empire largely fell into two categories, states such as those of Rajputana whose rulers, having submitted to his authority, he permitted to remain on condition that they paid him tribute; one ingenious monarch pointed out that if he was to justify his title of King of Kings he needed to have some kings to serve under him, and provinces directly administered from his Court.

To these last he appointed governors with the title of *nawab*. He had seen the peril of allowing great nobles to accumulate too much power and guarded carefully against it. According to Moghul law, all land belonged to the Emperor and was held at his pleasure. No prince of a subject state, therefore, could succeed without imperial sanction, and the lands of the great nobles in theory at least reverted to the state on their death. He maintained a strict control over his nawabs, moved them from province to province to prevent them from becoming too entrenched and appointed to them *diwans*, or chief ministers, who were personally responsible to him for collecting the Imperial revenues. Nor was this all. In the provinces he also appointed governors answerable only to himself to command important fortresses.

Initially he paid his great ministers of state, known as *omras*, lavish salaries from his exchequer, but later found it more convenient to allot to them the right to collect the revenues from appropriately sized districts, *jaghirs* as they were called. At this time all ministers were also generals, and with the jaghir went the obligation to supply the Emperor with a given number of troops on request; the holders of jaghirs were frequently referred to as the general of so many horse and foot. On the termination of the appointment or the death of the holder the jaghir reverted to the Emperor.

The nawabs and Muslim Indian princes possessed almost unfettered power within their provinces; separated from their subjects by religion they tended to recruit Muslim mercenaries, often from outside India, for their armies and had few ties with those whom they ruled. But as a result of Akbar's wise and liberal policies the Rajput princes and their fearless warriors for long supported the Emperor. At sea, Akbar hired ships, mostly manned by Abyssinian mercenaries, for his navy. These sailors were generally referred to as *sidis*, the title by which their admirals were known.

With this secure foundation through most of the seventeenth century the Moghul Empire expanded steadily southwards. The kingdom of Ahmadnagar succumbed in 1632. In Bijapur and Golconda the fighting was protracted and the issue for long in doubt. To the south the remnants of Vijayanagar came under attack both from Bijapur and the Moghuls. By the end of the century all these kingdoms had lost their independence and been largely dismembered. But as they declined a new power emerged in the Deccan, the Mahrattas.

They had hitherto been relatively passive subjects under the kings of Ahmadnagar and Bijapur. But under their leader, Sivaji, they not only threw off their old allegiance, but waged war against the Moghuls under the last of the great Emperors, Aurangzib. Aurangzib lacked the religious tolerance of Akbar, and by discriminating against the Hindus revived the old bitter rivalry Akbar had been anxious to dispel, alienating even the Rajputs. The Mahrattas were Hindu and, despite an always keen interest in plunder, at least initially fought a semi-national, semi-religious war against the Muslim oppressor.

They fortified strongholds in the Eastern Ghats, the rugged range of hills where the Deccan tableland dropped down to the eastern coastal plain. From these they practised guerrilla warfare, avoiding pitched battles, but raiding into Moghul-held territories, harassing their armies, cutting their communications and starving them into retreat. Aurangzib conceded them the right of *chauth*, the right to claim a quarter of the revenue from any state in southern India. It was a vitally important concession which the Mahrattas subsequently extended to central India; they levied it from any state on which they felt strong enough to impose their will. But still the unrelenting struggle, punctuated by infrequent patched-up truces, continued for the rest of the century, fatally sapping the strength of the Empire.

These were difficult times for honest, or moderately honest, merchants anxious to keep out of trouble and make a profit. The Portuguese, arrogantly remembering their feats of the previous century, sadly underestimated the strength of the Moghul armies and lost many of their possessions. The English, very conscious of their weakness in the face of Dutch and Portuguese hostility, shrewdly contrived to remain on friendly terms with whoever was their sovereign of the moment.

But wars for supremacy in the Deccan were not their only problem. In England, King and Parliament, tired of argument, were engaged in settling their differences with sword, pike and musket. Taking everything into account, it is remarkable that the Company survived its tribulations. Yet the sturdy English merchants refused to allow either the vicissitudes of war in the Deccan or in their native land to disturb the solid good sense with which they tackled their problems. At home Charles, having sold the Company's charter, now bought the Company's goods on credit; since there was no likelihood that he would ever pay for them he could afford a generous price. Parliament on the other hand demanded all the normal customs dues and suavely removed from the Company what little they had managed to salvage from the King.

Apparently unperturbed, the Company's merchants developed their little township on the Coromandel coast. In Madras, so long as the naik received an occasional present, their authority was virtually unfettered. As early as 1642 the tiny council there, consisting of Andrew Cogan, Henry Greenhill and John Browne reported to the President at Bantam that the body of a woman had been found floating in the sea. On investigation it became clear that she had been murdered by her husband and his 'consort'. The report continued, 'So we apprehended them and notified all the passages to the Naik, who gave us an express command to do justice on the homicides according to the laws of England. . . . We did justice on them and hanged them on a gibbet, where they hung till it was 11 December, when because the great Naik came to visit us for a present they were cut down.'

So over its three square miles of territory the Company had been granted almost unlimited jurisdiction. Although there had been guards at Surat, Masulipatam, and Bantam previously, only in Madras was British law paramount, and it seems fair therefore to take 1642 as the date when the Company's army was born. The garrison at this time numbered about thirty-five European soldiers, mainly Englishmen, and a slightly larger number of local Indian levies known as the Company's peons. From the European nucleus a unit developed which remained in continuous existence until 1922, becoming in turn the

Madras European Battalion, the Madras Fusiliers and finally
the Royal Dublin Fusiliers.

With the passage of time, it became evident that the Company's right to Madras needed to be confirmed by a more
exalted authority than a mere coastal naik. In 1645, Sri Ranga,
the Raja of the rump of Vijayanagar, had been forced by the
Muslim armies to take refuge in Vellore, about ninety miles
inland. Here he began to reassert his authority over the naiks
in the Carnatic. He threatened to besiege the strong Dutch
settlement at Pulicat, twenty-five miles south of Madras,
unless they acknowledged his authority and paid him tribute.
The English, weaker and therefore more discreet than their
European neighbours, thought it wise to despatch an emissary
to him to confirm the charter they had negotiated with the naik.
They explained to the Company:

'We have ofttimes been solicited by this King to give him a
visit which was never yet done to him or his predecessors since
our first arrival here which is now seven years almost. So if we
any longer deny his reasonable request we may suddenly expect
his just displeasure and peradventure have a siege about us, as
our friends the Hollanders on one side and Portugals of the
other which are seldom free notwithstanding their great power
and defence, which have twenty for one more than we; so that
if the like should happen to us, what can you expect of fifty well
and sick men to defend your estate and fort against the King's
power.'

The Raja, of course, expected more than just a social visit,
some suitable presents would have to accompany the embassy
and it was important that the dividend-conscious proprietors of
the Company in London should appreciate the need for such
expenditure. Mr Greenhill with an escort of four soldiers duly
went to the Raja's court, and since that potentate, now at war
with the Dutch, was not averse to allies and the English presents
were to his taste, Greenhill met with a genial reception.

The Raja confirmed the naik's grant, settled the tribute to be
paid and in addition 'for the better managing your business we
surrender the government and justice of the town to your
hands; and if any of your neighbours of Poonamallee [a town

some fifteen miles inland ruled by a troublesome naik] shall injure you, we promise you our ready assistance. . . . In confidence of this our *cowle* you may cheerfully proceed in your affairs. . . . This our *cowle* may stand firm as long as the Sun and Moon endureth.' A somewhat optimistic forecast for a raja whose rule was already doomed, and in due course the Company had to reopen negotiations with rather less celestial bodies; nevertheless the grant furnished a useful legal claim.

At this time the Company's army in Madras mustered about forty to fifty Europeans, including 'topasses', a name applied to Christians reputedly descended from the Portuguese settlers, large numbers of whom appear to have acted on Albuquerque's advice with great thoroughness. The Europeans, it may be guessed, all carried muskets, while the Company's peons, now about a hundred strong, probably carried only swords and bucklers. These troops acted under the orders of the Governor, at that time known as the Agent, with Lieutenant Jermin as their immediate commander. Uniform was not introduced until 1672, when the red coats, recently adopted by the newly formed British regular army, were adopted for the European troops.

The Company provided a chirurgeon for the medical care of their men, but their soldiers, never far from death by disease, clearly felt the need for spiritual care as well. Thomas Ivie, then Governor in Madras, wrote in 1645 to the Council at Bantam: 'We were presented with a petition from the soldiers for the desiring of a minister to be here with them for the maintenance of their "Soules health".'

Typically, the first action recorded by the garrison was against the Portuguese. In 1646 Mir Jumla, the chief minister and commander-in-chief of the King of Golconda – trimming his sails to the wind he ended his days as a viceroy of the Moghul Empire – had expelled the Raja of Vijayanagar from the Carnatic. Ivie with some skill confirmed the British concession with the Muslim General, but the Portuguese were less adroit and in due course Mir Jumla with a large army appeared before St Thomé. To the intense indignation of the Portuguese, Ivie lent Mir Jumla some gunners and infantry out of his scanty garrison. The Portuguese were forced to come to terms, but the memory of what they thought of as English perfidy lingered on. Some Madras citizens visiting St Thomé were assaulted. Ivie, not the man to tolerate such conduct, wrote sternly to the Portuguese on 27 October 1647:

'To the General and Council belonging to the city of St Thomay, we the Agent etc Council belonging to the Honourable English East India Company and now resident in fort St George upon the coast of Choromandel, send greeting . . . some of the inhabitants belonging to our jurisdiction being detained and most inhumanely beaten by some of their soldiers . . . for these reasons (according to the custom of Christians) we require satisfaction of you . . . which if you shall refuse to grant let no man wonder at it if, according to the Law of nations, we seek it by force of arms. We expect their answer and determination by twelve of the clock. Farewell. Thomas Ivie, George Travell, William Gurney.'

In a curious way the letter seems to have been partially written in the third person and Ivie does not substantiate his statements as to the correct behaviour for Christians.

The Portuguese appear to have disregarded the warning, for we later learn that the Agent with the lieutenant and twenty musketeers and the Company's peons sallied out to rescue some Madras citizens arrested in St Thomé. When the little force was returning the Portuguese 'shot at us with their missive weapons and killed of us three Englishmen'. The quarrel was referred to the British and Portuguese authorities at Surat and Goa, and was eventually smoothed over, perhaps because both the English and Portuguese had reason to fear the activities of the Dutch.

Such expeditions were, however, rare, and in general the duties of the garrison were to provide guards at the gates of the fort and to intervene in the town in the event of disorder. Madras, as a haven of peace in a distracted land, was growing fast and already its population numbered about 15,000. Jermin died and in 1649 the Court of Directors met to nominate his successor. A Captain Martin was called forward for interview on 13 March 1649. In the normal fashion of such affairs the Directors cross-examined him and it was recorded that 'several questions were demanded of him, where he had been bred a soldier, and in what quality, and whether he had not been on the King's side'. Charles I was not popular in the City of London. 'Martin did reply, that he did command some tenants of Mr the Archbishop's in Yorkshire, but that he was never a commissioned officer.'

This information gave the Directors pause; could they consider appointing a royalist? Presumably there was a dearth of applicants for a post in a strange faraway land, for in a couple of days they overcame their misgivings. Martin was posted to command the garrison of Madras with a seat on the Council. He duly sailed, going first to Bantam to present his credentials to the Council. He did not reach Madras until September 1651.

His career was somewhat chequered. He seems to have been indiscreet over voicing his views about the Lord Protector; it was subsequently charged against him that he 'hath invied [*sic*] against Governor Cromwell in this manner, how before the wars begun he was a poor cowardly fellow and would take a cuff on the ear from any man . . . '. In 1654 he fell out with the Agent and Governor Greenhill as a result of a complicated and not particularly creditable feud raging in the Council in which accusations of corruption were freely bandied about. Greenhill imprisoned him. This high-handed action brought Baker, the President at Bantam, to find out what was happening at Madras. What followed illustrated, if nothing else, the vigour of the early officials of the Company. Baker supported the soldier and ordered Martin's release on his guarantee of good behaviour. Greenhill far from satisfied with this action on 27 March forwarded a 'declaration' to Baker in which he asserted of Martin:

'It was not long ere the evil spirit of malice, faction, and contradiction repossest him and declared his devilish and corrupt disposition. . . . He hath violated your orders for the Government which he both as a Councillor and Captain of soldiers was most especially bound to perform by sending a private challenge to our chirurgeon, Edward Whyting, even at a time when sickness was most rife among us, and waiting without the town accompanied by his second William Wouters (for his valour durst not engage single). . . . When Thomas Price, a carpenter, complained to you for justice against the ditto Captain Martin he beat the poor man in your chamber. . . . He is an incendiary and factious person endeavouring to seduce men to his party, like the Devil, with large promises of preferment.'

Martin hit back trenchantly at Leigh, one of Greenhill's party:

'The said Leigh disbursed 200 pagodas odd and upwards in unnecessary expences in building . . . a great warehouse, only to put his own private gaine in, wherebye the Company received much damage. The said Leigh declared in the Hall of Madras-patam before myself, Anthony Baker [a nephew of the President] and others that there was no Parliament in England, since the presbyterians were suspended by force of the Army. And for the said Leigh . . . he is one that hath been known to be drunk near upon a month together. . . . It was Mr Leigh's custom to be drunk by nine of the clock in the forenoon and goes into the tanke where he falls asleep.'

Leigh apparently had the habit of punctuating Church services by emitting a loud series of amens at not particularly appropriate moments to show his devotion 'untile he fell asleep and so remained after all the Company were risen from their devotions'.

Baker however placed Greenhill, Leigh and Lieutenant Minors, who had officiated as garrison commander until Martin came out, under arrest. Greenhill related that when he was attending a soldier's wedding feast at first all was festive, then in the evening 'the scene strangely changed; myself basely abused by Captain Martin and confined, the garrison in general heated by strong drink ready to cut anothers throats. In which hurly-burly, yourself, sir, and ditto Captain Martin were in the dark night with drawn swords, while I patiently abode your doom without stirring up aloft.'

Whether it was the heat, drink or the excitement of arresting Greenhill is not clear, but Martin died soon afterwards. He must have been the prime mover in the feud, or perhaps the breaking of the monsoon cooled tempers as well as the atmos-phere, for except for some terse correspondence between Baker and Greenhill the matter was allowed to subside. Baker sailed for England on 20 January 1655, while Greenhill resumed his post as Governor and Lieutenant Minors took charge of the garrison, pending the appointment of a new captain by the Board of Directors in London.

Friction of this sort and what on occasion amounted to 'palace' revolution in the Council chamber were not to be unknown in the future. However, taking into account the distance of the Company's possessions from London it was surprising how few and in the end ineffective these were. Partly this was perhaps due to the intention of those in India sooner or later to return to England, partly it was the invariable refusal of the Company to surrender to blackmail, so that although it might be some years later a naval squadron from England would eventually arrive and the erring officials have the choice between submitting or becoming the enemies of their country.

Chapter 2

The Company Expands

In 1655 the European garrison at Madras sank to twenty-five officers and men, a number insufficient to mount a proper guard, let alone defend the fort in the perilous days that lay ahead. The numbers were augmented by recruiting sailors from ships to man the guns on the ramparts, but the total was still pitifully small. The dangers of an inadequate garrison were emphasised by the fate of the Portuguese settlement at St Thomé. In 1661, largely as the result of a Montague-Capulet style feud between the two leading families and the failure of a weak home government to impose its will on the warring factions, the Portuguese town was starved into surrender by an army under the orders of the King of Golconda. Some of the Portuguese migrated to Madras and noted bitterly how the English port, militarily far weaker than their own, continued to flourish.

In the autumn of the following year, 1662, Sir Edward Winter Bart (he appears to have conferred the baronetcy on himself, but it was well suited to his swashbuckling nature) became Agent and Governor. At this time relations with the King of Golconda gave cause for alarm. At Masulipatam, now a subordinate of its lusty offspring, Madras, the local Governor harassed the English factory, while the army that had triumphed over St Thomé hovered menacingly in the neighbourhood. The King threw out suggestions that he should appoint his own governor to Madras. Winter was determined to resist such an appointment, by force of arms if necessary. He was not unduly impressed by the threats of the King, who not only faced the likelihood of an invasion by the Moghul armies in the north, but had quarrelled with the Mahratta ruler of the state of

Tanjore to the south; moreover the Hindu naiks of the coast loathed their new Muslim overlords and might at any moment break out in open rebellion. Winter's characteristically bold front succeeded.

Now he embarked on a course of joyous living in the best cavalier tradition, which was to embroil him with the Directors in England, and lead to a bloody affray in Fort St George. He fell foul of some merchants in Madras and wrote home to the Directors that they devoted all their attention to private trading and neglected the affairs of the Company. They, on their part, counter-charged that their Governor wasted the Company's money on ostentatious buildings, that he showed an undue partiality for his relatives when it came to filling vacancies in the administration, that he spent far too much on entertaining and, perhaps worst of all, was so irregular in his attendances at church that there were dark suspicions that he contemplated becoming a papist.

The perplexed Directors sent out a commissioner, Nicholas Buckeridge, to investigate and report. Buckeridge sided with Winter's opponents; it is not improbable that there was some foundation in the allegations made by both sides. He recommended that Winter should be deprived of his post; despite the vigorous protestations of the baronet, the Directors acted on his recommendations, deposed Winter and appointed George Foxcroft to take his place. Foxcroft on arrival, at least in Sir Edward's eyes, turned out to be a pedantic, puritanical ex-roundhead, who displayed an unnecessary, even intolerable, curiosity about the accounts kept by his predecessor.

Whether it was uneasiness over what the new Governor might unearth, or merely distaste for his roundhead successor, is unclear, but Winter decided to unseat him. On 14 September 1665 he charged Foxcroft during a Council meeting with treason and speaking disrespectfully of His Majesty, Charles II. He then went to the guardroom to order the guard to arrest him. At this point matters took an unexpected turn, for the guard arrested Winter, as he somewhat ingenuously complained to the Directors, 'Without any reason so much as alleged for it'. However, he was not the man to submit lightly. Everything depended on the attitude of the garrison commander, called variously Lieutenant or Captain Chuseman; he succumbed to

Winter's persuasions, released him the next day, Friday, and agreed to arrest Foxcroft instead.

At about nine o'clock on the Saturday morning, Chuseman arrived with a file of musketeers at the Governor's house to arrest him for treason. Accounts vary as to what happened next. Foxcroft, his son and two Councillors, Samborne and Dawes, were apparently in an upper room that served as a private chapel. Hearing shouting in the hall below, they came down the stairs, according to Winter carrying drawn pistols and swords. He reported, 'Notwithstanding the said Francis Chuseman was [acting] in obedience to the charge given in his Majesty's name to keep the peace, yet they fired several pistols and made several passes at the person of Francis Chuseman against whom all the weapons were directed; who notwithstanding, behaved himself in such a sedate manner that he kept himself all the while on the defensive'. Some of Chuseman's men must have behaved in a less sedate manner, for while Chuseman and his men suffered no injury, all in the Governor's party were wounded and Dawes mortally. Proby in his statement said that he had met Samborne at chapel and came downstairs just after the affray was concluded. He related, 'I saw Mr Samborne sitting on the stairs all bloody, Mr Dawes lying on the ground, and the Agent's son bloody in face and breast, and the Agent carried away to a close chamber'.

At this moment Sir Edward appeared on the scene; he arranged for Foxcroft to be imprisoned and proclaimed himself Governor. The citizens of Madras were either uninterested or too cowed to protest, for Sir Edward reassumed his office without difficulty. He prudently kept back the despatches from Madras, and it was not until eighteen months later that the Directors heard what had happened through a despatch that Sir John Oxenden, their Governor at Surat, sent overland via Aleppo. The Directors at once referred the matter to Charles II, who instituted a lengthy inquiry into the whole affair; in consequence it was not until 24 January 1668, nearly two years after Winter's coup, that the King despatched a party of Commissioners bearing with them a royal letter instructing Winter to surrender Fort St George and reinstate Foxcroft. They sailed in a squadron of five ships including a frigate.

One morning in late August 1668, two ships flying the red

and white barred ensigns of the Company dropped anchor off
Madras. They acknowledged the fort with no salute nor did
they attempt to communicate with the shore. Proby and Locke,
two members of Winter's illegal Council, put off in a boat to
investigate and boarded one of them, the *Rainbow*. As they
clambered on deck they were promptly arrested and escorted
over to the other vessel, the appropriately-named *Loyal
Merchant*, in which travelled Joseph Hall, one of the Commissioners. Hall was in something of a quandary. He had lost
touch with the other three ships in the squadron, had no idea
when they were likely to arrive and was conscious that in a
month's time the northeast monsoon would break, making the
roadstead unusable.

As a first move he showed Proby the royal letter. Proby asked
if he could write to Winter and tell him of its contents. Hall
granted the request. While waiting for the reply, another boat
arrived with a missive from Foxcroft, who was clearly not guarded
too closely. He warned Hall against allowing any member of his
party ashore, for Winter would certainly keep them as hostages.
At about the same time Winter's reply was brought asking if a
member of the Commission would come ashore and meet him.
Hall assembled a Council of War which decided to ignore
Foxcroft's warning. Hall accordingly went ashore himself with
three companions. He afterwards described what happened:

'We went that night and got ashore two hours after candle
light. At our landing we were conducted up to Sir Edward's
house, where, after salutation, we told him we were come ashore
to take possession of the fort.' Winter asked if Proby accompanied
them. When he was told that Proby was held on board ship he
proceeded to scrutinise the royal letter very carefully. He had
with him Mr Smithes, the senior Anglican priest in Madras.
Mr Smithes suffered from no scruples about entering into a
temporal dispute and vociferously opposed the surrender of the
fort. After some discussion, Winter said that he would decide
what he would do next morning and offered Hall's party the
hospitality of his house. Hall, perhaps reluctant to try fortune
too far, declined and returned with his party to the seafront.
'But coming down to the sea-side we found it so dark and the
sea so much increased that no boat would carry us off.' Next
morning Winter offered to surrender the fort, provided that he

and his supporters were pardoned and none of their possessions were confiscated. Hall promised to consider the proposition and returned to the *Loyal Merchant* in 'another boat well manned, and a catamaran before us to take us up in case the boat overturned'.

On the *Loyal Merchant* he re-assembled his Council of War. Eventually it was agreed to accept Winter's terms on the grounds that the two ships lacked sufficient strength to enforce a decision and delay was dangerous as Winter might change his mind after discussion 'with that treacherous, pestiferous villain, Lieutenant Cheeseman [*sic*]'.

An emissary went ashore and told Winter his terms were accepted, but that if he and his supporters did not immediately surrender the fort they would be branded as traitors to their country. (The punishment for traitors was hanging, drawing and quartering, an extremely unpleasant way to die.) That ended the matter. Winter handed over the keys of the fort and marched his men out. The gates were then at once locked, an improvised garrison from the ship's companies installed, and Foxcroft released.

Perhaps understandably, after enduring nearly three years confinement, Foxcroft was incensed to find that his adversary had been pardoned, and the death of the unfortunate Dawes seemed to have been forgotten. Yet the conclusion of the affair reflected the realities of the situation. Quite apart from Hall's natural reluctance to risk shedding British blood, and the damage to prestige that an internecine conflict must cause, he lacked the military power to take Madras by force. On the other hand, Winter, since the verdict in England had gone against him, provided that he safeguarded his life and property, had much to lose if he defied the authority of his monarch. The agreement, whatever its limitations, preserved the peace and upheld the authority of the Crown.

Foxcroft reconstituted his council and resumed the governorship. Chuseman and Proby went back to England and were dismissed by the Company. Sir Edward Winter, magnificently indifferent to what had occurred, remained in India, trading as a private merchant between Madras and Masulipatam, while Foxcroft and his council speculated uneasily what further mischief he intended. However, he left India in 1672 without causing any further trouble. On arrival in London he sued the Company, presumably on the ground that he had been wrongfully dismissed when Foxcroft superseded him and was awarded £6,000 damages. He died in Battersea, where a fine monument was erected to his memory in the Parish Church. His coup had shown that where a deep rift existed in the Council the actions of the Garrison Commander would prove decisive, but only in the short term.

While on the east coast, despite its internal difficulties, Madras steadily increased in stature, on the west coast an important new English possession had been acquired. In 1661, as part of the dowry brought by Catherine of Braganza when she married Charles II, the Portuguese Government presented the port and island of Bombay to the English King, apparently on the assurance that the English would help them against the depredations of the Dutch. On 6 April 1661 the Earl of Marlborough sailed with a fleet which carried Sir Abraham Shipman and four companies of infantry to take possession. Each of the companies consisted of a lieutenant, an ensign, two sergeants, two drummers, three corporals and one hundred private soldiers; in addition there were two gunners and two gunners' mates. Shipman commanded the first company, and his second-in-command, Lieutenant-Colonel John Hungerford, the second; the remaining two were commanded by captains.

The first echelon of the ill-fated expedition, the first troops of the regular army to visit India, arrived off Bombay in September 1662. The Portuguese in India, furious with their own government for surrendering so rich a prize and deeply suspicious of the English intentions, refused to let them land. The fleet sailed on to the Company's factory at Surat, but Sir John Oxenden, the Company's Governor, asked them not to remain for fear that the arrival of so many English soldiers would arouse the wrath of the Emperor. By now Marlborough was bored with ferrying Sir Abraham Shipman and his soldiers round the Indian ocean. He dumped them on the tiny, unhealthy and virtually deserted island of Angediva, about fifty-two miles from the Portuguese stronghold of Goa; then, apparently unworried by their probable fate, he sailed home to England to report the Portuguese objections. On Angediva Shipman and most of his men died. It was not until 1665 that peremptory instructions came from Lisbon ordering the Portuguese Viceroy in India, as he was somewhat grandiloquently termed, to hand over the port of Bombay. On 8 February 1665, one hundred demoralised survivors of Shipman's regiment, under the command of Cooke who had been Shipman's secretary, took possession of Bombay Island. Oxenden, visiting them from Surat, was so horrified at their bearing and discipline that he hurriedly wrote home asking that some sober and well qualified officers should be sent out. By December 1667 the garrison numbered 93 English, 42 Portuguese and French and 150 Deccanis.

To Charles II in England the attractions of the fine-sounding dowry brought by Catherine palled almost as quickly as those of his wife, and while Catherine could be ignored Bombay made inordinate demands not only on his time but on his purse. He solved the problem with his customary indolent shrewdness and disposed of Bombay somewhat less expensively than some of his discarded mistresses. In 1668 he transferred it to the Company for an annual rental of £10 in gold. The Company put the new settlement under their Agent at Surat, and most of the few survivors of the original expedition entered their service.

At this time the so-called island consisted of two or three low-lying and heavily-wooded islands only connected with each other at low tide and stretching in all over an area about seven miles long and two miles at its widest. The island faced an excellent deep water anchorage, with beyond it the narrow coastal plain of the Konkan and the steep hills of the western Ghauts. Many travellers later exclaimed at the beauty of its setting, but this probably escaped the jaundiced eyes of its garrison, cooped up on their little island, which they were to find excessively unhealthy, even by the standards of that time. From October 1675 to February 1676, it is noted in the Records of the 2nd Battalion the Royal Dublin Fusiliers that no fewer than a hundred men died out of a garrison that can have numbered little more than 200. In consequence discipline was poor and unrest common.

Despite the natural advantages, the small English community was surrounded by dangers. The Portuguese, still bitterly hostile, held the larger island of Salsette, separated from Bombay only by a shallow neck of sea; they did everything they

could to harass their neighbours, at one time stationing a
guardship at the entrance to the harbour, which levied a duty
on every ship entering. Besides the Portuguese, the French and
Dutch, who hesitated to indulge in hostilities on Moghul
territory, had no such scruples about attacking what was now
legally English soil. However, the determined aspect of the
garrison proved sufficient to make them sheer off.

A greater peril was the feud between Aurangzib and the
Mahrattas. The Mahrattas held the western Ghats, just inland
from the island. Sivaji had organised a fleet to prey on Moghul
shipping. The Sidis, Abyssinian mercenaries manning the
Moghul navy, insisted on using Bombay harbour. The slender
English garrison dared not defy them, but they thereby incurred
the wrath of Sivaji. Fortunately the Moghul and Mahratta
fleets, composed chiefly of flat-bottomed coastal vessels, were
no match for the ocean-going ships of the Company, and
European style fortifications, backed by European-manned
artillery, excited the respect of both the contestants. But on
occasion it seemed unlikely that the British settlement would
survive.

The Council at Surat, still the superior authority to that at
Bombay, ordered the raising of a troop of forty European horse
who could move rapidly round the island to repel an invasion.
The troop was placed under the command of Captain Keigwin,
a dashing amphibious warrior, who after the fashion of the time
seemed equally at home on the back of a horse or the quarterdeck of a ship. He distinguished himself in an engagement with
the Mahrattas, when Sivaji sought to blockade the port in
revenge for allowing the Moghul navy to use the harbour.
However in 1680 matters were composed with Sivaji and
Keigwin returned home. He came out again in 1681 to take up
the appointment of garrison commander and third in council at
Bombay, an appointment that was to lead to a dramatic clash
between the soldiers and the officials of the Company. Life for
the small garrison on their constricted island, with a third of
their number on guard every night, was far from pleasant. It
was shortly to be made worse.

Like Charles II before them, the Directors were finding
Bombay a decidedly expensive luxury. They had to spend vast
sums of money on unproductive soldiers, and equally unpro-

ductive fortifications, far more than they received back in revenue. Orthodox financiers to a man, they drew their Governor's attention to this unhappy state of affairs and directed that Bombay must pay for itself. It happened that the Governor at Surat, John Child, was the brother of Sir Josiah, the Chairman of the Directors. He lost no time in carrying out his brother's instructions. He levied heavy taxes on the inhabitants of Bombay, ran down the strength of the garrison by the simple expedient of sending it no reinforcements, and insisted that the fortifications should go unrepaired; he also reduced the pay of the soldiers. It was widely believed in Bombay that he was deliberately weakening the defences, so that either the Mahrattas or the Moghuls could relieve the Company of its undesired liability.

Not unnaturally these measures caused intense hostility in Bombay, and Keigwin became the focus of disaffection. Shortly after his arrival his rank had been downgraded from Captain to Captain-lieutenant; this had the advantage, from the Company's point of view, that while he ranked as a captain he was paid as a lieutenant. Then the Governor of Bombay, Ward, deprived him of his seat on the local Council and the privileges and allowances that went with it. Keigwin petitioned to be given a subsistence allowance and Ward granted him one of 25 rupees per month (about £2 10s). In due course this extravagance was disallowed and the unfortunate Keigwin required to pay back what he had received. It was too much. On 27 December 1683 he imprisoned Ward and his few supporters, proclaimed the cession of Bombay to the Company was now annulled and that he ruled in the name of the King, and made all the inhabitants swear an oath of allegiance to Charles II. He then wrote to the King complaining that the Company ill-treated their servants, and by their foolish economies would deliver Bombay into the hands either of the Mahrattas or the Moghuls.

While the soldiers and citizens of Bombay rejoiced at the change of government, the curious anomaly that, except for a small bodyguard, all the troops were in Bombay, although the Governor resided at Surat, resulted in John Child having to content himself with writing plaintive or abusive letters and indulging in impotent fury. However, in London Sir Josiah, as chairman of a great Company, had the ear of the King. He whispered into it that Keigwin's professions of loyalty masked an intention to make himself independent and the Cromwell of Bombay. Perhaps, despite the absurdity of the suggestion, the name Cromwell could still strike terror into the heart of a Stuart, but more probably, having once unburdened himself of the expensive and troublesome island, Charles had no wish to acquire it again. He issued a commission under the Great Seal appointing John Child, now Sir John, Captain General and Admiral of the Company's sea and land forces, with Sir Thomas Grantham as Vice Admiral, and ordered them to take all necessary steps to recover Bombay. If it was done peaceably, all except Keigwin and his closest associates would be pardoned.

But Charles, whatever his other failings, was no fool. He had no intention of allowing a royal possession, even if it brought in a rent of only £10 a year, to be lost owing to the negligence, intentional or otherwise, of the Company. He therefore gave the commonsense order that the Company's headquarters on the west coast should be moved from Surat to Bombay and that the Company, at its own expense of course, should maintain there a garrison of three companies of infantry.

Sir Thomas Grantham came to Bombay and with considerable courage landed without escort or attendants. In view of what occurred it is difficult not to believe that his sympathies lay with Keigwin rather than the Company. Despite the opposition of some of his followers, Keigwin at once declared himself ready to obey the wishes of his sovereign. On 19 November 1684 he formally surrendered the island to Grantham as the representative of the Crown who then formally transferred it back to the Company. Keigwin returned to England, and, so little were the actions of the erstwhile cavalryman condemned, he was shortly afterwards appointed captain of a royal frigate in which post he died in 1690, gallantly leading his men in an attack. John Child characteristically disliked Grantham's generosity and testily observed of Keigwin, ''Tis a ten thousand pities he should escape the halter'.

Keigwin's revolt had one permanent result, it was no longer possible for the Directors to contemplate abandoning Bombay. The effect on the Child brothers was curious and to cost the Company dear. They exalted Bombay to the capital of the

British territories in India and Sir Josiah appointed his brother as 'regent'. Strange delusions of grandeur now afflicted the brothers. They had the audacity to declare war on the Moghul Empire itself. Possibly John Child, living so close to the Mahrattas, gravely underestimated the fundamental strength of Aurangzib's Empire. The strange and foolish war orginated from a quarrel in Bengal. The English had been slow to start trading with this prosperous province, but soon after its founding, the Council at Madras established subsidiary factories in the Bengal viceroyalty that included Bihar and Orissa. At first trade languished, owing to intransigent local officials and the crippling taxes and transit dues they imposed. At one time the Company contemplated closing down its factories, then an odd freak of fortune transformed the situation.

A daughter of the Emperor Shah Jahan (1628–57) was accidentally burned and her injuries refused to heal. At this time English medicine enjoyed a high reputation and the anxious Emperor asked the Company at Surat to send him an English doctor. A ship's surgeon named Boughton, whose ship happened to be in port, was selected to perform the task of healing the ailing Princess. Under his skilled administrations the Princess recovered completely; considering the medical theories of the day it is probable that nature had a hand in the cure, but Boughton received the credit.

The delighted Emperor asked him to name his reward, and Boughton, displaying an astonishing degree of altruism and patriotism, asked only that a firman should be granted to the Company, giving it the right to establish factories and trade in Bengal free of all taxes. The Imperial firman was duly issued, and Boughton personally accompanied it to Rajmahal, where the Viceroy, Prince Suja, a second son of the Emperor, held his court. By a happy chance the excellent doctor here cured a member of the Prince's harem to the gratified surprise of the Prince. Suja now agreed to execute the firman; he sanctioned the opening of a factory at Patna, the centre of a lucrative trade in saltpetre, and for the trifling annual payment of 3,000 rupees permitted the Company to trade throughout his viceroyalty free of all taxes and duties.

With such an advantage over its competitors the Company's trade expanded rapidly. Unhappily Prince Suja met the fate of all sons of a Moghul Emperor, either to reign or meet a violent death. In 1657 Shah Jahan fell ill and his sons at once massed their armies to contest the succession. Aurangzib emerged the victor and Suja, his army defeated and scattered, took refuge with the King of Arakan, whose unusual views on hospitality included murdering his guest and raping his wives.

Mir Jumla, after a quarrel with his master, the King of Golconda, had shrewdly linked his fortunes to those of Aurangzib; as a reward he received the vacant Bengal viceroyalty. At first his relations with the Company were far from cordial. The Council of Madras, mistakenly thinking that one of his ships lying off the coast contained treasure, compounded their error by seizing it. The enraged Viceroy vented his wrath on the English traders in Bengal, effectively blocking all trade. However, after receiving substantial compensation he relented and the Company was allowed to resume its former privileges.

Most commerce in India flowed down the great rivers and especially down the Ganges; the Company set up a factory at the port of Hooghly on the river of that name that formed part of the Ganges delta. Here goods were loaded onto coastal shipping and despatched to Madras. As trade expanded the Company's establishment at Hooghly rapidly increased in size and importance and in 1676 the Company raised it to the level of an Agency with the right to trade direct with England. With the appointment of the Agent, Madras's authority over the establishments in Bengal came to an end.

In 1663 Mir Jumla died; he was replaced by Shaista Khan, a nephew of the Empress Nur Jahan. By 1681 the number of English troops at Hooghly had risen to two companies, not so much to safeguard the warehouses from local officials as to protect its cargoes from the depredations of English merchants, generally referred to as interlopers, who, while not members of the Company, tried to trade in India. These were not above indulging in a little piracy, and their attentions were supplemented by professional pirates including the notorious Captain Kidd.

Shaista Khan was not convinced of the purity of English intentions and watched the growing English military strength with deepening suspicion. He peremptorily refused a request to allow the Company to fortify its establishment at Hooghly; then the English, with a distressing lack of diplomatic tact, appeared to harbour a pretender to his viceroyalty. To express his displeasure he imposed such heavy duties on the Company's goods that it soon became evident that unless these duties were rescinded the Bengal factories would have to close.

Protests proved unavailing, and Sir Josiah Child resolved to resort to force. A fleet of ten ships was despatched from England carrying six companies of infantry with subalterns but no captains. On its arrival in India, Job Charnock, the Agent at Hooghly, was to become Admiral and Commander-in-Chief and the members of his council were to command the Companies. A better formula for disaster could scarcely have been contrived but after his experience with Keigwin Child distrusted professional soldiers. James II, who had succeeded his brother Charles, with his usual lack of judgement, associated himself with this extraordinary enterprise and issued the fleet with a royal commission. Setting aside the fundamental stupidity of the whole project, the military planning was not entirely misconceived. Having concentrated all the available military resouces of the Company, the fleet was directed to capture the port of Chittagong on the east coast of Bengal, fortify it as a secure base for operations, and then seize the prosperous city of Dacca, the capital of Eastern Bengal; it was confidently expected that this would bring Shaista Khan to terms. Chittagong had some virtues as a base. It was close to the eastern border of the Empire with Arakan, now the west coast province of modern Burma. Chittagong had recently been wrested from Arakan by Aurangzib who, while ready enough himself to execute Moghul princes, was not prepared to extend that privilege to lesser monarchs, and it was thought the King of Arakan might be eager to help anyone who would restore to him his lost port.

But if the plan had some merit, its execution had none. The fleet lost three ships on the voyage out, but this was only the beginning of a catalogue of disasters. By a curious lack of imagination, the port of Hooghly had been selected as the rendezvous for the enterprise. The factory at Hooghly clearly had to be evacuated before hostilities began and the infantry companies had to meet their new commanders, but no one seems to have considered what Shaista Khan might do while the English forces assembled.

On 28 October 1686, shortly after the fleet from England had arrived, the inevitable happened. A brawl between some of the English soldiers and the Moghul garrison developed into a pitched battle. The English fleet bombarded the town and the Moghul troops were driven out. Charnock, anxious to avoid exacerbating an unfortunate situation, prevented his men from plundering the town, an act of restraint that in due course earned him a rebuke from the Directors. But now he was committed to hostilities, not in a distant region, but virtually in the centre of Bengal with an excellent waterway along which Shaista Khan could transport his army. While his army was concentrating, the expelled Governor of Hooghly opened a spurious negotiation designed to keep the English in the area. Charnock was still futilely trying to arrive at a peaceable settlement when he learnt that a powerful Moghul army had arrived in the neighbourhood. Hopelessly outnumbered, the English had no alternative but to beat an ignominious retreat. They found refuge on a fever ridden island at the mouth of the Hooghly, variously called Ingellee or Hijili. A Moghul assault was beaten off, but the conditions they were living under and the climate were deadlier foes.

Charnock now tried to reopen negotiations. At sea English naval supremacy had begun to make itself felt. Moghul ships were being captured, and perhaps worse, in the eyes of that fanatical Moslem, Aurangzib, the pilgrim traffic to Mecca had been halted. He was engaged in conquering the Deccan and poised to shatter the Kingdom of Golconda. He had no wish to be distracted by an extraneous quarrel for which his Viceroy was partially to blame. Negotiations followed the usual dilatory course. Charnock managed to extract about 100 survivors of the English force from the deathtrap into which they had been penned, and moved to the village of Chuttanuttee, about forty miles up the Hooghly.

In London the Directors, furious at the fiasco, determined to continue with their original plan. In October 1688, when Charnock seemed on the point of achieving a satisfactory settlement, Captain Heath arrived from England in a 64-gun ship of the line, accompanied by a frigate and a reinforcement of 160 soldiers. He carried peremptory instructions from the Directors to put the original plan into effect. Charnock expostulated vainly, pointing out the folly of such an action when he had every hope of effecting a satisfactory compromise. The pugnacious sailor would not listen.

After the incidents at Hooghly the Governor of Balasore had imprisoned the Company's servants there and impounded their goods. Heath now sailed to Balasore with his fleet, and demanded their release and the return of all the Company's property. The Governor refused. Heath bombarded the port, whereat the Governor retired inland with his prisoners, having first taken the precaution of burning all the Company's possessions. The baffled Captain had to content himself with plundering the defenceless town. He had achieved nothing save the destruction of the Company's property and a flagrantly hostile act that Aurangzib was unlikely to overlook.

Heath left Balasore on 13 December to carry out his original instructions and capture Chittagong. When he anchored off that port, however, it was clear that it was now strongly fortified. He held a Council of War which decided against an assault. He then made overtures to the King of Arakan for an alliance, which that monarch firmly rejected. Frustrated at every turn, Heath returned to find the Company's establishments all over India in jeopardy.

The attack on Balasore infuriated Aurangzib. The fortress of Golconda had fallen in 1687 and although his ceaseless war with the Mahrattas showed no sign of ending, he issued instructions that the English should be extirpated from the Empire. Heath, with Charnock and all the members of the Bengal staff not already captured or dead, sailed for Madras, but all over the Moghul's dominions the Company's property was sacked and its servants killed or imprisoned. Only Madras and Bombay escaped the general holocaust.

Since Winter's coup, despite occasional internal squabbles, Madras had prospered and grown. The Portuguese settlement at St Thomé was no more and by a shrewd stroke the Company had ensured that it would not be reborn. In 1672 a French fleet had appeared off the old Portuguese port. Annoyed by the refusal of the Governor to give them provisions, the arrogant countrymen of Louis XIV summarily stormed it. But they reckoned without the Dutch. When the King of Golconda sent an army to avenge the insult, a Dutch fleet, anxious to avenge the suffering inflicted on their country by the French King's army, cruised off the port. Blockaded from the sea and attacked from the land, after a brave resistance the French surrendered to the Dutch who granted them the honours of war and permission to return to France – to the intense annoyance of the King of Golconda, whom the Dutch had not thought it necessary to consult. Before the surrender, however, a small party of French had sailed to the south under M. François Martin, and these in 1676 obtained permission to build a bastion at a small village which they cultivated so well that the Indians called it Phulcherry or flower town, which the French corrupted into Pondichéry and the English into Pondicherry.

The Council in Madras were quick to see in the French reverse an opportunity to destroy St Thomé completely, and represented to the King the foolishness of leaving such a town with its fortifications as an open invitation to any unscrupulous European adventurer who might appear off the coast. The King agreed to destroy the town, but his general, not able to contemplate the destruction of so many fine buildings, merely dismantled the fortifications with the enthusiastic help of citizens from Madras.

By the time that Heath arrived with his unhappy convoy of refugees from Bengal, Madras was the foremost trading port on the Coromandel coast. But thanks to the folly of the Directors, the future looked gloomy. Golconda had fallen and now the news arrived that the factory at Masulipatam had been sacked and the English staff massacred, while a Moghul army under a general with the engaging name of Potty Khan was encamped nearby.

Aurangzib was now at the zenith of his power. He had crushed Bijapur and Golconda; his deadliest enemy, Sivaji, was dead; he had captured many of the Mahratta strongholds on the west coast; Sivaji's son and successor, Sambhaji, had been captured and executed; the last great Mahratta chief still in the field, Raja Ram, acting as Regent for Sambhaji's infant son, Shahu, had fled from the western Ghats and taken refuge in the nearly impregnable fort of Gingee in the Carnatic about eighty miles to the south of Madras. The Moghul armies, under one of their ablest generals, Zulfikar Khan, seemed set to extinguish the last embers of Mahratta resistance and sweep down to the Deccan to Cape Comorin. To the Moghul tiger, intent on stalking and killing the wounded Mahratta panther, Madras appeared like a curled hedgehog; there was nothing to fear from it, but to stamp on it might risk driving a quill into a foot that might become poisoned and cripple the hunter. Zulfikar Khan left Madras unmolested.

Bombay was not so fortunate. On 26 December 1688, nearly two months after Heath's ill-conceived attack on Balasore, the Governor of Surat confiscated the Company's goods, imprisoned two of the factors, and offered a large price for the capture of Sir John Child, dead or alive. In 1687 John Child, rather belatedly obeying the instructions of his monarch, had moved to Bombay. He now probably felt grateful for the fortifications, the expenses of which he had so often deplored. But on 14 February 1689, Sidi Yakub, the Moghul admiral, landed an army of 20,000 men on Bombay island and marched on the fort. Child, with greater optimism than military judgement, sent out two companies of the garrison under Captain Pean to drive them away.

Apart from the gross disparity in numbers, the discipline and skill of the garrison left something to be desired. Sidi Yakub and his men showed a firm front to the tiny English force, whereat, according to a British merchant, Hamilton, himself an interloper and no friend of the Company, 'The Captain betook himself to his heels and was the foremost man to the Portuguese Church, where he took courage to look behind him to see what had become of his men. . . . He was a fellow as well made for running as ever I saw'. It does not appear that Pean outdistanced his men by any substantial margin, although it is recorded that about a dozen stayed and fought and were cut to pieces.

The Sidi contented himself with blockading the fort. After vainly trying to bribe some high officials at the Imperial Court, John Child had no alternative but to throw himself on the mercy of the Emperor, then residing at Bijapur. By now Aurangzib's wrath had abated. The Company's ships still imperilled the sea routes and the loss of European trade affected his revenues; he considered the English had been sufficiently chastised. On 27 February 1690 he issued a firman couched in contemptuous language which masked the moderation of its terms. It ran:

'All the English having made a most humble submission that the crimes they have done may be pardoned, and the Governor of Surat's petition to the famous court, equal to the sky, being arrived, that they would pay the Great King with a fine of 150,000 rupees (£15,000) to his most noble treasury, would restore the merchants' goods they have taken away to the owners of them, and would walk by the ancient customs of the port and behave themselves no more in such a shameful manner, therefore His Majesty has pardoned their faults . . . they follow their trade as in former times and Mr Child, who did the disgrace, be turned out and expelled. This order is irreversible.' (Extracted from the translation in Bruce's Annals of the East India Company.)

Child died on 4 February 1690, before receiving the news of his humiliating dismissal. In Bengal, Aurangzib agreed to restore its old privileges to the Company and allow it to trade tax free on the old annual payment of 3,000 rupees. Charnock, who had no wish to renew his acquaintanceship with the Governor of Hooghly or come under the direct jurisdiction of any other senior Moghul official, obtained permission to organise an unfortified factory at Chuttanuttee. He stepped ashore there on 24 August 1690 to found the city of Calcutta.

In England the fiasco led to an outcry against the Company. Its identification with James II told against it, now that monarch was sampling the hospitality of the King of France and William III reigned in his place. There were besides many merchants in the City of London eager to break the Company's monopoly of trade with the East. In 1698, Parliament, with its usual happy ignorance of matters oriental, authorised a second company to trade with India. The resultant chaos nearly ruined both.

Aurangzib declared irritably that he did not know with whom he was expected to negotiate; his governors in western India solved the problem to their own satisfaction by making the two companies bid against each other for privileges of doubtful worth, and were not above imprisoning the loser of the contest for obviously failing to submit a reasonable bid. The anomaly was resolved by Godolphin in 1708. He decreed that the two companies should be united and trade with India under the title of 'The United Company of Merchants trading in the East Indies' and that his decision should remain in force until 1726. The most lasting effect of the ill-judged war was the impact it made on Company policy. It had been forcibly taught not to meddle in Indian politics, a rule it faithfully observed for close on fifty years.

Chapter 3

Peaceful Traders, 1690–1745

In 1707 Aurangzib died aged 89, a soured and embittered man. His earlier successes against the Mahrattas proved illusory. Gingee, it is true, fell after a desultory siege lasting eight years and Shahu, the infant son of Sambhaji, eldest son of Sivaji, and heir to the Mahratta kingdom, was captured, to be brought up at the Imperial Court. But Raja Ram, his uncle and Regent, escaped and the Mahrattas, fighting a religious and semi-nationalistic war, gradually wore down their opponents. At first the Moghul armies could march and invade where they chose, but even then they were like a man striking with a clenched fist into a vast sponge that, yielding in front, closed in on the wrist like a tourniquet, arresting the flow of blood. Wherever the Moghuls marched, whatever the success they attained, the Mahratta horsemen hovered on their flanks and rear harassing them and starving them into retreat.

As the war progresssed, the Moghul soldiers, never fighing their elusive enemy except at a disadvantage, lost heart, and the Mahrattas came to dominate the battlefield itself. Now only where Zulfikar Khan or Aurangzib himself commanded could the Moghul armies hope to be victorious. Raja Ram died; his widow, an intriguing termagant named Tarabai, ignoring Shahu's superior claim to the monarchy, proclaimed her young son Shivaji King of the Mahrattas and herself Regent. Under her guidance the struggle continued.

To add to the worries of the sick and melancholy Emperor, the Rajputs, alienated by his discrimination against the Hindus, staged a revolt that his generals seemed unable entirely to subdue, while his sons, following the pattern he himself had set, jockeyed for position ready to begin their fratricidal strife

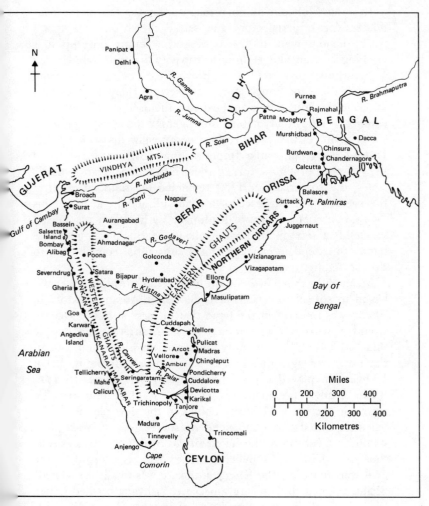

India in the eighteenth century

as soon as he died. His worst fears were soon to be realised. His successors inherited his ambitions but none of his talents. Between 1707 and 1720, eight Emperors reigned briefly, only one of whom was to know a natural death. During the incessant battles for the succession, Zulfikar Khan perished and the Empire slowly disintegrated.

In 1720 Mohammed Shah disposed of the last of the contenders for Imperial glory and seized the throne. He was a
weak, devious man, but he possessed a certain unscrupulous
cunning and an almost infinite capacity for survival. He led
a luxurious, dissipated life, preventing his generals from
accumulating too much power by setting them against each
other, in the hope they would exhaust themselves in internecine
conflict, a policy that enabled him to enjoy the corrupt pleasure
of Delhi in relative security for twenty-eight disastrous years.
During his reign, while Imperial power withered away and
the rulers of provinces turned them into independent dynastic
states, the Imperial Court yet remained the fount of legality;
the usurper who disposed of a rival still sought to invest his
usurpation with an aura of legitimacy by having it recognised
at Delhi, a recognition that Mohammed Shah was generally
happy to extend in exchange for a substantial contribution to
his ever-empty treasury.

Meanwhile the power of the Mahrattas steadily grew and
began to spread into Central India. After Aurangzib's death,
Shahu was released in the hope that his arrival in the Deccan
would provoke a civil war among the Mahrattas and cripple
their strength. Tarabai duly contested Shahu's claim, but in
the bitter struggle that ensued a Chitpavan Brahmin, Balaji
Vishvanath, played a prominent part in her defeat. In 1713
Shahu made Vishvanath his Peshwa, or chief minister. To
reconcile the great Mahratta nobles to the new régime, Vishvanath granted them independent sovereignty in their own
dominions, subject to the suzerainty of Shahu and his Peshwa;
thus the Mahratta Confederacy was born. As a result of the
civil war, however, the King's authority was fatally weakened;
Shahu reigned, but in large measure Vishvanath ruled. After
Shahu's death in 1747 Sivaji's royal line faded into insignificance and power passed into the hands of the Peshwa, now a
hereditary office.

Meanwhile the Deccan which Aurangzib had purported to
subdue became the scene of a violent conflict between the
Mahrattas and the Moghul Viceroy, who had arrogated to
himself the title of Nizam-ul-mulk, the old dynastic name of
the Kings of Ahmadnagar. The Peshwa and his vassal princes,
however, their gaze fixed on the rich states of Central India,

now slipping from the failing grasp of the Moghuls, were eager to disengage from a war in the south, and in 1731 concluded the Treaty of Warna with Nizam-ul-mulk. By its provisions, although Shahu was recognised in theory as sovereign of the whole of the Deccan, in fact that vast region was divided; the west comprising most of the old Kingdoms of Ahmadnagar and Bijapur fell to the Mahrattas, while Nizam-ul-mulk received the old Kingdom of Golconda, including the Carnatic; however he retained in the west Aurangabad, the capital of the Deccan that Aurangzib had named after himself, while on the east coast, the state of Tanjore, long a possession of a branch of Sivaji's family, remained part of the Mahratta Confederacy.

With the issue in the Deccan apparently settled, the Mahratta princes swooped down on Central India, intent on carving out independent realms for themselves. In 1737, alarmed by the extensions to their power, Nizam-ul-mulk put on the mantle of a faithful Viceroy to the Emperor, one that he had long since discarded, and went to Delhi to offer his services to his sore-pressed master. He led a Moghul army against the Mahrattas, but under their new Peshwa, Baji Rao, who had succeeded Vishvanath, they were proving too much for him when catastrophe overtook the crumbling Empire. In 1739, Nadir Shah, King of Persia, invaded India, carried all before him, paraded Mohammed Shah as his captive through Delhi, and plundered the Imperial city for fifty-seven terrible days before returning to Persia richly laden with booty.

After his conqueror had departed, Mohammed Shah hastily patched up a peace with the Mahrattas, ceding them most of Central India from Gujarat to the borders of Oudh. Nizam-ul-mulk, leaving his eldest son, Ghazi-ud-din, in Delhi to watch his interests, returned to the Deccan to find his vice-royalty in chaos. His second son, Nazir Jang, was up in arms against him and the Mahrattas swarming over the Carnatic, events that were to cast a long shadow over the activities of the British and French.

Dost Ali, the Nawab of Arcot, the title generally given to the ruler of the Carnatic, had been negligent in paying his dues to the Viceroy, absent in Central India, and in paying chauth to the Mahrattas, a right they claimed over all the states in

the Deccan. In 1737, after a discreditable intrigue, he installed
his son-in-law, Chunda Sahib, as Governor of Trichinopoly, a
state which had formerly acknowledged the authority of the
Mahratta kingdom of Tanjore, and which exercised the right
to receive tribute from the two southern states of Madura
and Tinnevelly.

Raghoji Bhonsla, a Mahratta prince who had acquired the
state of Berar for himself, seeing Nizam-ul-mulk locked in
combat with Baji Rao on the plains of Central India, seized a
splendid opportunity to chastise Dost Ali and recover Trichinopoly. In 1740 he invaded the Carnatic. At the pass near
Ambur, not far from Arcot, Dost Ali gave battle, was defeated
and killed. His son and heir, Safdar Ali, retired to Arcot,
while Chunda Sahib prepared to defend himself in Trichinopoly. Both sent their families to Pondicherry, placing them
under the protection of the French Governor, Dùmas. On
21 March 1741, after a siege of more than three months,
Trichinopoly fell and Chunda Sahib went a prisoner to Satara,
the capital of the Mahrattas in the northwest of the Deccan.
Raghoji now ordered Dumas to surrender the families of both
Chunda Sahib and Safdar Ali. Dumas politely declined,
manned the guns on his ramparts and sent in lieu a selection
of French liqueurs. The Mahratta Prince found drinking the
choice products of France an agreeable substitute for a possibly
protracted and expensive siege, and did not press his demands.
This successful defiance of the Mahrattas by the French made
a profound impression all over the Deccan.

Raghoji now appointed Safdar Ali, Dost Ali's son, as nawab
of the Carnatic provided he paid an enormous indemnity to
meet the costs of the Mahratta campaign, and Morari Rao,
a scion of the impoverished but famous Mahratta family of
Ghorpade, Governor of Trichinopoly with responsibility for
seeing that Safdar Ali met his obligations. He thereupon
retraced his steps to Berar, where his chief minister was engaged
on what he hoped would be a lucrative foray into Bengal.

On his return Nizam-ul-mulk at once took vigorous action
to restore order into his chaotic viceroyalty. He crushed Nazir
Jang's revolt, then in 1742, assembling a hugh army, he chased
Morari Rao and his Mahrattas out of Trichinopoly and the
Carnatic. By now the unfortunate Safdar Ali had been

assassinated by his cousin Murtaza Ali Khan, the Governor of Vellore, a fate soon to be shared by his infant only son. Nizam-ul-mulk appointed Anwar-ud-din, one of his generals, initially as guardian to Safdar Ali's heir, but after that infant's death he became nawab in name as well as in fact. His eldest son, Mafuz Khan, became deputy nawab, and his second son, Mohammed Ali, Governor of Trichinopoly. By these measures a certain, uneasy stability was introduced into the viceroyalty, which lasted until Nizam-ul-mulk's death in 1748.

But there was to be no such stability in Bengal. The second great Viceroyalty of the Empire, that of Bengal, Bihar and Orissa, had by now become the preserve of the descendants of the Viceroy Murshid Kuli Khan, who had renamed his capital Murshidabad after himself. His son-in-law, Suja-ud-daula, succeeded him unchallenged and died in 1739; but in 1740, after his heir, Sarafraz, had become Viceroy, a central Asian adventurer named Alivardi Khan, who had risen to high rank under Suja-ud-daula, rebelled, killed Sarafraz in battle and usurped the viceroyalty. A violent civil war erupted, and Raghoji's chief minister, seeing at the least an excellent chance to plunder, intervened on behalf of Murshid Kuli Khan's dynasty, initially without much success.

When Raghoji Bhonsla appeared, the alarmed Alivardi Khan appealed to the Emperor for help. Mohammed Shah had, of course, none to offer, but assistance came from an unexpected quarter. Balaji Rao had succeeded his father, Baji Rao, as Peshwa in 1740, but Raghoji had campaigned vigorously, if unsuccessfully, against his accession. Balaji Rao decided to adopt the unlikely guise of a Moghul general and, armed with the Imperial authority, discipline his unruly noble, in return, of course, for a fair price for his services. He agreed with the Emperor to drive his rival out of Bengal in exchange for the right to collect chauth from the province of Gujerat. The contemporary historian Ghulam Hussain has left, in his book, *Seir Mutakharin*, a vivid account of Balaji Rao's incursion into Bengal, showing that it was almost worse to have the Mahrattas as friends than as enemies:

'It was at this time that news came of Balaji Rao's approach with no less than forty or fifty thousand horse. And what added

to the terror of the inhabitants was that by this time it became
known that all along his passage he had exacted contributions;
and that whoever paid with a good grace had his person,
lands and country spared; but whoever had pretended to stand
on his defence had not failed of having his person plundered,
his country ruined and his tenants put to the sword. . . . What
are we to think of those generals and viceroys sent by an imperial
order to succour a province of the Empire; and what are we
to conclude from their treating everywhere that province as
an enemy's country? . . . A lady of distinction . . . having it
not in her power to provide otherwise for her safety resolved
to stand her ground and defend her honour to the last drop
of her blood. This heroine called her relations and dependants
together, exhorted them to perish rather than to behold their
women defiled or attempted, and finding them willing, she
shut the doors of her houses, barricaded her quarter and
arming her dependants with a small number of rusty muskets
then at hand she prepared to defend herself against that host
of mighty foes. All the inhabitants had fled, or had submitted
to defilement and sack and plunder; and it was only from that
cluster of ruinous buildings that some opposition was exhibited
and a report of firing heard. The plunderers, surprised at so
unexpected an appearance, surrounded the refractory quarter
and were in doubt whether they should force it or not; for the
firing went on and their men were falling. But meanwhile
intelligence of this strange event having reached the ears of the
Mahratta general [Balaji Rao], it excited a sense of admiration
mixed with curiosity; . . . he was informed that the widow of a
renowned general being through poverty unable to provide
herself with lodgings and subsistence the other side of the water,
had resolved to bury herself under the ruins of her house rather
than suffer any defilement, that she had barricaded her quarter
and with a handful of dependants whom her resolution had
aroused, she was defending it so well that the plunderers,
little accustomed to finding so much resistance, had not
dared to attempt it, and were only looking at it from afar. The
intelligence pleased Balaji Rao. He was astonished to find so
much daringness in a woman; and not content with praising
her resolution, he sent her a kind message which he accompanied with a present . . . and to put her house out of danger

he sent a detachment of his body-guards to take charge of it with orders not to stir from thence until the whole army should be gone and far off. He added they should answer to him for any insult she might suffer. After giving this order he continued his route by the hilly country; and the guards having strictly executed their orders, took respectful leave of the heroine and rejoined the army.'

Balaji Rao, having made Alivardi Khan agree to the payment of chauth and extracted a suitable back-payment, duly thrashed Raghoji Bhonsla, drove him out of Bengal and pocketed his reward. Then, having vindicated his authority, he accepted Raghoji Bhonsla's submission, and in return granted him a free hand in Bengal. The war there dragged on until 1750 when Alivardi Khan purchased peace by ceding the province of Orissa, except for the district of Balasore, and agreeing to pay chauth. For a brief period there was tranquillity in Bengal.

During these confused and troubled years which were profoundly to affect it in the decade to come, the Company avoided political entanglements and quietly prospered. After the award by Godolphin the United Company divided its possessions into three equal ranking presidencies, those of Bombay, Madras and Calcutta, each controlled by a President selected by the Company, but who was approved as Governor by the Crown. He was assisted by a council among whom he was only first member without the right to overrule a majority decision. He moved in considerable state generally with a military escort.

The three Presidencies developed their little armies quite independently; each was jealous of its own authority; any attempt to transfer an official from one to assume an appointment in another was deeply resented. The senior soldier in each garrison, for long a captain, was appointed by the Directors, the remaining officers normally by the Governor. The ranks of the ensigns were generally filled by commissioning suitable sergeants; a soldier who had ability a little above the average of his fellows, was reasonably diligent in his duties, was healthy enough to survive a number of years in India and kept on good terms with his seniors, might expect to rise to the rank of lieutenant or even, exceptionally, captain-lieutenant.

The largest garrison was maintained in Bombay, presumably

because of its formidable neighbours. Perhaps as a result of being a royal possession, unlike his brethren in the Presidencies of Madras and Calcutta, the Governor of Bombay had the right to inflict the death penalty. After an attempt to seize power had miscarried, it is recorded in the history of the 2nd Royal Dublin Fusiliers that James Forke was condemned to death for attempting to corrupt Ensign Kennedy; Sergeant Cross and Corporal Powle were to throw dice for their lives on a drumhead under the gallows, the loser to die; presumably it was expected that the goddess of chance would dispense justice, but it is rare to find the phrase 'dicing with death' interpreted quite so literally. Sergeant Sands and Private Powle were publicly to confess their guilt on parade and be banished and Private Cole was to run the gauntlet backwards and forwards between the two companies. Those condemned to death petitioned that they might be shot like soldiers and their wish was granted.

In March 1673 an officer of the garrison was condemned to death for mutiny and striking his superior officer and was 'to have been shot to death, in order whereunto all the soldiers were under arms and those persons which he chose to be his executioners had their muskets laden with balls and were ready to perform their duty, but owing to the intercession of ladies of quality on the island the Governor was moved to grant a reprieve'. Most punishments, however, consisted of flogging, and thirty-nine lashes administered outside the Church appeared to be a popular sentence. On rare occasions a soldier might be made to run the gauntlet, but the humiliation caused by such an experience was considered to render the soldier unfit for further service; the sentence therefore had to be followed by dismissal and the Company could ill afford to lose any men.

The strength of the garrison varied between four and eight companies, five normally being stationed in Bombay and the remainder scattered as detachments in out-lying factories. The soldiers were drawn from varying nationalities, and the so-called European companies often had few full-blooded Europeans in their ranks. In 1675, for instance, the total English population in Bombay only amounted to 300. In a return of 1742, the European garrison is shown as amounting to 1,593 all ranks, but of these only 346 were Europeans, the remainder being locally recruited and over 1,000 of them Topasses; the

Europeans were divided between all the companies so as to
have a leavening of them in each; only one captain was carried
on the strength, who commanded the first or senior company;
the remainder were commanded by lieutenants with two or
three ensigns serving under them. The companies are shown as
very strong, one amounting to no fewer than three hundred
soldiers. At one time the officers complained that owing to the
parsimonious refusal of the Company to pay for an adequate
number of officers their companies were far too large and
unwieldy, but it may be suspected that the figures quoted were
grossly inflated, possibly to increase the amount of pay and
allowances that might be drawn. In addition to the so-called
European companies, bands of Indian mercenaries under their
own commanders were recruited, but no attempt was made to
train them, and if they were required to fight in a battle they
almost invariably misbehaved.

The European companies wore uniform after the pattern of
the regular British army, but probably about twenty years out
of date. In the records of the 2nd Dublin Fusiliers a letter
written on 16 December 1675 is quoted about the wearing of
red coats: 'As for red coats they blush to own the refusal of
them, considering how cheap they were . . . the soldiers are in
general well content to wear them, but we are become wary how
we deliver them any more, for the frequent mortality which
happens among the soldiers and the long time before they pay
for them make the Honble Company rather sufferers than
gainers from this practice.' Red coats in the humid atmosphere
of Bombay must have contributed materially to the horrifying
deathrate that this remark reveals so unemotionally.

It was not to be expected that the scratch mixture of Europeans, Eurasians and Topasses would be formidable on the
battlefield, particularly as they spent an inordinate amount of
time on guard duty. Hamilton, that staunch critic of the Company, records of an action fought at Karwar in 1718:

'When all was ready we landed 1,250 men without the least
hindrance from the enemy . . . but our freshwater land officers
were so long in drawing up their confounded hollow square that
the enemy took courage and with horse and foot came running
towards our men firing and wounding some as they marched in

their ranks; which our commandant seeing, pulled off his redcoat and vanished. Some other as valiant captains as he took example and left their posts, and then the soldiers followed and threw down their arms . . . later about 80 sailors went to the field of battle and brought on the "Commodore" about 200 stand of arms, most of them loaded.'

Apart from the Mahrattas the main problem confronting Bombay was the numerous nests of pirates that had sprung up along the west coast of the Indian Peninsula. Aurangzib, accepting philosophically in his latter days the inevitable superiority of the Europeans at sea, neglected his own naval forces, preferring to compel the Europeans to safeguard the sea-routes by enforcing fines on their settlements if any Moghul merchantmen were captured on the high seas. The Sidis, therefore, abandoning their ships, took to erecting forts on the Konkan along the western coast. The Mahrattas resented this activity and their Admiral, Kanhoji Angria, captured a number, notably one at Gheria, some 170 miles south of Bombay. To meet his expenses Angria began to levy chauth on all shipping sailing off the coast. Having stopped a ship to value its cargo it became obvious that it was simpler to confiscate the whole rather than to levy a tax on it. Soon Angria, ably supported by a number of English pirates, instituted a reign of terror all over the Arabian sea. In 1717 the Governor of Bombay sent a force which included 300 men from the Bombay garrison to destroy Gheria. The attempt failed miserably. Another attempt on a fort Angria had established at Khanderi met with a similar fate. In despair the Directors petitioned George I for assistance and a naval squadron of four warships under Commodore Matthews assembled in Bombay harbour in 1721. Hostilities nearly began prematurely between the Governor and the Commodore, and the naval officers themselves, disdaining to have any truck with the Company's staff, amused themselves by fighting duels with each other. The long-suffering citizens of Bombay consoled themselves with the thought that if they displayed a similar savagery against Angria, that pirate's days were surely numbered. Eventually an Anglo-Portuguese force of 5,000 men, convoyed by Commodore Matthews, sailed against Alibag, at that time Angria's headquarters.

The expedition proved abortive. Matthews, superintending operations on land, was wounded in the thigh by a lance and the Portuguese, so the British asserted, ran away uncovering the British flank. Matthews in a fury accused the Portuguese of treachery and assaulted their commander with his cane. The Portuguese retired in high dudgeon while Matthews re-embarked the Company's troops and returned to Bombay. Angria was left triumphant. The Governor of Bombay had to resign himself to the prospect that any convoy that sailed without a strong escort, did so at its peril.

Kanhoji Angria died in 1731, the same year as the Treaty of Warna, which confirmed the titular supremacy of Shahu over the whole of the Deccan. In a curious way his death worked somewhat to the advantage of the Company. The succession to his fleet and territory was disputed between his sons in the customary manner. Bombay wisely refrained from interfering, but the Portuguese supported one of the claimants. Baji Rao, fresh from his triumph over Nizam-ul-mulk, settled the matter as leader of the Mahratta confederacy, then rebuked the Portuguese for their interference. Portuguese arrogance em-bittered the dispute, and Baji Rao despatched a large army to seize Salsette Island and the Portuguese stronghold of Bassein. The Portuguese fought valiantly but by 1739 were utterly defeated. The crafty Council at Bombay were the true victors. A dangerous European trade rival had been eliminated, while the Mahrattas, reputedly having lost 12,000 men in the struggle, became extremely chary of attacking fortifications mounting artillery manned by Europeans. When the hostilities ended the Council at Bombay sent a delegation to the Mahratta court at Satara to emphasise their good intentions. Shahu received them at first with a display of coldness to impress on them their insignificance; finally he became extremely cordial, and granted the Company permission to trade free of all duties and taxes. Nadir Shah had taken Delhi and the Mahrattas, uncertain of the Persian monarch's intentions, wanted to avoid any un-necessary distractions in the Deccan. The Council at Bombay was happy to oblige him; noting the fate that had overtaken the Portuguese, they intended at all costs to avoid antagonising their dangerous neighbours.

In Calcutta, four years after its founding, so Broome in his history of the Bengal army declares, the garrison consisted of a guard of two sergeants, two corporals and twenty privates. In 1695 a rebellion in the district of Burdwan, sixty miles away to the north west, was used to justify a request to build some form of fortification, and subsequently Sir Charles Eyre, appointed in 1699 as the first President, cautiously built a small bastion which, after the Company's unfortunately close relationship with James II, he thought it wise to call Fort William.

As with Aurangzib's impending death the skies darkened over India, it was considered prudent quietly to extend the bastion into a fort, with the ramparts forming the sides of a pentagon, designed to accommodate all the British in Bengal. By 1705 the garrison had swollen to about 150 European soldiers including gunners. The town grew steadily in size and importance and with the progress of the fortifications the inhabitants became a little over-confident. A dispute with a local official over the passage of a ship was settled by force. The Viceroy of Bengal, generally termed for some reason the 'Nawab', took offence and imposed a blockade on all British establishments. The point was taken; the Governor apologised and substantial compensation was paid.

Thereafter the Council took care to avoid giving any grounds for offence. When Alivardi Khan usurped the nawabship and began his long drawn out struggle with the Mahrattas, permission was obtained to dig a ditch some seven miles in extent round the city, as it had now become. It was an absurd precaution in view of the size of the garrison, and it was never completed. The defences of the fort were, however, improved.

The Mahrattas never penetrated to eastern Bengal, and Calcutta as a secure haven on the fringe of the desolation they wrought attracted many Indian merchants. The Company, however, thought it wise to abandon its factory at Patna until the times were more settled. By 1746 the garrison was organised in three companies under a captain-and-chief-engineer with a salary of £200 a year; there was a second captain at £150, a captain-lieutenant at £100, a first lieutenant fireworker (an artilleryman) at £75, a second lieutenant fireworker at £60; ensigns received £50 per year, sergeant bombardiers 2s per diem, corporal bombardiers 1s 6d and gunners and drummers 1s.

Despite the presence of a Dutch settlement at Chinsura,

twenty-two miles up the river, and a French one at Chandernagore, about three miles closer, there was little friction
between the European trading communities, a happy state of
affairs that persisted despite the wars waged by their respective
nations in Europe, and a convention grew up that the Hooghly
should be treated as a neutral waterway, open to all. Alivardi
Khan did not trouble the Europeans so long as they did not
trouble him, but he died in 1756 and the period of prosperity
and tranquillity came abruptly to an end.

Madras, too, was little affected by the wars raging inland.
One further important acquisition the Council made before the
end of the seventeenth century. In 1690 Raja Ram, seeing the
Moghul armies under Zulfikar Khan closing in on his refuge in
Gingee fort and being desperate for money, offered to sell the
Company a semi-ruined fort at the village of Tegnapatam,
about two miles from Cuddalore and sixteen from the new
French settlement at Pondicherry. The Council decided to buy
it; they proposed to renovate it and use it to keep an eye on the
French whose activities they viewed with considerable mistrust.

In addition to the fort itself Raja Ram sold 'all the ground,
woods and rivers round the said fort within random shot of a
great gun'. The Council sent to Tegnapatam the largest gun
in Madras, manned by the most skilful of their gunners. Fired
with great ceremony at maximum range the shot actually landed
on the far side of Cuddalore; no doubt in those troubled times a
single shot hurtling over their town caused little alarm to the
citizens. The new fort was christened Fort St David. Raja Ram
found it advisable to leave Gingee secretly and hurriedly, but
after scrutinising the deeds of sale Zulfikar Khan confirmed the
Company in its new acquisition.

At the turn of the century Madras, although as a Presidency
merely the equal of Bombay and Calcutta, had become, for all
practical purposes, the centre of British power in India. Its
garrison, somewhat smaller than that of Bombay, varied
between two, three or four companies of infantry, excluding a
couple that were normally stationed at Fort St David. The
companies included a substantial number of Topasses which the
Directors thriftily noted 'are cheaper by one half' than European
soldiers. In a letter of 13 February 1685, the Directors suggested
to the Governor 'that he should raise a mounted militia. If you

could persuade all the rich men of Fort St George to the number of 100 English, Jews, Portuguese and Hindus to keep each of them a horse and arms at their charge . . . it might be a brave additional strength upon any sudden occasion. And you may appoint a captain and officers to exercise the troop once in two or three months as a militia or city troop.' One was duly raised, but its efficiency seems to have matched the remarkably small number of parades the Directors thought adequate.

In 1709 the Council recommended the promotion of Lieutenant Roach to the rank of Captain-Major, so that he would have unquestioned authority over all the garrisons on the Coromandel coast. The need for a proper central military authority was clearly demonstrated in 1713 when Robert Raworth, the Deputy Governor of the Presidency and Commander at Fort St David, aware that his warehouses in Madras were lamentably deficient of the silver bullion they ought to contain, declared himself independant. He fired on troops sent from Madras and for three months deadlock ensued. A number of his soldiers deserted him and eventually he agreed to yield the fort in return for a safe conduct to Pondicherry. Raworth sailed to France and died shortly after arriving in Paris. Had there been a clearly designated Commander-in-Chief at Madras, the duty of the troops in Fort St David would have been clear beyond any doubt and any who refused to obey his orders would undoubtedly have been guilty of mutiny.

On 21 October 1717 in the Consultations at Madras it was recorded that the President 'constitutes Lieutenant John Roach major of all the Honbl Companies forces on the coast of Choromandell and Island of Sumatra. Agreed that his pay as major be 20 Pagodas per mensem' (£8). Roach was soon in trouble. He was accused of abducting a young girl but managed to clear himself on the grounds he had been appointed her guardian. He went on sick leave to Calcutta, but instead of returning at its expiry he decided to sail on to Manilla. The Councillors, angry at this casual treatment of his military duties, resolved in the Consultations for 31 January 1719: 'The manner of Major Roach's quitting the service here appears to the Board to be no better than desertion. Agreed that Major Roach be discharged of his military commission and of the Honble Company's service under this Presidency.'

Later in the year Ensign Clarke was discharged on the grounds of 'incorrigible sottishness and being on two successive occasions drunk and incapable while commanding the guard'. Nothing more is heard of Clarke; Roach, however, knew the answer to the instructions of mere Councils. He returned to England and convinced the Directors so strongly of his earnest devotion to duty that in 1724 he was re-appointed Major of the Madras Garrison with an allowance of two servants 'to support the grandeur of a field officer'. He appears to have been the first field officer in the Company's service officially appointed by the Directors.

If the quality of the officers was poor, that of their men was worse. In 1721 the Council wrote to the Directors that the total garrisons of Fort St George and Fort St David amounted to 545 all ranks, only 245 of whom were Europeans 'of whom the greater part are infirm'. The remainder were Topasses, 'most of whom we are obliged to take tho' good for little'. Recruiting adequate numbers of English soldiers proved extremely difficult, especially in view of the high deathrate from disease. The Council at one juncture remarked plaintively that while it was perhaps unavoidable that the Company should find most of their recruits from the prison at Newgate, they thought it injudicious to plunder the lunatic asylums and suggested that enlistments from Bedlam should be stopped.

Opportunities for training the men in much more than how to stand to attention when the Governor passed by were hard to find. In 1719, for instance, the garrison officers pointed out to the Governor with some justification that as their troops had to find sixteen guards daily, their men suffered excessive fatigue and there was no time for any kind of training. At any one time two of the three companies stationed in Madras were on guard and the third resting, a state of affairs that in any climate would have placed an intolerable physical strain on the men. On the other hand the Council found it necessary to decree that soldiers should be permitted to run public houses only when the ships of the Company were in port. At this time, as in Bombay, the European soldiers wore red coats, the three companies being distinguished by red, yellow or green facings.

The standard of the gunners whose skill and courage would be crucial in the event of a siege was little better. Known as the

gunroom crew, they served under a chief gunner and appeared
to be organised mainly as a form of relief for needy sailors who
had probably been discharged from their ships for good reason.
In the paymaster's report for 1724 it was stated that the gunroom 'was lookt on as a lodging workhouse to relieve poor
sailors and at the same time be of use to the garrison'. At that
time the gunroom crew consisted of 46 Europeans, 52 Portuguese (an interesting distinction) and 30 lascars. In 1740 when
Raghoji Bhonsla and his Mahrattas came storming into the
Carnatic the Council made a hurried review of the defences
and discovered that 100 gunners had to man 200 guns, a
handsome allowance of two guns to each man. They dismantled
some outlying redoubts, but otherwise did little effective to
remedy this astonishing disproportion. Admittedly the guns
were mostly naval 24-pounder cannon and virtually immovable,
so that the gunners would only have to man at one time those
actually in a position to engage an enemy.

In addition to the Europeans the Company maintained a
force of about 300 peons. These were, in practical terms,
nothing more than armed contract labour hired under their own
local leaders; they manned the custom posts and policed the
town outside the walls of Fort St George. One Governor,
horrified by their slackness and indiscipline, directed that British
officers should give them some training, but if the order was ever
obeyed it was soon conveniently forgotten; the European officers
had neither the time nor the inclination for such a task.

During the first part of the eighteenth century this polyglot
force of seedy mercenaries appeared adequate. The Indian
princes, anxiously trying to preserve life and property amid the
chaos surrounding them, did not worry overmuch about peaceable European traders who might be unduly independent, but
who gave no offence and paid their rent promptly. The
Company prospered, paying dividends of up to 10 per cent, and,
as one of the few places in the Deccan where law and order still
prevailed, Madras continued to grow in wealth and importance.

On the Coromandel coast, as in Bengal, the European trading
communities, whatever the feuds of their nations in Europe,
contrived to remain on good terms with each other. When
after a dispute with a local magnate two British officers were
incarcerated, the French governor at Pondicherry interceded

for them and helped to obtain their release. Only on the high seas might the navies and privateers of nations at war prey upon each other's shipping. The Dutch, it is true, on one occasion attacked and captured Pondicherry, but at the Treaty of Ryswick, 1693, it was handed back to the French, proving the uselessness of such a proceeding.

Now in 1740 when the War of the Austrian Succession was about to break out the Company's affairs appeared peaceful and prosperous, as they had been for the past forty years. On the west coast the Council at Bombay was on good terms with the Mahrattas, although the depredations of Tulaji Angria, who had succeeded his father Kanhoji, caused losses to the Company's shipping that gave rise to some concern. In the Carnatic, the newly appointed nawab, Anwar-ud-din, ruling in the name of Nizam-ul-mulk, appeared to be, if not popular, at least firmly seated. In Bengal a devastating war raged between Alivardi Khan and the Mahrattas, but Calcutta and eastern Bengal were little affected. Among the European trading nations the Portuguese had lost most of their influence, while the British, Dutch, French and small Danish settlements lived together in remarkable amity.

The Company's armies, although almost totally untrained in any field manoeuvres, appeared sufficient to maintain internal order and man the ramparts; it was unfortunate that the ramparts themselves in places had fallen in and that houses encroached on them to a dangerous degree, but they were sufficient to repel marauders and keep out the ill-disposed. In London the Directors, watching the storm clouds gathering over Europe, felt some uneasiness. They sent out an experienced engineer officer, Major Knipe, to report on the state of the fortifications and take over the vacant appointment of Garrison Commander at Madras. Unfortunately he died a few months after he landed.

Lieutenant Eckman, a Swede who had joined the Company's army in 1706 as a private soldier, officiated as garrison commander, pending a replacement from England. In 1741 (when the War of the Austrian Succession broke out in Europe) it is unlikely that any in India foresaw the tremendous changes impending, not even the young Robert Clive, unhappily engaged in learning the Company's system of accounting in Madras.

Chapter 4

Anglo-French Rivalry in the Carnatic

In Madras the morning of 3 September 1746 drew on like any other September day. The sea breeze died away and the hot sun climbed the brassy blue sky, burning down fiercely on the humid atmosphere and bathing the whitewashed buildings in a glaring light. By the half circle platform of the seagate bulging out from the rusty red laterite walls of Fort St George, the lolling red-coated, white-gaitered sentries, clutching their long muskets and probably sweating profusely into their heavy clothing, could gaze out at the sapphire rollers, glittering almost diamond-bright in the sunlight, and watch them break in a white surf on the golden sand at their feet. The anchorage before them was empty save for one small East Indiaman, the *Princess Mary*, sporting the red and white barred ensign of the Company and swinging to her anchor, perhaps three-quarters of a mile from the shore.

Just outside the north wall of the fort lay Blacktown, an area about 1,000 yards square, bounded on the south by the ramparts of the fort, on the east by the sea, and inland on the west by a narrow canal dug for its protection. Here prosperous Armenian, Portuguese – many had migrated from St Thomé – and Hindu merchants lived; the minarets of a mosque and the steeple of the Portuguese Church rose above their substantial, verandahed, white-walled houses, while in the streets below the merchants went about their affairs, perhaps congregating at the great open square at the foot of the north rampart of the fort where much of their business was transacted.

To the north and west, beyond the boundary canal, came a strip of open ground and gardens and then the densely populated native city divided into two large quarters, the Pedda

Naik's petta (or suburb) and the Mutial petta. Along their teeming streets patient bullock carts would be seen slowly threading their way through a noisy jostling throng of men, some clad in loose white garments, others wearing only a loin-cloth, while in the bazaars the shopkeepers in their little one-roomed shops squatted behind their wares, or bargained noisily with prospective purchasers. Down the street might come some wealthy man reclining on a palanquin borne by two stout men, followed perhaps by two or three armed followers to emphasise his dignity and importance, or a servant with a horsehair whisk to keep the swarming flies off his noble countenance.

Beyond the native city the streets led to the spacious garden suburbs, where the wealthier British merchants had their garden houses and where no doubt some, emerging into the blinding daylight outside, regretted the copious drafts of claret and madeira with which they had whiled away the previous night. In all, at this time the population of Madras was estimated to amount to about 150,000 persons, of whom only three or four hundred were British.

In Fort St George itself, sometimes called 'White Town', perhaps a few off-duty soldiers and Company officials would be strolling down its narrow streets, flanked by tall white houses with pillared verandahs in front to keep out the worst of the sun; as they went they might gossip with friends leaning down from the upper verandahs, for the airless ground floors were frequently relegated to the role of warehouses. In his palatial mansion in the central square of the fort Nicholas Morse, the Governor, had much on his mind. The business of the year was slowing to a halt and in a few weeks the north-east monsoon would close the anchorage to shipping. It could not come too soon. The French under their tiresome Governor, Joseph François Dupleix, had been behaving oddly of late. When, two years earlier, the news came of a war in Europe between their two countries, Dupleix had written suggesting that in accordance with past practice there should be no hostilities 'east of the Cape' (presumably he meant the Cape of Good Hope). Morse would have been happy to oblige him, but he knew a naval squadron under Commodore Barnet, consisting of three ships of the line, third raters, and a frigate of 20-guns, had been sent out by the British Government with the express purpose of capturing Pondicherry, and he could only reply that he had no authority to speak for the actions of His Britannic Majesty's officers. Dupleix then appealed to the Nawab, Anwar-ud-din, and that high official wrote forbidding any hostilities on the territory of the Great Moghul.

Fortunately, when in 1745 Barnet appeared, the sailor proved amenable and agreed not to attack Pondicherry, although with its crumbling fortifications, in little better shape than those of Madras, it must have fallen an easy victim. But the Commodore, with some justice, refused to deny himself the prize money to be derived from capturing French merchantmen on the high seas, and later that year, before he sailed to spend the monsoon months at Mergui on the Burmese coast, he seized some rich merchantmen belonging to the 'Compagnie des Indes'.

Dupleix resented their loss. In January 1746 French troops from Pondicherry made a threatening demonstration towards Fort St David and only withdrew when Barnet's ships appeared. After this episode Morse wrote to Anwar-ud-din to protest, and the Nawab assured him that in no circumstances would he permit hostilities on Indian soil. Since then the situation had worsened. In the spring Barnet, a brave and energetic seaman, died of a fever and command devolved on the next senior officer, Captain Peyton. Peyton seemed uneasy about his sudden elevation and only interested in repairing his ships which, after two years in tropical waters, were cranky and far from watertight. In June Peyton, with his squadron now enlarged to six, sailed away to the port of Trincomali in Ceylon, the only east coast harbour where he could careen and refit his ships. On the way he encountered a French squadron of nine ships carrying some 2,000 French and 1,000 African soldiers under François Mahé de La Bourdonnais, Governor of the French-held island of Mauritius. The French squadron, except for a single line-of-battle ship, the *Achille* of seventy guns, consisted of warships the Frenchman had improvised by arming merchantmen. Despite the disparity of numbers, Peyton should have been able to give a good account of himself, but he contented himself with a long range cannonade and went on to Trincomali. With the way open La Bourdonnais wasted no time in bringing his ships to Pondicherry.

In June, after his refit, Peyton sailed again northwards. La Bourdonnais came out to challenge him, but, avoiding action, Peyton passed by Madras, anchored off Pulicat, paused there briefly, then set course towards Bengal, intending apparently to spend the monsoon months in the mouth of the Hooghly. With the French now free to sail where they wished, Morse fervently hoped that the monsoon would break early, or that they would respect the Nawab's prohibition against indulging in hostilities on land. Ominously enough, in August La Bourdonnais appeared off Madras with his ships, bombarded Fort St George for a brief period, and then sailed away. It seemed a pointless gesture unless he was seeing how Peyton would react. By now he must know that the timid British sailor had left the Coromandel coast.

Before the day ended Morse had his worst fears confirmed. Lookouts reported sails to the southward and soon ships with the golden Lilies of France fluttering from their mastheads came to anchor opposite St Thomas's Mount. Then boats started ferrying men and equipment ashore while a marching column joined them from the direction of Pondicherry. Clearly a full-scale French attack impended. To meet it Morse could call on the regular garrison amounting to about two hundred so-called Europeans, about one hundred gunners under a corpulent and middle-aged chief gunner named Smith, whose honesty was not above suspicion, about two officers and thirty-five ratings from the *Princess Mary*, the local militia composed of some 150 able-bodied European civilians and four to five hundred peons armed with matchlocks, swords and shields. The senior soldier in the garrison was still the ageing, incompetent and pugnacious Peter Eckman.

Morse called a conference of his council and the principal soldiers, including Eckman, Smith and the two other company commanders, de Gingins, a valiant but muddle-headed Swiss, and Holland. Morse knew nothing of things military and soon had good reason to believe his experts knew little more. A heated argument developed between Eckman and the Chief Gunner, Smith. Eckman wanted to man the ramparts of both Fort St George and Blacktown, but Smith, supported by most of the others, objected that the numbers of garrison were insufficient for such an extensive perimeter, especially as the ramparts of Blacktown were so dilapidated that in places only the houses built against them prevented them from collapsing. The garrison would undoubtedly be dangerously thinly spread if both Blacktown and Fort St George were held, but on the other hand there was no source of drinking water in the fort and the French could cut off the supply. In the end it was decided to evacuate Blacktown, whereat Eckman left the meeting in a rage; as he passed the main guard he threw his sword on the ground, declaring he had no use for it as he could not defend Madras as he wished; he was subsequently charged with mutiny for his gesture, but it appears that it was finally accepted as no more than justifiable pique.

On the 4th, while bitter arguments distracted the garrison, La Bourdonnais methodically entrenched a camp the far side of the Triplicane lagoon near the sea-shore, about a mile to the south and out of range of the guns of the fort. On the 5th he moved a number of troops round the landward side of Madras and began to construct a camp and some batteries in the open ground between Blacktown and the Pedda Naik's petta. His move seemed to offer a chance to strike back at the Triplicane camp which it was judged must now be nearly empty. On the morning of the 6th, with considerable optimism, the peons were despatched to assault it. Grateful for the chance to escape from an unpleasant siege, they sallied out with great dash, fired a few random shots and disappeared into the countryside to become interested spectators of the battle.

On the morning of the 7th La Bourdonnais opened fire with five mortars from a battery near the bank of the lagoon to the south and ten more he had emplaced in the gardens to the west. The guns on the ramparts that could bear gave reply. But after a few ill-aimed rounds their gun-carriages, which had been made of inferior wood, fell to pieces, putting the cannon irretrievably out of action. That day the Chief Gunner, Smith, died of a heart attack. Hallyburton in the journal he kept of the siege observed caustically: 'Mr Smith our Chief Gunner, having by this time discovered that he was ill-used by his wife, and likewise that much would be laid to his charge for having hardly anything that belonged to his province in that readiness that had all along been expected of him, died

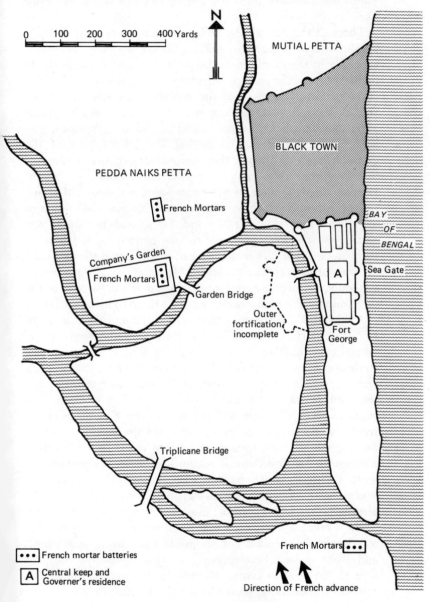

The First Siege of Madras

the day the enemy landed.' (Cole in his journal observed that
Smith died the day the siege began, and this seems the more
likely.)

Through the daylight hours the French maintained a steady
bombardment, firing salvoes of mortar bombs every half-hour,
generally in the direction of the central square of the Fort. As
night drew on, the slow, unrelenting fire continued, and under
cover of darkness most of the remaining peons and all the
Indian servants of the Europeans clambered down the ramparts and vanished into the night, as did the Topasses, gun
lascars and Portuguese composing the greater part of the
gunroom crew. Although they did not desert, the conduct of
the European soldiers gave considerable cause for alarm.
Despite the daily issue of good provisions and drams of arrack
and punch with which to keep up their spirits, Cole noted in
his journal that when Mr Monson, the second-in-council, was
passing by the main gate guard, two privates seized him by
the arm and told him in an insolent manner that the cup used
for measuring tots was too small. He observed of the garrison
generally, 'so drunken and mutinous was the behaviour of the
garrison that their officers did not trust them to make a sally'.

All through the 8th came the dull thudding of the discharges
from the mortars followed by the high pitched scream of the
bombs curving through the air before falling to the ground to
sizzle for a few moments before exploding with a crash. They
were reasonably easy to avoid, and casualties were few, but
the damage was considerable. By the evening, with the fort
running short of water and cut off by the French from the
fresh water springs, the guns silent and the garrison unfit to
make a sally, Morse thought it time to call a halt. He sent a
message to La Bourdonnais asking him if he was prepared to
treat. La Bourdonnais had no wish to prolong the siege; he
was afraid that Peyton with his ships might reappear; there had
already been one false alarm; in such circumstances, with most
of the French ashore, even that timid sailor could scarcely fail
to triumph. He replied that he would cease firing between six
and eight o'clock next morning so that emissaries could be
sent to the French camp. Meanwhile, to prevent the British
resolution hardening, he continued the bombardment.

Punctually at six o'clock on the morning of the 9th the

French mortars fell silent and Monson and Hallyburton went out to the French camp to discuss terms. La Bourdonnais told them as translated, 'Gentlemen, you'll give up your town and all within it. I will put you in possession again upon you paying the ransom.' Monson pressed him to say what the ransom would be. La Bourdonnais was not to be drawn into naming a sum, but he hinted broadly that it would not be excessive, and with this Monson had to be content. He returned to Fort St George to explain the proposals to Morse, and at eight o'clock the French mortars boomed out again. All through the day the firing continued and the night was once again punctuated by sudden vivid flashes of light followed by the heavy crump of the bombs. By morning on the 10th Morse had had enough; he decided to accept La Bourdonnais' terms. In the text of the capitulation it was agreed that,

'Fort St George and the town of Madras with all their dependencies shall today, 10 September, at two o'clock in the afternoon be put in the hands of La Bourdonnais . . . all the garrison and in general all the English who are in the fort and town shall remain prisoners of war; . . . the garrison shall be conducted to Fort St David prisoners of war; and if the town of Madras be restored by ransom the English shall be free to take possession again of their garrison to defend themselves against the people of the country. . . . Made and drafted in the French camp, 10 September 1746.'

The French duly marched into Madras, being met by Governor Morse at the watergate. Morse offered La Bourdonnais his sword and the Frenchman politely returned it. During the siege, out of a total of 500 Europeans about six of the garrison had been killed. La Bourdonnais had with him an army of about 3,400 French and Africans, of which he disembarked 1,800. The disproportion in numbers was not such as to justify the poor showing of the British. But with his guns out of action and his garrison either drunk or mutinous, or both, Morse was probably wise to surrender while he still had something with which to bargain, rather than to wait until the hopelessness of his position threw him naked into the hands of the French.

The next few days were spent haggling about the amount of the ransom. A sum of 1,100,000 pagodas (£400,000) was finally agreed, but now Dupleix interfered, and began to reveal his true aims. The ransom would have amply compensated the French for the loss of the cargoes captured by Barnet, but Dupleix wanted much more than merely to square his accounts. He had married a widow who had been born and bred in India; he probably knew more about the internal stresses that wracked the Moghul Empire than any other European in India; and his ambitions were unbounded. It was his weakness that he lacked the moderation and dispassionate sense of reality that his great rival – it might almost be said, pupil – Clive was later to display. He now set in motion a train of events that in due course was to bring disaster to the French and make the British, to their surprise and almost against their will, the foremost military power in India. He wrote curtly to La Bourdonnais telling him he had no right to make a treaty without his consent, and that he had in any case promised to give Madras back to Anwar-ud-din.

La Bourdonnais treated the letter with derision; as Governor of Mauritius he was not prepared to admit that Dupleix had any authority over his actions and could not, with any semblance of honour, repudiate the conditions agreed with Morse as the price of surrender. He continued to negotiate how the ransom should be paid. Dupleix, furious, resolved to supersede the obstreperous sailor; he ordered d'Esprémémil to take charge of Madras and sent three commissioners under an elderly general, de Bury, to enforce his decisions. He did not understand the nature of the man with whom he was dealing. La Bourdonnais ordered all the Pondicherry troops on board his ships, clapped them under hatches and arrested the Commissioners. Deadlock ensued and Dupleix had begun to give way when the weather intervened. On 2 October a storm blew up that scattered the French fleet. Hallyburton noted in his journal, 'The *Duc d'Orleans* and *Yanam* vessel which had on board bombs and mortars destined against Fort St David were lost also the *Phoenix* . . . they lost 1,200 men in the storm'. Four more of the French ships were dismasted. Now La Bourdonnais was anxious to be gone before the monsoon broke in earnest. By 10 October he signed a detailed capitulation with Morse and sailed away, writing to the Council at Pondi-cherry: 'Gentlemen, this is the capitulation which I thought proper to make with the English for the ransom of the town and its dependencies, the evacuation of which (by the French) must be at the furthest in January next.' He handed over charge of Madras to d'Espréménil, took his battered ships to Pondicherry, exchanged some heated words with Dupleix, then departed for Mauritius. He had accepted from Morse the sum of 100,000 pagodas as a small token of personal esteem and with the 80,000 that had been paid in cash he took ship for France never to return. Owing to his losses in shipping, he left some of his troops behind, but his departure robbed Dupleix of command of the sea, a loss that for the rest of the war was fatally to compromise his plans. A storm and a clash of personalities saved the British on the Coromandel coast and perhaps in India.

On 24 October 1746 Paradis, a Swiss Engineer officer in the service of the French, came to the wide and shallow estuary of the Adyar River just south of the old Portuguese settlement of St Thomé. He had with him 300 French soldiers and 700 sepoys. These were very different from the Company's peons; they were locally recruited, but Dupleix's predecessor, Dumas, had made the experiment of training and equipping them as fully fledged European infantry. As he peered across the muddy waters he could see a host of cavalry and a long row of the large and unwieldy guns beloved by the Indian princes lining the far bank.

Anwar-ud-din, angry at the way Dupleix had ignored his instructions and deeply sceptical of his professions to return Madras, had sent his eldest son, Mafuz Khan, with 10,000 men to take possession of the city. The French garrison refused point blank to surrender it without express orders from Dupleix; they tried to avoid a clash, but while awaiting orders from Pondicherry they found it necessary to drive away some Indian cavalry who had seized the fresh water spring from which Fort St George drew its supplies. Their action precipi-tated hostilities, but it is doubtful if Dupleix ever seriously intended to deliver Madras to the Nawab. Malleson, in his book *The French in India*, contended that Dupleix proposed to hand over Madras to the Nawab after he had first razed its fortifications. Whatever Dupleix may subsequently have written, events do not seem to bear this contention out. He now despatched Paradis with his men to reinforce the garrison.

Mafuz Khan, learning that Paradis with his little army was approaching, deployed his army along the banks of the Adyar to intercept it. As he gazed across the shallow waters at the Indian host, Paradis realised his force was in no small danger; it is significant that he made no attempt to negotiate a crossing, as might have been expected if Dupleix intended to achieve a compromise with the Nawab. Instead he decided to force his way through to Madras some four miles to the northward.

Mafuz Khan, on his elephant, watched with stupefied surprise as the French infantry, with the sepoys deployed on either flank, formed a long thin three-rank line and began to wade across the water. His heavy, slow-firing cannon belched out a single ill-directed salvo which the French disregarded, then as they neared the far bank a new sound broke on his ears. The French infantry began the steady rolling musketry that was already a familiar sound on the battlefields of Europe, but which at that time was unknown in India. The ill-organised mátchlock men of Mafuz's army loosed off an irregular and ragged volley and fled, leaving the cavalry to endure a fire to which they could make no effective reply; a charge into water, however shallow, could scarcely be thought of. After a few minutes the front ranks of the horsemen gave back, disordering the ranks behind; the backward movement gained momentum and soon there was an unruly rush back to the shelter of St Thomé. The French line, pouring out its deadly fire, pressed forward and a panic set in. A disorderly mob of horsemen galloped back through the narrow streets; then as they emerged from the far side another blast of musketry smote them. A detachment sent from Madras to escort Paradis and his men in had taken up positions just short of the old Portuguese settlement. Fired at from front and rear all control broke down and the fugitive horsemen streamed away westwards in hopeless disorder, leaving their artillery behind them. Little more than 1,000 French and French trained Indian infantry had routed an army ten times their size.

As soon as he heard the news a jubilant Dupleix directed that La Bordonnais' treaty with the British should be repudiated.

Barthélémy, now commanding at Madras, considered such conduct dishonourable and refused to obey the order. Dupleix replaced him with the victorious Swiss, and Paradis promptly declared that the treaty was void. Clive, and some others in Madras on parole not to carry arms against the French considered that the French breach of faith released them from their undertaking and escaped to Fort St David in disguise. They were soon to see more action.

Dupleix now determined to capture Fort St David and root the British out of their last stronghold in the Carnatic. He nominated General de Bury to command the expedition. It was a fortunate choice for the small British garrison at Fort St David, only about 200 strong. De Bury was old and lethargic, as Dupleix knew well, but he feared that if he gave command to the comparatively junior foreigner, Paradis, the rest of his senior officers would refuse to serve under him. De Bury, with a force of about 1,700 men, on 8 December 1746 marched by night to Cuddalore, intending to attack the British fort the next day. Next morning, feeling fatigued by their exertions of the previous night, they settled down to cook their morning meal on the outskirts of Cuddalore, and Mafuz Khan and his brother, Mohammed Ali, who, at the invitation of the British, were lurking in the neighbourhood with their troops, caught them unawares. As the mass of cavalry suddenly erupted in front of them the French threw down their cooking pots and tried to snatch up their muskets; it was too late; all attempt at an orderly resistance soon vanished and a mad race developed back to the sheltering walls of Pondicherry about sixteen miles distant. Fortunately for the French, Mafuz's men found their baggage train almost irresistibly attractive, and most of them managed to escape. A small part of British infantry tumbled out after them from Fort St David but were hopelessly outdistanced. Unpressed by the cavalry the pace of the flight soon slackened and the French formed a battle line too strong for the British to attack; then both sides returned to their respective bases. Dupleix was compelled to recognise that he could not hope to attack Fort St David successfully until he had made his peace with Anwar-ud-din.

But already that month Commodore Thomas Griffin with two ships from England had arrived at the mouth of the

Hooghly; he relieved the pusillanimous Peyton and at once prepared to take the British squadron back to the Coromandel coast. Meanwhile Dupleix opened negotiations with Anwar-ud-din and with his usual diplomacy, assisted by a present of 150,000 rupees, convinced the Prince that his best interests lay in supporting the French. The Nawab withdrew Mafuz Khan but, as time was to show, cherished little affection for the victors of the battle of St Thomé.

However, the way was now clear for another attempt on Fort St David. On 3 March 1747 Paradis led a substantial French force on Cuddalore. But as he drew near to the town against light British resistance, to his mortification he saw the masts of British warships coming up over the horizon, and as the full British squadron came into view he had no alternative but to beat a hasty retreat to Pondicherry. Admiral Griffin, as he became, landed 500 sailors and 150 marines as a temporary reinforcement to the garrison of the fort and placed one of his ship's captains, Gibson, to take command. During the rest of the year he cruised off the coast while a stream of reinforcements steadily reached the British stronghold.

In the face of British naval supremacy Dupleix was helpless. He wrote home urgently for ships, and a French naval squadron early in 1748 managed to elude the blockading British squadron and anchor off Pondicherry. Although they were too weak to engage the British ships with any chance of success, the French succeeded in luring Griffin away from the coast. Dupleix struck at once. A French force numbering 800 Europeans and 1,000 sepoys on 27 June marched out to Cuddalore. Convinced the British had evacuated the town they sought to occupy it after dark. They fell into a well-laid British ambush; in the darkness the French panicked and once again were well on their way back to Pondicherry before they could be rallied. Their defeat was largely due to the new British commander, Major Stringer Lawrence, a recently retired and experienced regimental officer in the regular army who had arrived from England on 1 January 1748 and in six months had done something towards turning the Company's ill-disciplined set of ruffians into soldiers.

Dupleix had lost his last chance; in July warships from England started to fill the sea opposite Cuddalore; by the 30th a fleet of thirty ships under a famous Admiral, the Hon. Edward Boscawen, swung to their anchors; among them were thirteen whose long hulls, chequered by a double line of black gun ports, revealed them to be ships of the line. Such an armada had never before been seen in Indian waters. The news of its arrival filtered through to Anwar-ud-din in his palace at Arcot; he wondered if the moment to take his revenge on the French might not have arrived.

Boscawen carried out with him a large number of soldiers. The British Government was determined to avenge the French capture of Madras by meting out a similar fate to Pondicherry. Boscawen had been given the title of Admiral, General, and Commander-in-Chief of all forces in the East Indies, and must rank as one of the earlier of interservice theatre commanders. When he had assembled all the available land forces, Boscawen, according to his despatches, organised them as follows:

Unit	Officers	Men	Total
Marine Battalion	32	818	850
1st Battalion Indep. Coys	33	591	624
2nd Battalion Indep. Coys	34	593	627
Company's European Battalion	28	725	753
Artillery			148
Seamen's Battalion			1,097
		Total	4,099

In addition he had 2,000 semi-trained sepoys, and subsequently Anwar-ud-din contributed some 1,500 cavalry of dubious value. Before an army numbering about 7,500, including 4,000 European troops, Pondicherry appeared doomed.

But there existed some weaknesses. The Company's Europeans, about half of whom came from the Bombay European companies, could still be considered only semi-trained and unused to acting as an infantry battalion. The independent companies were formed from the rejects of British regular battalions in England and Ireland, stiffened by a number of Jacobite rebels who had been offered the alternatives of serving in India or hanging in England. In a siege the most important component of a force was its artillery; it may be significant that Boscawen made no mention of any artillery officers, although some must have been present; no doubt it was expected that sailors could fire the cannon as well as any land-lubbers, but firing broadsides at sea was very different from the type of precision shooting needed to breach a rampart; nothing is said about engineer officers, although in that most technical of land operations, a siege, their role was the most important of all. In his later despatches Boscawen mentions his engineer officers, but only to complain of their inexperience and in-eptitude. The sepoys do not appear to have made any serious contribution to the operations; it may be conjectured that they were still little better than the Company's peons, and that the British officers supervising them had yet to understand how to handle them. John Hallyburton, commanding a troop of Indian cavalry, was murdered by one of his own troopers, apparently aggrieved by a reprimand. The gravest drawback of all was the lack of time before the monsoon made the coast dangerous to shipping.

Boscawen, however, wasted little time in organising his troops and on 8 August they set out for Pondicherry sixteen miles to the north. They do not appear to have hurried, for it was not until 12 August that they came to a minor fort guarding the ford where the coastal road crossed the Ariancopang river which formed the boundary of French territory and was about two miles from Pondicherry itself. Boscawen, hearing that the fort was lightly held, resoved to assault it at dawn the following day. The storming party consisted of the piquets, normally half a company per battalion, and the grenadier companies and therefore cannot have been more than 500 strong. The stormers rushed at the fort with great dash, to find themselves confronted by a dry ditch backed by walls too high to clamber over. Without ladders and unable to assault, they exchanged fire for a short time with the defenders, who amounted to more than a 100 French troops firing from behind cover and supported by artillery. The one-sided battle could have only one conclusion; their commander, Major Goodyer, was killed and the attackers, abandoning a hopeless task, withdrew, suffering heavy casualties. This fiasco was bad enough, but to compound their folly the British started to besiege the little fort in due form, digging trenches to allow an assault party to approach the walls under cover and erecting batteries with which to breach the walls.

In this way a fortnight was wasted during which a troop of about fifty horse that Dupleix had organised charged a forward trench and captured Stringer Lawrence, fuming furiously at his nimble infantry, who had made a hurried departure. Boscawen was now deprived of his only two officers with any experience of land warfare. Eventually a lucky shot caused the magazine of the fort to explode and the French garrison retreated to Pondicherry. As Clive observed afterwards, the fort should either have been bypassed or masked by a small force while the main British army closed in on Pondicherry.

The limits of French territory were marked by a high and virtually impenetrable thorn hedge, called the boundary hedge; it was pierced in four places to admit roads, each entrance guarded by a redoubt. Boscawen, for some unexplained reason, marched round the hedge, neutralising the redoubts, and began to dig trenches and erect batteries to attack Pondicherry from the northwest. All supplies therefore had to be conveyed round the hedge or else be landed on beaches to the north of the town. Dupleix at once constructed batteries which could sweep these beaches with their fire.

Owing to the inexperience of the engineer officers, the approaches were begun 1,500 yards from the French fortifications and more time was expended on a laborious advance. At last on 25 September two batteries, one mounting six 24-pounder and two 18-pounder guns, the other two 24-pounder, two 18-pounder guns and five large mortars, opened fire. The mortar bombs all fell short of the French defences and it became apparent that the range to the ramparts was 800 yards not 600, as Boscawen's engineers had calculated; at 800 yards the British roundshot rebounded from the walls doing very little damage. Dupleix contemptuously mounted guns on the wall that was meant to be breached and silenced the British batteries.

Time was running out; in the hot, sticky, insanitary trenches the troops had begun to fall sick in alarming numbers. It became difficult to find a sufficient number of fit men to man them. An assault could not long be delayed. But now the British engineer officers regretfully had to acknowledge that they had selected an impossible approach. The ground in front was marshy; it could not be entrenched, and the perfidious French had made matters worse by flooding it near the walls. The approach would have to be abandoned, and there was no time to begin another. Boscawen's fury at this news can well be imagined. As a last restort he ordered the fleet to bombard Pondicherry; he wrote, 'I found nothing left but to endeavour to annoy them as much as possible and therebye reduce them to the necessity of surrendering'. The ships warped in to about 1,000 yards of the shore, but were then stopped by the shallowness of the water. During the whole of one day there was a prodigious expenditure of ammunition by both sides; the British ships lost two men and a bowsprit; Dupleix remarked that his only casualty was a Malabari woman who selected an unfortunate moment to cross a street.

The last hope had failed. The monsoon was about to break; on 30 September Boscawen called a council of war which decided to raise the siege. There was no panic withdrawal. From 1 to 4 October stores were backloaded onto the ships, and cannon too damaged to be moved were blown up. Then at dawn on 6 October 1748, with drums beating and colours flying, the British marched away, challenging the French to pursue them, an invitation that Dupleix declined. The French garrison had numbered about 1,800 Europeans and had not escaped unscathed. In one sally Paradis had been killed, a grave loss for Dupleix. Out of the 4,000 Europeans besieging the French town it was stated by Robert Orme that 1,065 were either killed or died from sickness. This number, assuming the normal proportion of wounded and convalescents, would imply that virtually none of the attackers were on their feet at the end and must be an exaggeration. Probably the casualties from all sources totalled about 1,000; this figure would be heavy enough and suggests that it was lack of skill not of courage that led to the British reverse.

The monsoon brought all prospect of operations to an end; then in November the news arrived that the preliminaries of a peace treaty had been signed between France and England at Aix-la-Chapelle on 19 April, that hostilities were to cease in India within six months of that date, and that the French had undertaken to restore Madras. On 28 November Stringer

Lawrence returned from Pondicherry speaking well of the treatment he had received, but ever after manifested a marked dislike of his captors. Discussions over the arrangements for the return of Madras to the British dragged on, and it was not until 21 August 1749 that the Union Jack was once more hoisted over Fort St George. Many of its citizens had left Madras, and the French had done some damage to Blacktown, clearing fields of fire for the fort and improving its defences. The Directors in London decided to keep Fort St David as the capital of the Presidency and reduce Madras to the status of a subsidiary. Otherwise it appeared that the conflict in the Carnatic had accomplished nothing and that the two Companies, having indulged in an expensive and futile war, would once more settle down to their true role of trading and amassing satisfactory dividends for their proprietors at home. But Dupleix thought otherwise.

Chapter 5

Dupleix's Great Design

On 1 May 1749 Stringer Lawrence contemplated Devicotta fort 500 yards away across the muddy estuary of the Coleroon river. Flanked by copses of coconut palms and standing about 100 yards back from the low river bank, its high vulnerable walls studded by towers at irregular intervals looked an easy target to his experienced eye. The day before he had disembarked a force of 800 Europeans and 1,500 sepoys at the mouth of the river which ran into the Bay of Bengal about twenty miles south of Fort St David, and marched four miles up its northern bank, as he thought, to camp opposite the fort. As he scrutinised his objective some of his officers came to report that they were camped not on the river bank but on an island formed by two branches of the Coleroon. He shrugged off the news. It would make sallies by the garrison more difficult and guard his rear against interference by the Tanjore army; on the other hand it would undoubtedly complicate an assault on a breach, but the prospect did not worry him. Judging the distance with care he marked out a site for a siege battery about 500 yards away from the fort across the water.

At this time Stringer Lawrence was fifty-two years old. His portrait by Sir Joshua Reynolds reveals him as a stocky, strongly-built man standing four-square on sturdy legs, planted wide apart. His face was solid and broad, the eyes steady and honest, the mouth strong and determined. His body was inclined to corpulence and his waistcoat bulged gracefully in the fashion common in that age. His early history is obscure; his father was probably an apothecary in Hereford and it is likely that he enlisted as a private soldier. At the age of thirty he was gazetted as an ensign in Clayton's regiment, later the 14th Foot. He was thirty-eight before he reached the rank of lieutenant and forty-eight that of captain. His progress depended solely on merit in a system where merit counted for less than money or influence. No doubt he witnessed many a young man buy promotion over his head, but during his long service as a regimental officer he had the opportunity of learning the basic essentials of soldiering, an opportunity it is evident he did not neglect. The slowness of his promotion appears in no way to have embittered him, although by the time he became a captain he knew the rank of major in the regular army to be outside his reach.

He saw service in Flanders, Spain and the rebellion of 1745, then in 1746 he applied to the Directors of the Company to be appointed Major and Garrison Commander of Madras, the appointment made vacant by the death of Major Knipe in 1743. He was accepted, retired from the army and stepped ashore at Fort St David to take over his first independent command at the age of fifty. Now with twenty years and more of soldiering behind him, he was the complete professional. He knew every facet of handling an infantry battalion, the basic skills of the battlefield and how the British soldier thought and reacted. His detailed mastery of his profession gave him a quiet and composed self-assurance; he accepted dictation from no one in matters that he considered his own province and was prepared to resign if his wishes were not respected. He was able through his own unassailable competence to impose his authority on his juniors without effort or needless self-assertion, and in consequence received the unstinting affection and loyalty of his subordinates. He was perhaps a little unimaginative, impatient of paper or politics, unable to understand the point of view of men who knew nothing of soldiering, or to persuade them to understand his; but his integrity shone from him; he was an Englishman and proud of it, a soldier and proud of it. He would never do anything to demean himself, his profession or his country.

Such was the obscure regimental officer who now began a career that was to imprint his name indelibly on the history of the Company he served. Immediately after his arrival at Fort St David he set himself to turn the Company's courageous but

ill-disciplined ruffians into soldiers on the model of the regular
army he knew so well. He divided them into seven companies
each consisting of three officers, a captain, lieutenant and an
ensign, four sergeants, four corporals, three drummers and
seventy private soldiers. The companies, however, retained
their independent status, being grouped together to form an
infantry battalion only while actually on service.

He adopted a similar organisation for the sepoys, turning
their leaders into officers with properly defined duties and
responsibilities, and arming them and drilling them after the
European fashion. He did not place them permanently under
British officers, but allotted them to British commanders for
specific tasks. There are no documents showing their organisation at this time, but a muster roll of a sepoy company in 1755,
as quoted by Lt-Col Wilson in his history of the Madras army,
shows it as consisting of a subedar company commander; four
jemadars, eight havildars (sergeants), eight naiks (corporals),
two colour men, and eighty-four privates. Probably this
organisation evolved over a period of time, and much had to be
done before the new traditions were understood and absorbed.
Sepoys played no significant part at the siege of Pondicherry,
and it was to be some time before they could be relied on in a
crisis, but regular pay and a proper system of organisation and
subordination gradually had their effect.

His officers were young and inexperienced, but numbered
some of great promise. In particular he noticed a newly commissioned officer, Robert Clive. Clive, like himself, was of
rather heavy build and not particularly prepossessing; he had
a heavy face, apt to appear sullen in repose, but an almost
overmastering personality smouldered within him. He could be
moody and irascible, impatient of restraint; he was not particularly popular with his fellows, not an easy man to get on with.
But beside the immense driving force caged within him could
be sensed a powerful mind. He was not merely a leader fit for
any enterprise, but one who would think and calculate, be
second to none in daring, but neither foolish nor rash. Of course,
despite his readiness to advance his own opinions, he knew
nothing of real soldiering, but Lawrence marked him down as
a man who from his character had to lead, one who if guided
gently and allowed the free exercise of his talents promised

achievements above the ordinary. He subsequently wrote of him: 'This young man's early genius surprised and gained my attention as well before as at the siege of Devicotta.'

The wise old soldier was one of the few of those set over him who ever succeeded in controlling Clive and gaining his respect. But then the 'old gentleman', as his irreverent juniors called him, by his steadfastness, his justice and his unshakeable good sense earned the respect and affection of all who served under him. Now he had to capture the fort of Devicotta, garrisoned, it was said, by 5,000 men from the army of the Raja of Tanjore.

That state was ruled by a Mahratta descended from a branch of the great Sivaji's family. Three brothers had ruled it in turn, then the succession had been disputed. Sahoji, a son of the last ruler, asked the French Governor at Pondicherry, Dumas, for help. Dumas agreed to assist him if in return he would cede the French the useful port of Karikal, situated on one of the mouths of the Cauveri delta. Sahoji accepted these terms, but triumphed without French assistance; he saw no point in paying for a service he had not received and refused to hand over the port. The French did not share his viewpoint. After a tortuous series of intrigues and with the help of Chunda Sahib, then Governor of Trichinopoly, the French caused Sahoji to be deposed and replaced by his illegitimate half-brother, Partap Singh. All this had happened some seven years before.

Now that the British and French were at peace, but nevertheless scarcely friends, Sahoji thought he might obtain British aid with which to regain his kingdom. He promised the Council at Fort St David to give them the town of Devicotta at the mouth of the Coleroon river and to pay all their expenses, if they lent him a detachment of British troops. He asserted that he had but to appear and a popular revolt in his favour would sweep him to power.

Admiral Boscawen, who feared the dangerous anchorage at Madras with good reason, hoped that after excavating a channel across the bar at the mouth of the river it would be possible to use its mouth as a safe harbour and strongly supported Sahoji's request; the Council with a large number of idle soldiers, who were not to be denied their pay on that account, concurred with the Admiral, and in March 1749 Captain Cope, with a force of 800 Europeans and 1,500 sepoys, set out for Tanjore. Cope speedily discovered that the local inhabitants had no love for Sahoji; he also disliked the appearance of Devicotta fort, and as owing to an inexcusable muddle, despite the presence of British warships off the mouth of the river from which he could borrow them, he possessed no siege artillery, he decided the fortifications were too strong for him and returned to Fort St David empty-handed. The mortified Council, with no prospect of receiving payment for the cost of the expedition, now sent Stringer Lawrence with orders at the least to capture Devicotta.

Cope's experience troubled Lawrence not at all. He knew Cope to be an amiable, courageous blockhead. By 8 June he had completed his battery and mounted in it four 24-pounder cannon. He then ordered three rounds to be fired. The shot carried well, smashing into the mud-faced ramparts. Having demonstrated the power of his guns, he wrote to the fort commander giving that officer an opportunity to surrender without wasting any more time or risking an unnecessary loss of life. He concluded his letter, 'as my batteries are now ready to open fire I send this to let you know that if you open your gates and receive the troops under my command into the fort your persons and effects will be safe and your persons well treated, but if on the contrary you obstinately hold out the place I will beat down the wall, enter your town and then no man need expect quarter'.

The enemy commander, startled by this insolent demand from the small force at his gate, replied to the effect that he would be failing in his duty if he surrendered the fort, that he had a high sense of duty, and that anyway the fort was impregnable. Lawrence unemotionally ordered his battery into action, and by 12 June 1750 blew a large breach in its walls. There remained the problem of crossing the 300 yards of water to the far bank. A ship's carpenter had built a raft capable of transporting 400 men and moored it by night in a hiding place opposite the fort. He now swam across the river and attached a line to a tree on the far bank unperceived by the garrison.

At two o'clock on a hot and overcast afternoon, as Stringer Lawrence dared not delay for he feared the heavy sky portended a storm, the British force crossed the river under a heavy fire from the fort. Despite casualties, all were over by four o'clock.

The garrison, without attempting to block the breach, had thrown up an entrenchment to its left to enfilade its approaches, and some Tanjore horse had been seen in the neighbourhood. Stringer Lawrence now ordered Clive with 30 Europeans and 400 sepoys to assault the entrenchment and cover the left flank of the stormers, and detached a further 300 sepoys to safeguard the right.

Clive nearly met with disaster. When he was about fifty yards from the enemy position he stumbled on a wide, muddy nullah. He crossed it with his Europeans, but his sepoys hung back. Then some Tanjore cavalry whirled round the end of the entrenchment, came in on his flank and rear and cut his little platoon to pieces. Clive, nimbly ducking away from a sword cut, was lucky to reach the nullah alive. Lawrence at once sent a reinforcement which carried the entrenchment without difficulty. Then, while the stormers approached the breach, he personally led two platoons of Europeans to support the sepoys guarding his right who were threatened by another body of Tanjore horse. After receiving a couple of volleys, these made off while the rest of the stormers rushed up the breach and into the fort against a feeble resistance. By five o'clock, for the loss of thirty Europeans and fifty sepoys, the fort was in the hands of the British.

The little army spent the night manning the ramparts, their arms beside them, ready for a counter-attack; none came, but as the hot, humid dawn came up Lawrence saw about five miles away a pagoda and sent Cope with a small force to occupy it. The Indian temples, known as pagodas, were surrounded by high walls and made useful improvised strongpoints. The Tanjore army, horrified to think of infidels desecrating their holy places, attacked it that night, but were beaten off without difficulty.

Now negotiations were opened. Partap Singh was ready to cede Devicotta if in return the British withdrew their support for Sahoji and gave back the pagoda. The Council at Fort St David accepted. Sahoji was pensioned off to Madras and a probably more secure way of life; but the Company, by abandoning their protégé while obtaining benefits for themselves, however realistic their decision, made the whole operation appear little better than the blackmail of a weaker state. Partap Singh's readiness to treat owed something to his anxiety about events elsewhere in the Deccan. In 1748 the great Nizam-ul-mulk had died and it was now apparent that the succession would be disputed. In the chaotic days that almost certainly lay ahead it might be an advantage to have the fort at Devicotta garrisoned by friendly British soldiers, and the European trade in any case would bring extra revenue into his country.

The ease with which Stringer Lawrence triumphed over a very superior enemy and the apparent invincibility of European infantry, a characteristic soon to be shared by European-trained sepoys, merits further consideration; it was to be of paramount importance in the years to come. Indian battles at this period in some ways resembled the encounters of the ancient Greeks as related by Homer. The issue of a battle was often settled by the heroes of either side engaging each other in single combat. Once a commander had left the battlefield or was slain, his troops would either flee or surrender.

The armies themselves, after the pattern of those of mediaeval Europe, were composed of nobles and chieftains, each, as was his duty, bringing a contingent of retainers and hired mercenaries to the banners of his overlord; the chiefs fought mounted on elephants, surrounded by their followers generally on horseback. After the immediate need for an army had vanished, the nobles returned to their estates and the mercenaries were disbanded. Except among the Mahrattas and in some Rajput states there was little continuity of service or attempt to study the techniques of the battlefield. The soldiers, individually courageous enough, lacked discipline and were incapable of any but the simplest of manoeuvres; since most were mounted, armies lacked the stability imparted by the slower moving infantry. At night, so R. O. Cambridge asserted in his contemporary account of the war in Hindustan, sentries were seldom posted and most of the troops, having consumed an inordinate quantity of rice or stupefied themselves with drugs or alcohol, were virtually incapable of fighting, a characteristic the Europeans were quick to exploit.

There were of course exceptions; Sivaji introduced a proper system of subordination by appointing a commander to every ten men, every hundred, and every thousand, and paying them a regular salary; but even before he died the system had begun to collapse, for his payments often became irregular and the Mahratta generals preferred to be granted estates rather than depend on money from a treasury not infrequently empty.

In Europe, on the other hand, standing professional armies had existed for more than a century. Manoeuvres and the military arts were studied, and a system for the disciplined devolution of authority had emerged. This in itself did not give European arms a decisive advantage, as the reverses suffered by the British and Portuguese during the seventeenth century illustrated. But towards the close of the seventeenth century and during the beginning of the eighteenth technical advances in the design of fire-arms occurred which added immeasurably to this superiority in organisation. Artillery had become light, mobile and quick firing. The heavy cumbersome cannon of the Indian army made a brave show, but, owing to their bulk, were excessively slow to move, load or aim; in consequence their rate of fire was, perhaps, one round in ten or fifteen minutes, whereas a well-trained detachment firing the light European field cannon could expect to fire two aimed rounds in a minute, or some twenty rounds in the time taken to fire one by an Indian gun detachment. Against troops in the open the far heavier cannon balls of the Indian artillery compensated little for their slow rate of fire; any advantage in the weight of shot was outweighed by the comparative ease with which European guns could be moved about the battlefield. It was probably not too much to say that one European manned gun was worth twenty manned by Indian gunners.

Nor was this all. The European infantry, rigidly trained and disciplined, had a further great advantage in the weapons they carried. During most of the seventeenth century the fire-arm of the infantry soldier had been the matchlock musket. As implied in the name, to fire it the soldier had to apply a burning match to the powder in his priming pan which in turn ignited the charge that propelled the musket ball. The infantryman had to go into battle swathed in yards of slow burning match; he could fire about three rounds in two minutes, the weapon was difficult to aim – the European musketeer often carried a crutch on which to rest it – the match might go out or the priming powder fail to ignite, and misfires were almost as common as successful discharges. During this period the musketeer was little more than a useful adjunct to the artillery; men armed with pikes were needed for close-quarter fighting and the issue of battles was generally decided by the cavalry.

The introduction of the flintlock musket that gave its firer an easy and far more reliable firing mechanism and the ability to fire two or three aimed rounds in a minute altered all this. Misfires still occurred, but were far less frequent. Now the musketeer could defend himself, the need for the pikemen disappeared, and steady infantry began to wrest pre-eminence on the battlefield from the cavalry. In the British army, the flintlock tower musket, affectionately known as 'brown Bess', was introduced at the beginning of the eighteenth century, and for the remainder of that century was to prove one of the best fire-arms in general service with the infantry.

This dramatic change had passed unnoticed in India. The Indian foot-soldier, it would do him more than justice to call him an infantryman, still carried only the matchlock, if he carried fire-arms at all. The cavalry man despised him and looked down on him as a vile mechanic who disgraced an otherwise gentlemanly and often profitable profession. Thus the highly trained and disciplined European armies, quick to manoeuvre and able to produce a devastating volume of fire, introduced a new dimension into Indian warfare. Their success, by creating a mystical aura of invincibility, bred success. Already, although the Mahrattas were still treated with respect, European soldiers had begun to refer to the Princely armies as 'that rabble'. European or European-trained infantry were rapidly becoming the decisive element on the battlefield.

When Nizam-ul-mulk died there were three major contenders for his inheritance. His eldest son Ghazi-ud-din, whom he had left to represent him at the court at Delhi, had risen to Bakshi, or paymaster-general, an appointment that made him the second most powerful minister in the Empire. He waived his claim to the Deccan and supported that of his younger brother, Nazir Jang. But Muzaffar Jang, a favourite grandson of Nizam-ul-mulk, claimed that his grandfather had willed the Deccan to him, and indeed Nizam-ul-mulk had little reason to look favourably on a son who had rebelled against him. Nazir Jang,

however, at Aurangabad when his father died, at once proclaimed himself viceroy and seized the treasury and the
administrative apparatus of government. Muzaffar Jang's
situation looked hopeless. But now an intrigue Dupleix had
already initiated took an unexpected turn which that experienced
statesman was quick to put to profit.

He knew that in the long run Anwar-ud-din would never
forgive the French for the humiliating defeats they had inflicted
on him, and had embarked on an ambitious scheme to replace
him. In Satara, Chunda Sahib, the ex-governor of Trichinopoly
and son-in-law to the old Nawab of Arcot, languished in a
Mahratta prison. Anwar-ud-din had defaulted on his payments
of chauth to the Mahrattas, and Dupleix now offered to ransom
the captive, an offer the Mahrattas were happy to accept.
Chunda Sahib once freed wandered through the Deccan trying
to induce the great nobles to back his claim to rule the Carnatic
and furnish him with troops. About this time Muzaffar Jang
went to Satara, hoping to enlist support from the Mahrattas.
They gave him fair words but nothing more. Then he heard
that Chunda Sahib was trying to raise an army to recover the
Carnatic and had a valuable link with the French. He approached
him and the two princes agreed to make common cause.

After some vicissitudes they managed to assemble an army
and when they approached the Carnatic, Dupleix sent d'Auteuil
with 400 French soldiers and 2,000 sepoys to assist them.
Anwar-ud-din opposed them with an army by the fateful pass
near Ambur. Largely owing to the gallantry of the French on
23 July 1749 he was defeated and killed. His eldest son Mafuz
Khan was captured, but Mohammed Ali made good his escape
to Trichinopoly.

The day after their victory the two princes entered Arcot in
triumph and the Carnatic lay at their feet. They went on to
Pondicherry to receive a magnificent welcome from Dupleix.
The French governor feasted them, but counselled caution.
Boscawen with his powerful fleet still cruised off the Coromandel coast and Dupleix was disinclined to trifle with that
redoubtable sailor. The Council at Fort St David, however,
seemed oblivious of the peril developing before their eyes. The
Devicotta expedition just ended gave them no appetite for
further adventures; they had, moreover, no desire to embroil

themselves against princes who might secure recognition from the Emperor and had not fully realised that the days of Aurangzib and Imperial greatness were finally ended.

They sent a token force of 120 men under Cope to aid Mohammed Ali at Trichinopoly. But when Boscawen, with a surer judgement, offered to remain off the coast, although his orders were to return to Britain as soon as Madras had been surrendered by the French, they refused his offer. The Admiral, leaving behind some 300 of his soldiers who had volunteered to take service with the Company, sailed for England on 21 October 1749.

Dupleix at once urged the two princes to capture Trichinopoly and settle the fate of Mohammed Ali, once and for all. They, however, lacked money with which to pay their troops and Dupleix had none to spare. They therefore advanced on Tanjore, intending to hold the Raja to ransom; it was rumoured he had a full treasury and was in no position to offer serious resistance. It was an unfortunate move. Accompanied by 800 Frenchmen under Law, they camped by the city. Partap Singh must have wondered what he had done to deserve so many tribulations, but nevertheless he was equal to the occasion. He alternately temporised and resisted. The French, growing impatient, blasted a breach in the walls of the city, but hesitated to storm, while the Raja at once offered to come to terms and pay a large indemnity. Now the wily Partap Singh procrastinated over the method of payment. Bargaining continued into the month of December, when Dupleix, driven to distraction by this wanton frittering away of time, wrote to tell the two princes that Nazir Jang with an immense army was approaching the borders of the Carnatic, adding acidly that they had better hasten the capture of Tanjore, as soon they would be needing a secure place of refuge. The alarmed princes, contenting themselves with what money they had managed to obtain, broke off the siege and hurried back to Pondicherry.

In late January 1750 Nazir Jang entered the Carnatic and made a stately progress towards Pondicherry, demanding as he went his dues in money and men as the legal viceroy of the Deccan. Mohammed Ali left Trichinopoly and joined him in February at his camp at Valdavur, a little more than ten miles from Pondicherry. Here the Viceroy haughtily desired to know

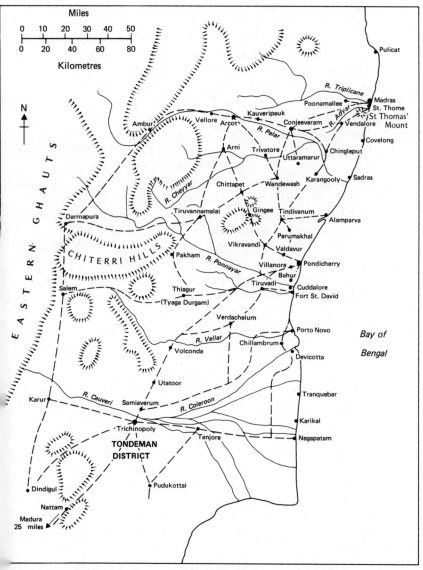

Southeast India, the Central and Southern Carnatic

what present he had been brought. The impecunious but quick-witted Prince pointed to Cope and his 120 European soldiers. Nazir Jang condescended to appear pleased and confirmed him as Nawab of Arcot and therefore the ruler of the Carnatic.

Dupleix tried to negotiate with the Viceroy without success, and then at the end of March prepared to give battle, supporting Chunda Sahib and Muzaffar Jang with 2,000 French soldiers. At Fort St David, the Council, satisfied with the legality of Mohammed Ali's claim and impressed with the size of the Viceroy's army, decided to support him. Stringer Lawrence with 600 Europeans marched to Villanore only four miles from Pondicherry and there joined Nazir Jang on 2 April. By this time the opposing armies were within cannon shot of each other and a battle appeared imminent. Stringer Lawrence related, 'We joined him at Villanoure and were very graciously received, suitable to the dignity of an Eastern Prince at the head of 300,000 men, of which he declared me genalissimo'. By now Stringer Lawrence understood the correct way to address an Indian prince. 'I told him in eastern style that he must be sure of victory wherever he fought, yet the attack might be attended with some difficulty, and cost him the lives of many brave men, as the enemy was strongly posted and had with them a large train of artillery. But that if he pleased to march between them and Pondicherry, he might, by cutting their communication, oblige them to fight at a greater disadvantage.'

His advice was not to the taste of the arrogant Viceroy. He replied, 'What, shall the son of Nizam-ul-mulk, even for an advantage, seem to retreat before so despicable an enemy?' Stringer Lawrence thought it wise not to press his point and next day the two armies formed up for battle; a cannonade ensued but no serious fighting occurred. That evening Lawrence received a message from d'Auteuil saying, as Lawrence related, that 'Although we were engaged in different causes, yet it was not his design nor inclination that any European blood should be spilt; but as he did not know our post, should any of his shot come our way and hurt the English he could not be blamed'.

The situation between the French and British troops was not a little ambiguous at a time when their countries were at peace, and d'Auteuil doubtless thought it judicious to safeguard himself if their respective governments came to investigate why the French and British were shooting at each other in India. Lawrence firmly replied that he carried the English colours on his flag-gun, that he was equally loathe to shed European blood, 'but that if any shot came that way, he might be assured I would return it'.

That night the French army, their pay in arrears and many of their officers in dispute with Dupleix, mutinied and returned to Pondicherry, leaving some of their guns and gunners behind them. Next day, 4 April 1750, Nazir Jang attacked. Without their French allies the armies of the two princes made little resistance. Muzaffar Jang threw himself on the mercy of his uncle, having been led to believe that their quarrel could be composed; Nazir Jang at once placed him in chains and stationed an executioner to decapitate him if any attempt was made to rescue him or threaten the safety of his uncle. Chunda Sahib, less trusting, fled to Pondicherry. In the battle the activities of the British were confined to rescuing the French gunners from the savagery of Nazir Jang's followers. Dupleix, to Lawrence's indignation, instead of thanking him, wanted to know by what right he took captive subjects of Louis XV. Morari Rao, the Mahratta chieftain Raghoji Bhonsla had appointed Governor of Trichinopoly, had thrown in his lot with Nazir Jang, and now pursued Chunda Sahib's army to the gates of Pondicherry.

Beaten in battle, Dupleix resorted to intrigue. He suborned Shah Nawaz, the Viceroy's prime minister, and opened a correspondence with some of his nobles who thought that their services had not been adequately rewarded. He refused to surrender Chunda Sahib. Stringer Lawrence watched developments with some uneasiness. Under the pretence that he was coming to terms with the Viceroy, Dupleix developed his conspiracy to unseat him. Lawrence pressed on the Viceroy the need to blockade Pondicherry and force the French to submit, but such basely commercial measures had little appeal to Nazir Jang. He had crushed the rebellion and now wished to enjoy the leisure he deserved in his two favourite pursuits, hunting and women. He authorised Lawrence to take possession of the districts round Madras, promised to the British as the price of their assistance. But Shah Nawaz, anxious to engineer a breach between his ruler and the British, thwarted all attempts to put the transfers into execution. By the end of April, bored with life in camp and convinced he had little to fear from the French, despite all Lawrence's protests, Nazir Jang returned to Arcot.* He asked the Englishman to accompany him, but Lawrence, according to his own account, afraid of a sudden move against Madras and aggrieved over the failure of the Prince to meet his obligations, refused. Probably the straightforward soldier found the hot-house atmosphere of the Viceroy's court increasingly distasteful and was glad of an excuse to leave it. He, however, made a serious error in leaving – it was one Clive would never have made.

With Nazir Jang safely in Arcot, Chunda Sahib quietly reformed his army. Dupleix restored order among the French soldiers and redoubled his endeavours to seduce Nazir Jang's nobles from their allegiance. Then he began to move. In early July he despatched a force by sea to reinstate the French factory at Masulipatam which Nazir Jang had sacked. The French took the city without loss. Emboldened, he struck at a weak garrison holding Tiruvadi fort about fourteen miles east of Fort St David. Nazir Jang, happily engrossed in the diversions offered by Arcot, took little notice. Mohammed Ali, however, at Arcot with the Viceroy, became apprehensive. He assembled an army of 20,000 men, most of whom he begged off his master, and asked the British to furnish him with a contingent, saying he would pay all their expenses.

Stringer Lawrence on his return found himself officiating as Governor at Fort St David. The Directors had dismissed the pleasure-loving Floyer and his replacement, Saunders, from Vizagapatam, had yet to arrive. Lawrence ordered Cope with 400 men to join Mohammed Ali. Cope stumbled into an engagement with some French near Tiruvadi, and as was customary with that officer, suffered a reverse. Mohammed Ali, meanwhile, had become embarrassed by lack of money and refused to pay the expenses of the British contingent. Lawrence,

* Fortescue, probably on the authority of Malleson, suggests that Nazir Jang retired because the French surprised part of his army. Stringer Lawrence, who was present, makes no mention of the incident, and as Nazir Jang disbanded much of his army after he arrived at Arcot, it seems highly unlikely that any significant engagement occurred.

without taking into account the possible longterm implications, and perhaps nervous of leaving Cope with an independent command, withdrew the British troops. It was the opportunity the French had been waiting for. On 1 September 1750 Chunda Sahib, with the aid of a powerful French detachment under d'Auteuil, attacked Mohammed Ali's army. That Prince's unpaid troops dispersed almost without a fight, and he himself fled to Arcot with only three attendants.

Chunda Sahib and the French at once followed up the victory. The able French soldier Bussy by a brilliant night assault carried Gingee fort to the astonishment of those who remembered that for eight long years it had defied the armies of Aurangzib. At last Nazir Jang realised that the hours of roses and wine were over. Much of his army had disbanded, but he marched with 60,000 men to recapture Gingee fort, unaware that most of his generals planned to betray him. By now the monsoon had broken and for some two months the two armies confronted each other without attempting an engagement. Then on 5 December 1750 the French attacked by night. Nazir Jang, asleep in his splendid pavilion, was woken at dawn to be told the French had broken into his camp. Contemptuously remarking that they must be drunk, he climbed onto his elephant without even bothering to don his body armour. As he rode over to the scene of the fighting he came upon the Nawab of Cuddapah, one of his vassals, sitting on his elephant with his men drawn up beside him, but apparently content merely to watch the conflict. The Viceroy rode over to expostulate. The Nawab, a Pathan, coolly told his companion in his howda to shoot the Viceroy. Perhaps made nervous by his august target, the man missed; the Nawab picked up another musket and did the job more efficiently. Then, decapitating Nazir Jang and mounting his bloody head on a spear, he sent it round the camp as a sign that the conspiracy had succeeded. All fighting at once ceased and amid universal acclamation Muzaffar Jang was released from his chains and proclaimed the new Viceroy – presumably his executioner had thought it discreet to withdraw.

In January 1751, Muzaffar Jang, supported by Bussy with 500 Europeans and 2,000 sepoys, marched for Aurangabad. As the French disappeared into the mysterious interior of the sub-continent, many in Madras thought that they would never be seen again. Fortunately for them, in Bussy they had a commander of rare ability. On the way Muzaffar Jang was killed in a skirmish with a rebellious chief who thought his services to the conspiracy had been inadequately rewarded. Bussy was equal to the emergency. He proclaimed Muzaffar Jang's uncle, Salabat Jang, the new Viceroy and resumed his march on Aurangabad. Salabat Jang arrived safely at his capital and seized the reins of government, but for the next two years, menaced by the Mahrattas, the traditional enemies of his father, he was to need all the assistance Bussy could give him to retain his position. Neither he nor Bussy were to have any men to spare for affairs in the Carnatic.

Stringer Lawrence was no longer at Fort St David. Politics, and Indian politics at that, had no appeal to the sturdy old soldier. He found the climate of Madras unpleasant, his pay and allowances insufficient, and now to crown all he was informed that some of the regulations he had issued for disciplining his troops were disallowed by the Directors in London. Disgusted, he resigned the Company's service and departed for England in October 1750. It is difficult to believe the patriotic old soldier would have left had he understood that the whole British position in India was about to be placed in jeopardy. Fortunately the new Governor, Saunders, was a dour, able and determined man, not one easily dismayed. During the coming year of 1751 his courage and determination were to be tested to the uttermost; he was not to be found wanting.

Chapter 6

The War in the Carnatic – the Opening Stages

While a French protégé departed to become Viceroy of the Deccan and Chunda Sahib set about imposing his rule on the Carnatic, Saunders pondered some exceedingly difficult problems. In August 1749, shortly after the defeat and death of his father, Mohammed Ali had written, 'I suppose I have a right for several reasons to claim your assistance in my affairs, as by the blessing of God and my assistance Fort St David was preserved'. During the past year the British had honoured their obligations, but now it was vital to preserve Mohammed Ali's authority intact to counterbalance the influence of Chunda Sahib.

When during the previous year French troops, on the pretext of recovering their property, seized Masulipatam, they had sacked the British factory there for good measure. If Chunda Sahib became Nawab of the Carnatic, he would never forgive the British for the help they had given Nazir Jang and Mohammed Ali. At the very least he would enforce a boycott of British goods, and by strangling their trade compel the British to close down their establishments on the Coromandel coast.

But this would only be the beginning. Firmly based in the Carnatic and with the Viceroy of the Deccan a complaisant tool in his hands, Dupleix would surely extend his influence to cripple the trade of Bombay and Calcutta. The Dutch the previous century had compelled the British virtually to withdraw from the Spice Islands; the French would not hesitate to impose a similar fate on them in India. Saunders might lack the flair and foresight of a Clive, but he possessed a steely determination and was firmly resolved to thwart the ambitious and far-reaching schemes of the great French Governor.

His first aim was to ensure that Mohammed Ali, who had taken refuge in his old capital, Trichinopoly, relinquished none of his rights. The ruler of that small state had suzerain rights over the southern provinces of Madura and Tinnevelly, and in theory at least Mohammed Ali ruled territory that extended almost to Cape Comorin. His situation was by no means desperate. Saunders sent Cope with 280 Europeans and 300 sepoys to Trichinopoly, as an earnest of British support and in exchange for the cession of Poonamallee; the Company, after all, was a commercial concern.

Much now depended on Mohammed Ali. The Prince was a good looking man of middle height. Brought up in princely splendour, an air of dignity and graciousness came to him naturally. He was no man of action and the arts of administration, generally despised by the Moghuls, he never attempted to master. He lived in the style he thought appropriate and made little effort to establish even a tenuous connection between income and expenditure. If no warrior or administrator, he yet possessed skills in the arts of intrigue, dissimulation and the management of men, and an instinctive political awareness that enabled him to survive where abler men perished.

He tried to negotiate a pact with Chunda Sahib, offering to recognise that Prince's rights in Arcot if in return he was permitted to keep Trichinopoly; his offer met with a scornful rejection. The unhappy Prince vacillated. Without British help he knew himself doomed. He wrote in a letter received at Fort St David on 16 January 1751: 'I desire you will let me know what you can do and what are your designs and resolutions?'*

Saunders hastened to reassure him. On 18 January he replied: 'You may depend on us as a true friend . . . I hope you are convinced of our friendship.' On 19 January in a burst of somewhat ill-founded optimism, 'I have had a letter from Mr [*sic*] Cope who informs me he is in so good a situation that if the united forces of the French and all our enemies were to march

---

* All the letters quoted from the Prince are taken from the translations from the Persian kept in the records of Fort St David and Madras. About this time, to confuse honest historians, he changed his name to that of his father and in contemporary British documents is sometimes called 'Annivardi Cawn'. In this narrative he will retain his original name.

against Trichinopoly they would not have it in their power to take it'.

His fears set at rest, the Prince wrote back cheerfully that he expected assistance from the rulers of Mysore and Tanjore and from numerous poligars – semi-independent feudal chieftains – and in particular from the poligars of Tondeman and Maravar. 'My intention is to strengthen Trichinopoly and by-and-by I shall think of retaking Arcot province.'

At first the news was good. On 13 February 1751 Muzaffar Jang was killed and, although Bussy proclaimed his uncle Salabat Jang the new Viceroy, he had not the remotest legal right for his action. Mohammed Ali informed Saunders that he had learned that Ghazi-ud-din, Nazir Jang's elder brother, was marching on the Deccan. He 'set out from Delhi for the Deccan on 18 January with 50,000 horse. It is two months since he set out . . . I believe he must have arrived at the River Nerbudda by this time.' The news was false, but the possibility of such an attack remained and Balaji Rao, the Peshwa of the Mahrattas, objected so strongly to Salabat Jang's elevation that later in the year, although without success, he took up arms against him. It was evident that in 1751 Dupleix could expect little help from the newly installed Viceroy.

Now, however, the political skies for Mohammed Ali began to darken. In March Madura revolted and its Governor, Allum Khan, declared for Chunda Sahib. This was a heavy blow. Madura, about eighty miles south of Trichinopoly, commanded the routes to Tinnevelly; its loss deprived Mohammed Ali of all the revenues he could hope to collect from the south. Cope, with his usual ill-timed optimism, volunteered to recapture the city. He happily marched out with 200 European infantry, 2,000 of the Prince's cavalry, of little use in a siege, and no siege guns. Fortunately a breach existed in the walls of Madura that the garrison had been too languid to repair. Hearing of Cope's approach, however, they hastily constructed an entrenchment behind it.

Cope managed to procure a single, aged siege gun and blasted away with it. Unfortunately his gun ran out of ammunition. Undeterred, although the entrenchment had suffered little damage, he determined on an immediate assault. As the stormers clambered up the breach they discovered three

champions who, after the style of Horatius Cocles, were prepared to dispute their passage. One, Orme noted, 'was a bulky
man clad from head to foot in armour'. The three died bravely,
but not in vain. Despite a courageous attack, in which the sepoys
behaved with conspicuous gallantry, the entrenchment proved
too strong. As they recoiled Cope had no alternative but to
retreat to Trichinopoly. On the way, discouraged by the
reverse, most of Mohammed Ali's troops deserted.

That Prince sent urgent appeals for more British troops with
which to recover his lost provinces, while urging on Saunders
a simultaneous advance on Arcot where he hoped to obtain
assistance from Murtaza Ali Khan, still Governor of Vellore.
But while the Prince and the British had been corresponding
and Cope failing before Madura, Chunda Sahib with the help
of the French had been quietly asserting his authority. Saunders
wrote to the Prince on 30 April 1751, that Chunda Sahib was at
Arcot and that the Governors of Chittapet and Vellore had
come to terms with him; he added, ''Tis my opinion if you
don't attack Chunda Sahib in this province he will attack you
in yours'.

Mohammed Ali, with some reluctance, discarded his plans
for the south and agreed to send his brother, Abdul Wahab,
with his army to Utatoor, about twenty-two miles north of
Trichinopoly on the Arcot road, to meet a British force and
then jointly to march on Arcot. At Fort St David Saunders
prepared to take decisive measures to remedy a fast deteriorating
situation. On 8 May he wrote to Mohammed Ali: 'I now send
Captain Gingins with a large command to consult measures and
act jointly with you in opposing the enemy.' Saunders, as was
to happen on other occasions, appeared to give scant consideration to the reactions of the French. Dupleix for his part thought
the time had come to put an end to Mohammed Ali. He
confidently told Chunda Sahib, 'think nothing of the British'.
So despite the peace officially existing between Britain and
France, in India the two companies drifted slowly but inexorably
towards an open armed conflict, one which in the end nearly
led to the financial ruin of both.

Captain de Gingins, the senior officer of the Company in the
absence of Stringer Lawrence, in mid-May set out with an army
of 500 Europeans, 50 European dragoons, 100 Africans, 1,000

sepoys and eight guns to join Abdul Wahab. He marched inland from Fort St David for some thirty miles to strike the Pondicherry–Trichinopoly road by the Verdachelum Pagoda which was held by a small garrison for Chunda Sahib. He fired at the Pagoda for most of a day and when in the evening stormers carrying scaling ladders drew near, the garrison prudently surrendered. De Gingins had scored an initial success, however paltry the opposition, and now held a useful strongpoint with which to safeguard his communications with Fort St David.

At Verdachelum he learned that Chunda Sahib had assembled an army at Arcot and was contemplating a move towards Trichinopoly. He arranged with Abdul Wahab to meet at Volconda, about forty-five miles north of Trichinopoly on the road to Arcot and there to concert plans for an advance on the central Carnatic. De Gingins, a Swiss by birth, had been a company commander at Madras for a number of years and his men had done better than most at the undistinguished defence of that port some five years before. He was personally courageous and no doubt knew how to post a sentry or parade a company; but conducting a campaign or commanding an army was completely beyond him, and, perhaps unfortunately, he knew it.

He duly met Abdul Wahab and his men at Volconda, but now his problems began. Volconda commanded the vital Arcot–Trichinopoly road. Its citadel had been constructed on a precipitous rock 200 feet high with a masonry wall at its foot, another half-way up and a third at its summit. The river Valam, dry at this time of year, ran along the western face of the rock; on its eastern bank, extending northwards from the base of the rock, a small stone fort had been constructed in which the principal citizens lived. Projecting a little northwards from this fort and enclosing its eastern side lay a larger, poorer quarter, known as the pettah, protected only by a thin mud wall.

The petty nobleman who governed the town and owned the citadel refused point blank to admit the British. He had heard that Chunda Sahib was moving southwards, bound apparently for Trichinopoly. He cared for neither side and only wished to enjoy his property in peace; he declared he would remain neutral until one or other side emerged victorious from a battle. Dalton, a cheerful and gallant ex-marine who had transferred to the Company's service and commanded the grenadier company of the Europeans, thought his attitude in those difficult times not unreasonable, sentiments unlikely to have appealed to de Gingins who was deeply perplexed by the difficulties confronting him.

He camped his army in the shade of a large copse about a mile or so to the south of the fort and discussed endlessly with his officers what he should do. Some were for an attack; but the position was strong and Abdul Wahab was convinced, erroneously as it turned out, that the Governor secretly sympathised with Mohammed Ali and could be won over. De Gingins posted sentries by the closed and barred gates of the town who soon struck up a pleasant acquaintanceship with those on duty from the garrison, and waited on events.

Inaction fostered discontent. The weather was hot, living conditions uncomfortable and food extremely expensive. His officers, not remarkable for their political insight, began to question why they should be living in expensive discomfort. If the Company was hiring out its troops at a handsome price to put a particular Nawab on the throne, it seemed only justice that some of the profit should be paid to those who suffered the discomfort and danger involved in the enterprise. Then on 5 or 6 June Chunda Sahib arrived with an army consisting of 15,000 cavalry and 5,000 infantry of dubious value, and a French battalion 500 strong under d'Auteuil, and camped about four miles to the north of the town beyond a range of low hills.

Despite his superior numbers, Chunda Sahib displayed little eagerness to attack, while de Gingins for his part, overawed by the size of his adversary's army and the strength of his camp, was equally reluctant. Possibly neither the French nor the British commander relished bringing on a battle which would inevitably lead to a violent clash between the two European contingents. News of such a clash might have unpredictable results when it came to the ears of their respective governments in Europe. In addition neither probably welcomed fighting fellow Europeans over what appeared to be a quarrel between two Indian princes. The two armies for the next fortnight remained inactive content merely to patrol each other's camps.

The British officers, possibly feeling that the presence of an enemy strengthened their position, now addressed a formal letter of complaint to their commander.

'To,
Rodolfus De Gingins Esq
Commander of the Honourable Company's troops
At Walgonda [Volconda] Camp

Sir,
It has always been customary for the Honourable Company's
troops in the service of the Moors to have from them an
allowance of 15 Rupees per day to the captains and to each
subaltern 10. . . . We find it impossible to live on the Company's
allowance. You are therefore, Sir, requested by all the under-
signed officers under your command and now in the service of
the Nawab to apply to him on their behalf and to let him
know that they do all and everyone insist upon the same they
formerly had . . .

7 June 1751   J Dalton
               W Richards
               Jas Killpatrick
               and 14 others.'

Not a pleasant missive to appear on the office table on a hot
and sweaty morning. De Gingins, temperamentally incapable
of dealing with such a matter himself, simply forwarded the
letter to Saunders at Fort St David.

Saunders sent a stinging reply on 12 June. 'Such behaviour
at such a time is greatly extravagant and unreasonable.' He
continued pertinently, 'Rewards are certainly due for service
performed, but what have we done for the Nawab? Is Chunda
Sahib conquered or Mohammed Ali in possession of his
government? When this is effected I am fully persuaded he will
not be wanting in showing a generous regard for merit.'

The answer was to no one's liking, but de Gingins received
another letter, equally unpleasant, tersely telling him that the
Council could not understand why he had done nothing to
bring Chunda Sahib to action and instructing him to take
immediate steps to do so. Again Saunders appeared conveniently to ignore the presence of the French. De Gingins
dared not ignore such an injunction and on 19 June convened
a council of war to discuss what should be done. Abdul Wahab
advocated a straightforward attack on Chunda Sahib's camp;

he was confident that at least one of the enemy generals was disaffected and would come over to the attackers. Most of the British officers demurred; Dalton related, 'our army made a very despicable figure in comparison with that of the enemy, and there was [*sic*] two rivers to cross and a steep hill to ascend to get at 'em . . . we thought it would be imprudent to march to them under these difficulties'.

So positive an action probably filled de Gingins with horror. He ruled against an attack on Chunda Sahib's camp and finally directed that Dalton with two mortars and a detachment of men should bombard the citadel and at the same time break through the mud wall into the petta, plunder it and set it on fire. He hoped this would induce the Governor to surrender; but if not, either Chunda Sahib would leave him to his fate and be discredited, or else march to his assistance and give the British a chance to bring him to action in the open.

Dalton thought little of the plan, 'It was not very probable that the few shells we could fire would make the governor surrender the fort, particularly as Chunda Sahib's army lay so near who, it was not to be doubted, would take advantage of our having commenced hostilities to march to its assistance and gain admittance'. He had a more subtle plan; he wanted to carry the stone fort at the foot of the citadel rock by escalade; rigid precautions against plundering should be taken and the Governor told that if he did not interfere the citadel would not be harmed. With most of the principal citizens in the power of the British, Dalton felt 'he would have gladly accepted these terms, not to be molested in the citadel, and in all probability we should have gained our point and obliged the enemy's army to retire'.

As escalade of the stone walls of the lower fort would be far more risky than breaking through a thin mud wall, de Gingins, with the obstinacy of a weak man uncertain of himself, refused to alter his decision.

At eight o'clock that night Dalton with his men entered the petta without difficulty, set fire to the houses and lobbed mortar bombs into the citadel. He lost only one man, but a number of the inhabitants, caught in the cross-fire, lost their lives. 'This piece of cruelty answered no sort of purpose, except possibly to frighten the Governor a little for a while' Dalton afterwards observed.

At dawn on 20 June 1751, since the citadel showed no signs of surrendering, he rejoined the main body of the army which was drawn up on a plain to the west of the town and just out of cannon shot of its walls. At eight o'clock mounted men could be seen, widely separated, coming over a low gently-sloping hill about a mile away to the north, then Chunda Sahib's army, spearheaded by the French, came into view marching for the dry river bed that offered them a covered approach to the north gate of the town. It was presumably what de Gingins wished to see, but now with his usual lack of decision he summoned a council of war while precious minutes slipped by.

Dalton and some others clamoured for an immediate attack and finally de Gingins assented. The officer with the African company, Dalton with his grenadier company, a company of topasses and three companies of sepoys, moved swiftly to check the French advance. The Africans, for whom all had a great respect, Dalton related, 'Ran all the way as fast as they could, and attacked the French grenadiers and sepoys who led their van in so daring a manner that they made them give way and abandon their advanced guns so precipitately that they threw the French main body into confusion'.

While Dalton and the Africans held the French advance, the European battalion advanced in line to their left to clinch their success; Abdul Wahb with his cavalry took post to the left again to cover the British flank against a charge by Chunda Sahib's horsemen. 'The Nabob's [Mohammed Ali's] horse', Dalton afterwards said, he never 'saw so animated as they were that day, and tho' few, seemed to despise Chunda Sahib's numbers.' He thought that 'never was there a finer prospect of complete victory'.

Two guns the French hastily brought into action and a few guns from the fort, although the range must have been considerable, opened fire on the advancing red-coated line. Seven or eight men fell, then, to Dalton's stupefaction, the line hesitated, wavered and splintered into little groups of fugitives running back towards the British camp the far side of the town. Abdul Wahab's cavalry, unperturbed by the cannonade, kept their station and, shouting contemptuous remarks after the fleeing British, covered their retreat. The French, however, showed no eagerness to quit their cover, and Chunda Sahib's men, who all along had held well back, made no noticeable effort to follow up the success. Dalton extricated his men and returned to the camp.

Here, all was confusion. The European soldiers protested they had been left without orders and the officers that de Gingins was nowhere to be found. Later, under Stringer Lawrence the battalion was to fight with splendid spirit, illustrating how an uncertain commander can have a baneful effect on his men. Equally it is difficult not to suspect that the officers, deeply dissatisfied with their treatment by the Company, failed to do their duty. (Orme speaks of Dalton, de Gingins and Clive vainly trying to rally the men, but Dalton by his own account was not there, nor would there have been any reason for Clive, at that time a non-combatant in charge of supplies, to have left camp.)

There was little thought of retrieving the situation. Abdul Wahab, disgusted with the behaviour of his allies, announced he was returning to Trichinopoly, and de Gingins, apparently feeling unwell, determined on a speedy retreat.

Camp was struck that evening and the British marched twenty miles the same night, to arrive at the little town of Utatoor by four o'clock next morning. Here the road ran through a rugged defile flanked by low rocky hills. It was an excellent position for defence and blocked the main approach to Trichinopoly. De Gingins halted and waited for his enemy to appear. Several days passed without any sign of Chunda Sahib and the French, and the officers took advantage of their leisure to raise again the matter of their field allowance or 'Batta' as it was known. They wrote a letter to Fort St David in such terms that the Council, hardly gratified by their efforts, exploded. In their Consultations it was recorded, 'agreed that Captains Richards and Killpatrick and Captain-Lieutenant Murray, who we are informed are the ringleaders', should be ordered back to the fort, put under arrest and shipped back to England, 'there to answer to our masters for their mutinous behaviour'. Their orders were duly executed. Richards died soon after arriving at Fort St David, Murray absconded to Pondicherry while Killpatrick remained awaiting a ship.

The advance-guard of the French arrived at Utatoor on about 11 July 1751. They spent two days skirmishing with the advanced British posts under Dalton and were firmly repulsed. De Gingins, with twelve troopers recklessly charging after an enemy cavalry patrol, fell into an ambush, narrowly escaped capture himself and caused Dalton to lose a sepoy company and Lieutenant Maskelyne while rescuing his commander. Maskelyne was received kindly by Chunda Sahib, parolled, and allowed to go back to Fort St David. Now de Gingins concluded that the enemy cavalry would cut him off from Trichinopoly, and on 13 July he withdrew to that city. Chunda Sahib and the French followed him and camped nearby.

Mohammed Ali saw the war drawing near him with unqualified dismay. On 9 June, Saunders received a letter from him. 'I must acquaint you that the countries towards Arcot are clear of the enemy's forces. If your forces, jointly with Mohammed Khan and Amuldars [petty noblemen] take possession of these districts it will throw the enemy into great confusion.' And on the 22nd, 'Please order a disturbance to be raised in the Arcot country as fast as possible to create uneasiness in the enemy'.

Saunders had no troops for so risky a diversion. He wrote instead to Allum Khan at Madura and Partap Singh at Tanjore urging them to move against the French. Not surprisingly they showed no enthusiasm. Partap Singh, while pledging his support, pointed out that he dared make no move while there were French forces near Trichinopoly and a French garrison at Karikal.

As de Gingins remained supinely camped by his city walls and the French made preparations for a siege, Mohammed Ali's agitation increased. He was now master of nothing outside the confines of Trichinopoly itself; his exchequer was empty and he greatly disliked looking at the tents of Chunda Sahib's army. He wanted his enemy drawn away elsewhere. On 29 July Saunders received a long letter in which he freely voiced his anxiety.

'After Muzaffar Jang was taken prisoner by Nazir Jang I undertook the government of the Carnatic on the advice of the English. After the death of Nazir Jang, Muzaffar Jang took upon himself the government of the Deccan country and many acknowledged him as such, but I, depending on the assistance of the English, followed their advice and lived in this place with a firm resolution. I lately sent my troops to Wolganda [Volconda] under the command of my brother and you are very sensible of what passed at that place. We thought of possessing ourselves the Arcot country, but by the contrary the enemy are in possession of Tinnevelli, Medera [Madura] and Trichinopoly districts and are on the point of besieging this fort. . . . If a disturbance could be raised in the Arcot country towards Madras, it would in all likelihood confound the enemy and break their hearts. . . . I am ready to deliver up the countries of Trichinopoly, Medera and Tinnevelli entirely to the English provided they allow me two lakhs of Madras pagodas yearly for my expenses. . . . If this is approved they shall be the sole masters of the said countries to dispose of them as they will. . . . Write to your officers to exert themselves in a better manner. Please raise as great a disturbance as possible in Conjeeveram and countries.'

It was a despairing cry from a very frightened man. Saunders replied on 3 August regretting that the Company only allowed him money for the purchase of goods. He added:

'In consequence of the mortgage you sent me of Trichinopoly country dated 15 July 1750, I have wrote to M. Dupleix to tell him to withdraw his troops as the place belongs to the English and our colours are there. . . . Since I sealed my letter to you I have reflected that we have 1,000 men in the field and wrote to Captain Gingins if he thinks himself strong enough to engage the enemy; if not he should consult with you how many men may be sufficient to defend Trichinopoly and with the rest, joined to your horse he make a diversion into the Arcot country and raise contributions for you.'

Saunders himself must have realised that his proposals were quite inadequate in view of the situation that had arisen. A few days after he had written, Clive returned to Fort St David from running a convoy of supplies to Trichinopoly. As the humid heat drenched them with sweat, in a lofty room of the Governor's house the two men discussed the situation. Clive had no comfort to offer. The British troops at Trichinopoly were dispirited; the men had no confidence in their commander and the officers passed the time quarrelling among themselves; nothing could be expected of them. But what then? Mohammed Ali would soon be bankrupt, when his army, already disaffected, would disperse and Trichinopoly fall. The ruin of the British on the Coromandel coast would then only be a matter of time.

There were, however, some gleams of hope. Partap Singh of Tanjore hated the French and Chunda Sahib; Nanj Raj the Regent of Mysore* (the King was a helpless puppet), had promised Mohammed Ali assistance. On the borders of the Carnatic the roving Mahratta chieftain Morari Rao lay with an army of 4,000 horse watching for an opportunity to make a quick profit. None of them, however, would move unless the British displayed some sign of being able to fight the French. Something dramatic had to be done and it had to be done quickly. Nothing could be hoped for from de Gingins; a raid towards Arcot seemed the only possible resource open to them.

But with what troops? If Fort St David and Madras were stripped bare perhaps 200 Europeans and 300 sepoys could be scraped together, but there were hardly any officers – volunteers would have to be called for from among the young *writers*, the junior civil servants of the Company. To send such a hetero-geneous handful of soldiers adventuring towards Arcot seemed a fearful risk. On the other hand it might shake Chunda Sahib's nerve and lessen the pressure on Trichinopoly.

Clive volunteered to command the expedition and moreover to capture Arcot. There must have been some quality in the smouldering young man in front of him that impressed Saunders. He assented to the proposition, and persuaded his Council to back his decision. It was an act of great moral courage on his part. If the expedition failed the ruin of the British would be complete and his disgrace certain.

Clive took 130 Europeans from Fort St David and sailed with them in the *Wager* to Madras. By stripping that garrison down to a mere fifty men he augmented their number by some eighty more Europeans. On 27 August 1751 he marched out of Madras with about 200 Europeans and 300 sepoys. In the

* Often referred to by the British as the 'Dalloway Sahib'.

humid heat that preceded the monsoon he did not hurry his men, and took four days to cover the forty-six miles to Conjeeveram, the most important town on his route and some twenty-five miles from Arcot. Here he received the unwelcome news that the garrison of Arcot fort amounted to about 1,100 men; he sent back to Madras for two 18-pounder siege cannon; however, he did not await their arrival. Next day when he resumed his march a tremendous thunderstorm broke over his men, but they trudged on along the muddy road, disregarding the lightning and the drenching rain. When he camped that night ten miles from the city, he received the astonishing news that the garrison, apparently assuming that an army that marched unscathed through a thunderstorm must be in league with the devil, had abandoned the fort.

On 1 September he rode into the city at the head of his little red-coated column. As they threaded their way through the narrow streets, the curious throngs parted before them in an almost friendly manner. Clearly the citizens of Arcot, numbering about 100,000, regarded the claims of either Chunda Sahib or Mohammed Ali to rule them with complete indifference, so long as they themselves were not molested. Clive occupied the empty fort and enforced stringent orders against plundering. He proclaimed Mohammed Ali the Nawab of Arcot and levied taxes in his name; he also laid in provisions and repaired so far as he was able the dilapidated ramparts of the fort.

During the next week he skirmished with the ex garrison; he finally managed to surprise them by a night attack on a camp they had set up near the city and dispersed them. Then he went to Conjeeveram to escort in the two 18-pounder guns which were reported en route to join him. During his absence a feeble attack was made on the fort, which the skeleton garrison he had left behind beat off without difficulty.

The enterprise had succeeded beyond all reasonable expectation. Saunders considered that now was the time to exploit it politically before any of the dire possibilities had time to mature. He wrote to Chunda Sahib on 8 September, 'Desist from molesting Mohammed Ali and let him enjoy the Districts of Trichinopoly and I shall not molest you in Arcot'. It was a confession of British weakness; Chunda Sahib disdained to reply.

At Arcot Clive awaited events with a growing sense of uneasiness. De Gingins gave no indication of sending any troops to help him, there was no news from Mysore, and Morari Rao seemed unmoved by what had occurred. Richard Prince, the Commandant at Madras, wrote to him on 8 September that a detachment of 150 French soldiers and as many sepoys had left Pondicherry, apparently destined for Arcot. Clive knew that if he was besieged Saunders had no troops with which to relieve him. The countryside swarmed with the adherents of Chunda Sahib; they already possessed Conjeeveram and were harassing his communications with Madras; the situation was becoming excessively dangerous; he had scored the success hoped for, and he wondered if he ought not to return to Madras while he could. He wrote to Prince asking his advice. Prince replied on 10 September that, politically, a withdrawal must have a most unfortunate effect, but that, 'we don't know what turn the expedition may have given affairs'. He thought Clive best placed to judge the situation and told him to decide for himself.

Clive stayed on, and soon he had no real alternative. On 23 September 1751, Chunda Sahib's son Raja Sahib entered Arcot with an army of 4,000 men and 150 French and occupied the Nawab's palace, a splendid edifice not far from the fort. Next day Clive attacked it, but in the narrow streets his men met with a bitter resistance and were forced back into the fort with the loss of two officers and thirty Europeans, heavy casualties for so small a force. But in the skirmishing round Arcot Clive had gained the confidence of his men, and undismayed by their reverse they prepared to withstand the rigours of a siege.

The British situation looked so hopeless the Governor of Vellore, the cowardly and treacherous Murtaza Ali Khan, thought it advisable to join Chunda Sahib, his first cousin's husband. Typically he suggested to Clive that if he made a sally he would attack Raja Sahib's army from behind. Clive declined a proposal that was probably made to lure him out of the fort. Affronted by the refusal, Murtaza deployed his men to complete the encirclement of Arcot fort, ensuring that no supplies could reach the garrison, although Clive's messengers experienced little difficulty in slipping through the lines of a somewhat indolent enemy.

Initially Raja Sahib, lacking siege guns with which to bombard the fort, posted sharp-shooters in houses overlooking the ramparts to snipe the defenders. Clive on his rounds had many narrow escapes, and on three occasions the sergeant accompanying him was shot. Then on 24 October French-manned heavy guns came into action. One of Clive's 18-pounder guns was dismounted almost immediately, and he withdrew the other to preserve it for the critical time when an assault was launched. He had collected ample rations* and watched the progress of the siege with quiet confidence.

At Fort St David Saunders laboured desperately to relieve his beleaguered little army. He wrote fruitless letters to de Gingins instructing him to instal the minimum garrison necessary to hold Trichinopoly, an exceedingly strong fortress, and to march with the rest on Arcot. Hearing Chunda Sahib and the French were making overtures to Partap Singh in Tanjore, thirty miles east of Trichinopoly, he wrote to him picturesquely on 16 October: 'I have heard of a snake that charms birds into his mouth and then devours them. . . . If the enemy should prove successful both yours and the King of Mysore's country will be ruined.'

He sent a handful of sepoys under Lieutenant Innis to reinforce Clive, but they were checked at Conjeeveram and forced to turn back. He pardoned James Killpatrick, still awaiting his ship, and tried to hire more sepoys. Killpatrick, despite a certain eagerness to see that his services were properly rewarded, was an excellent officer. Major Corneille of the 39th Foot subsequently wrote of him that he, 'Behaved to the satisfaction of all on many occasions . . . being cool in danger, in even the greatest possessing a presence of mind which did not let him miss the least advantage that might be taken. He was greatly loved by his soldiers, making it his business always to see them done justice to, and, as far as circumstances allowed, supplied with necessities.'

At last matters began to move, and Clive's spirited defence

---

* The quantity of goods available has been disputed. Orme states that Clive had supplies sufficient for sixty days and there is no reason to doubt his figure. Clive is later reported to have said that the sepoys gave up their rice to the Europeans, but the statement is at best second-hand, and Clive was not adverse to embroidering a good story.

to have its effect. In Mysore, Nanj Raj committed himself to Mohammed Ali, and while assembling his army sent money to that impecunious Prince, a point not missed by the eagle eye of Morari Rao. Clive had written to the Mahratta chief asking for his assistance; now he graciously replied that he would not leave to his fate so courageous a man as Clive. The pendulum of fate had begun to swing against Chunda Sahib.

By 30 October a wide breach yawned in the walls of the fort. Yet, even so, Clive's overmastering personality seemed almost to intimidate his foe. Raja Sahib hesitated to attack; he offered Clive terms and a large bribe if he would evacuate the fort. Clive scoffed at the offer. Still the Prince hesitated. Another breach was blown. Then on 9 November a party of Mahratta horse entered the city and plundered a few houses, but finding their progress checked by barricades in the streets rode off again. Killpatrick with 200 sepoys was reported near and bands of Mahratta cavalry roamed the neighbourhood, cutting off supplies. Raja Sahib steeled himself and on 13 November 1751 issued his orders for a storm. At dawn next day two armoured elephants, followed by a party of stormers, were to charge and break down the gates of the fort, while other parties assaulted the two breaches.

At this time of the garrison only about eighty Europeans and 120 sepoys remained on their feet but their determination remained unconquerable. The Europeans in the oft-quoted words of the sergeant diarist of the siege, 'solaced themselves with the pleasing reflection of having maintained the character of Britons in a clime so remote from our own'. And the sepoys, under the command of a man they admired and trusted, showed no less resolution.

Shortly after dawn on 14 November the assault began; it failed at every point. The elephants panicked under musketry fire and never reached the gates; at one breach a raft, designed to enable the attackers to cross the wet ditch in front of it, overturned with the leading troops on board; at the second, where the ditch was dry, the stormers with great gallantry attacked again and again, but could make no impression on the entrenchment Clive had thrown up to seal it off. Their leader died in the breach and one of his men, unheeding a hail of musket balls, carried away his corpse. By ten o'clock it was all over. That night Raja Sahib retired to Vellore, his army melting away as his despondent soldiers deserted. Of the garrison forty-five Europeans and thirty sepoys had been killed in the course of the siege.

It was reputed to have lasted fifty days, if anything an underestimate. Killpatrick arrived with his troops and a detachment of Mahratta horse on 15 or 16 November. Clive, neither his energies nor those of his men apparently impaired by the ordeal they had undergone, left Killpatrick to hold the fort while he followed up his victory by advancing on Vellore. The Mahratta cavalry, however, seeing little prospect of loot, refused to accompany him and Clive concluded that on his own he lacked sufficient strength to attack Raja Sahib's camp.

Dupleix reacted to this dramatic reversal of fortune with his customary energy and resolution. He despatched a mixed force of French soldiers and sepoys to reinforce Raja Sahib. It surprised the Mahrattas, who lost only about twenty men, but, far more calamitous, most of their baggage. Clive wished to intercept the French before they joined Raja Sahib, but the Mahrattas declined to budge, maintaining that the prospect of plunder was still insufficient. When they learned the French carried with them a large treasure chest to pay for the raising of more troops, they changed their minds but by then it was too late to prevent the junction between the French and Raja Sahib.

On 14 December, hearing that Raja Sahib with the united army was at Arni, a fortified town sixteen miles to the south of Arcot where the Arcot–Trichinopoly road crossed a tributary of the Cheyyar River, Clive marched that night to engage them with an army composed of 200 Europeans, 700 sepoys, 1,000 Mahratta horse and four guns.

At eight o'clock on the morning of 15 December 1751, as Clive rode down the highway, here slightly raised above the flat waterfilled rice-fields dotted here and there with copses of coconut palms, a message came back from his advance guard that Raja Sahib's army had been seen assembling near Arni. Clive continued his march and about ten o'clock, noticing some rising ground on the left of the road, he trotted over to it, hoping to have a good view of the country in front. In the clear, cool winter sunshine he could see in the distance the outlines of Arni fort, but nearer at hand, and about two miles away, a long column of horse and foot snaked along the road towards him. Raja Sahib was boldly advancing on Arcot. He was believed to have with him an army of 300 French, 2,500 sepoys, 2,000 horse and four guns.

Clive looked round him; the ground appeared well suited for defence. To his right the road ran through a small mud village then continued across water-logged rice-fields which extended for some six or seven hundred yards towards Arni; beyond the paddy the ground, firm and open, rose gently for a few hundred yards. To the right of the little village a broad wet ditch ran forward parallel to the righthand side of the road; any force trying to go round the right flank of the village would be in danger of becoming dangerously isolated from the rest of the army; clearly the village could form an excellent strongpoint on which to anchor his right. To the left of the road, across the front of the ridge on which he stood, the paddy fields continued, to end in a large coconut palm copse a little forward of him and about 150 yards to his left.

Clive issued rapid orders; the sepoys were to hold the village on the right, the Europeans with the guns to line the ridge in the centre and the Mahrattas to take station in the copse on the left. The columns filed on to their positions, then they waited. About midday the French guns came into action on the firm ground the far side of the paddy and opened fire on the ridge. The range was long, and the European infantry, taking cover behind the banks of an artificial pond, known as a tank, suffered little harm. At the same time long irregular lines of enemy cavalry started to move towards the coconut palm copse. The Mahrattas at once charged out, but some platoons of sepoys had been deployed among the enemy horsemen and the Mahrattas flinched before their musketry. Three or four times they charged forward, but each time pulled up before coming to close quarters.

Meanwhile the battle had flared up by the village on the right. To close the range the French pushed their guns forward along the road which here had a carriageway only about twelve feet wide. Then their infantry sprang forward towards the village. An advance post of the British sepoys ran back, but on the edge of the village the French were checked; the front was impossibly narrow; they had masked the fire of their guns and most of the infantry were strung back along the road, making an excellent target for the British guns on the ridge; it was clearly hopeless to attack the village straight down the road.

To their right the Mahrattas had started to give back and Raja Sahib's cavalry seemed to be gaining a footing in the copse. The French commander, noting their success, ordered his men to form line across the rice-fields, link up with the cavalry in the copse and storm the ridge in front. Clive on the ridge had been calmly watching developments. Now he sent two platoons of infantry and two guns to the copse to stiffen the Mahrattas. Then as he saw the French streaming off the road to flounder in the soggy paddy he ordered two platoons of Europeans to the village with orders to rush the French guns, now left virtually unprotected on the road. This they did with great spirit, storming the guns before the Frenchmen had time to fire a single shot.

Now the wretched French infantry, splashing about in the rice-fields, were in an unenviable situation. Clive's two platoons of Europeans and some sepoys formed along the road and enfiladed their left while the British guns on the ridge plied them with shot from in front. Demoralised by their helplessness, the French made little effort to advance, but soon turned round to struggle back to the dry land behind them. Clive thought the French infantry fought with less than their usual spirit that day.

Raja Sahib's cavalry, seeing the French recoiling, started to ride back themselves. Nothing pleased the Mahrattas more than to see the backs of their foes. They galloped down on them turning the withdrawal into a desperate race to escape.

The French infantry eventually rallied, and under cover of darkness Raja Sahib marched the remnants of his army through Arni and over the river. Clive averred the French did not halt until they reached the safety of Gingee fort thirty-two miles to the south.

The Mahrattas captured the treasure chest and most of the enemy baggage. Next morning the Governor of the fort at Arni discovered himself to be a firm supporter of Mohammed Ali, and even returned to Clive some of the booty he had thoughtfully removed from the French during the course of their hurried retreat the previous night. The British lost only eight sepoys and the Mahrattas fifty men. The French lost fifty men and Raja Sahib 150. Neither side had endured crippling losses but the effect of the battle on the morale of the French sepoys was marked; they deserted to the British in such numbers that Clive, taking only those still carrying their arms, formed a sepoy battalion 600 strong.

The political results of this victory were considerable. Arcot was now secure, Raja Sahib's army largely dispersed and the fort at Arni held by a supporter of Mohammed Ali. However, a party of some French and sepoys, having reoccupied the Conjeeveram pagoda, were interrupting communications between Madras and Arcot. Clive turned northeast, came to Conjeeveram and summoned the garrison in the pagoda to surrender. They refused. It took two days to bring up some breaching cannon from Madras and another three to blow a hole in the pagoda wall. The garrison vanished in the night without waiting for an attack. Clive ordered 200 Europeans and 500 sepoys to join Killpatrick in Arcot and took the remainder back with him to Madras, arriving towards the end of the year; he himself then went on to Fort St David to report. Saunders must have received him with open arms. Almost single-handed he had transformed the situation. At the beginning of September Mohammed Ali's days seemed numbered, now it was Chunda Sahib who faced a steadily worsening situation. And in Clive the Company had found a soldier whose feats of arms were already becoming a legend among the Indians, but not among some of his brother officers, who jealously preferred to attribute them to luck.

Chapter 7

The First Battle for Trichinopoly

In March 1752, M. Law, commanding the French troops besieging Trichinopoly, received yet another petulant letter from Dupleix in Pondicherry, demanding to know why he had not yet captured the city; but this one contained a sinister addition – the British were assembling a considerable force at Fort St David reportedly destined for Trichinopoly. Dupleix instructed him not to relax his blockade of the city, but at the same time to march with the bulk of his army to intercept and defeat the British reinforcement before it could link up with Mohammed Ali's supporters now camped around Trichinopoly. In Law's opinion, excellent though these instructions might be in theory, or viewed from the comfortable security of Pondicherry, they completely ignored the realities of the situation he faced.

He was a gallant soldier and an intelligent man, able without difficulty to envisage half a dozen excellent schemes, but lacking the self-assurance and resolution to choose the right one or carry it out successfully. Like de Gingins he found his circumstances beyond his military capacity and like that warrior he took refuge from his perplexities by eschewing any action that might be construed as risky. After the battle of Volconda he had pursued de Gingins in so leisurely a fashion that his opponent had retired to Trichinopoly virtually unmolested. Since the end of July 1751 he had been gazing not too hopefully at that city, more aware of his difficulties than how to overcome them. And in truth his difficulties were considerable.

The city was situated in a flat, open plain about a mile and a half south of the confluence of the Cauvery and Coleroon rivers. The plain was covered by rice-fields and seamed with

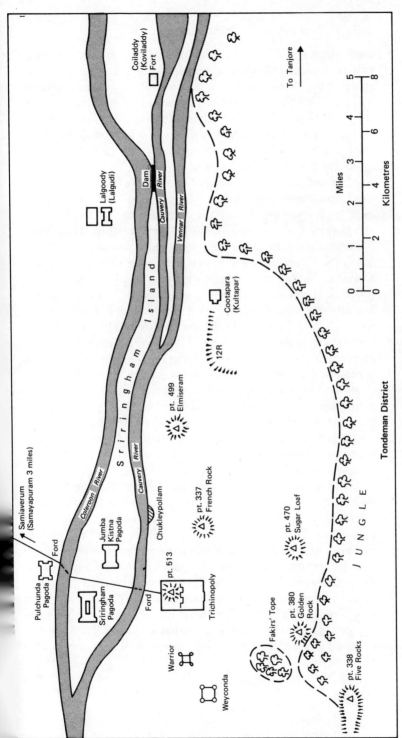

Trichinopoly and environs

Tondeman District

To Tanjore

Miles

Kilometres

Coiladdy (Koviladdy) Fort

Lalgoody (Lalgudi)

Cauvery River

Vennar River

Dam

Srirringham Island

Cootapara (Kultapar)

12R

Coleroon River

Samiaverum (Samayapuram 3 miles)

Ford

Pulchunda Pagoda

Sriringham Pagoda

Jumba Kistna Pagoda

Cauvery River

Chukleypollam

pt. 499 Elmiseram

pt. 337 French Rock

Ford

pt. 513

Trichinopoly

Warrior

Weyconda

Fakirs' Tope

pt. 380 Golden Rock

pt. 470 Sugar Loaf

pt. 338 Five Rocks

JUNGLE

watercourses and irrigation channels; it was marshy and difficult to entrench. Copses of coconut palms and banyan trees
studded the landscape, while here and there curious, isolated,
and precipitous rocks towered up 100 feet or more to dominate
the fields at their feet. The city of Trichinopoly had grown up
round one such rock about 250 feet high. Around its base,
some 1,200 yards in circumference, a town developed, enclosed,
as always in that troubled part of the world, by a rampart. The
site, a focal point for a number of waterways to the ports on
the Coromandel coast, favoured trade; the town grew into a
city; its houses overflowed the original rampart to the south
and that part of the rampart was allowed to decay. Thus it had
become oblong in shape, the long sides running north and
south (Stringer Lawrence asserted the long sides ran east and
west, but he had not consulted his own map). It was strongly
fortified. Twin masonry walls, about eight yards apart, surrounded it; outside them was a formidable wet ditch thirty
feet wide and fifteen deep. In the mediaeval fashion the outer
wall eighteen feet high and four feet wide had been built to
protect the inner one from battering rams or any other type of
bombardment. The inner rampart was truly formidable; it was
thirty feet high and thirty feet wide at its base, tapering to ten
at the top with a loopholed parapet and towers at irregular
intervals. On the top of the rock in the northern part of the
city a pagoda had been built, and from it a look-out with a
telescope could see the surrounding countryside for distances
of up to twenty miles.

About a mile and a half northwest of the city the Cauvery
forked; its two arms ran eastward and close together for nearly
fifteen miles to enclose a long, slender wooded island, called
Sriringham Island; at the eastern end of the island a high dam
had been built to prevent the two arms reuniting. The southern
arm, passing only half a mile to the north of the city, retained the
name Cauvery, while the northern, now christened Coleroon,
as already mentioned flowed out into the Bay of Bengal by
the port of Devicotta. The dam, just within the borders of
Tanjore, vitally affected the irrigation canals of that state and
to guard it a fort had been constructed at the nearby village
of Coiladdy.

Near the western end of the island the walls of two pagodas

showed over the trees. The more westerly of the two was the famous Sriringham Pagoda, from which the island took its name; it was a large edifice containing seven concentric walls and much revered by the Hindus. The other, about 800 yards to its east and considerably smaller, was called the Jumbakistna Pagoda. The far side of the Coleroon and nearly opposite these were two more, the Pitchunda Pagoda, which commanded the ford where the main road to Arcot and the north crossed the river, and the Lalgoody Pagoda, which dominated a minor ford a little to the east and was used for storing grain.

When he arrived on the island towards the end of July in the previous year, Law put small garrisons of Indian troops in all four pagodas, effectively blocking all the approaches to the city from the north. Then he pitched his camp at the little village of Chuckleypollam on the south bank of the Cauvery some two miles northeast of Trichinopoly, and proceeded to try to close the eastern approaches by taking Coiladdy fort and occupying two commanding rocks, the Elmiseram rock about two miles to the east of the city and another, subsequently christened French rock, about 1,500 yards south of his camp. But now his problems began. Chunda Sahib's army, reputedly numbering 15,000 horse and 20,000 foot, except for 1,000 Rajput mercenaries was of indifferent quality. Both the British and the French sepoys at this time modelled their conduct on the behaviour of the European troops and, in terms of real fighting power, Law confronted 600 British troops with 900 French; with so small a superiority in numbers he could not hope to storm a strongly fortified city. He adopted a plan, which, despite the recriminations of Dupleix, was probably the only one open to him. He erected batteries sited too far from the city to blow a breach in its walls but which were safe from a sudden sally, should de Gingins ever contemplate so rash an undertaking; from these he could shell the city. He directed Chunda Sahib to deploy his cavalry to the south and west of the city and cut off all supplies, while he sealed off the approaches from the north and east. Then he waited for Mohammed Ali to capitulate.

During September and October 1751, while de Gingins remained supinely in his camp under the city walls, it looked as if the policy might well succeed. But Clive's successful defence of Arcot and victory at Arni shattered his hopes. In

December Nanj Raj assembled a large army at Karur on the borders of Mysore, forty miles to the west, and Morari Rao's Mahratta horsemen came swarming in from the north. Now that Mohammed Ali's star seemed in the ascendant, numbers of minor chieftains came flocking in to join him with their bands of retainers. In January the Mysore army descended on Trichinopoly, driving Chunda Sahib's cavalry before it, although the unfortunate Cope lost his life in a skirmish while assisting its advance. From Tanjore, Partap Singh, anxious to revenge the humiliations Chanda Sahib had inflicted, sent an army under his Commander-in-Chief Manoji.

In Pondicherry, Dupleix, still sternly urging Law to accomplish the impossible and storm Trichinopoly, realised he had to strike elsewhere to retrieve a rapidly deteriorating situation. Raja Sahib had re-assembled his army and he ordered the Indian prince to ravage the Carnatic west of Madras, but to avoid a pitched battle; he hoped that by destroying British trade he might induce Saunders to come to terms. Raja Sahib acted energetically. He established a camp at Vendalore, about seventeen miles southwest of Madras, raided Poonamallee and plundered some of the British country houses on the slopes of St Thomas's Mount.

Saunders had no intention of allowing the Frenchman to blackmail him into abandoning his protégé. He sent Clive to Madras with instructions initially to safeguard British property by the Mount and then, when he could muster sufficient men, to drive the Indian prince away. With a handful of sepoys and about thirty Europeans Clive fortified a position near the Mount, recruited more sepoys and awaited reinforcements from Arcot and Bengal. Both sides proceeded to build up their strength. By February 1752 Raja Sahib commanded 400 Europeans, 2,000 sepoys, 2,500 native horse and nine guns. A company of Europeans arrived by sea from Bengal and on 20 February Killpatrick joined Clive from Arcot, bringing the strength of his army up to 400 Europeans, 1,300 sepoys and six guns. He now decided to take the offensive. He proposed to fetch a circuit round Raja Sahib's camp and attack it from behind. On 22 February, as he was about to set out, he learned that the camp was empty. He marched straight to it, then for twelve hours paused, uncertain where the Indian prince had gone and suspecting that he had gone south to rejoin his father outside Trichinopoly.

But Raja Sahib had more ambitious plans. He had suborned one or two members of the garrison at Arcot, now depleted by the troops taken by Killpatrick to reinforce Clive, and he resolved to capture the capital by a surprise attack. To conceal his intentions he dispersed his army into small detachments with orders to reassemble at Conjeeveram and proceed to Arcot. News that the prince's army had been seen at Conjeeveram reached Clive probably late on 22 February. He at once guessed Raja Sahib's plan and marched in the early hours of the 23rd for Conjeeveram thirty-two miles away, arriving there at 4 a.m. on the morning of 24 February 1752. A small enemy garrison in the pagoda at once surrendered to him and he found a message awaiting him from the commander of Arcot fort, telling him that Raja Sahib was expected there at any moment. His men were utterly exhausted and Clive rested them until midday, before demanding from them another herculean effort to reach Arcot, twenty-five miles distant.

That same morning Raja Sahib penetrated into Arcot and came up to the walls of the citadel, but the conspiracy had been detected, the traitors arrested and the gates remained barred against him. Raja Sahib, possibly with the intention of ambushing Clive who, he knew, would be hastening towards Arcot, returned down the Conjeeveram road some nine miles and camped near the village of Kauveripauk. He put his guns and most of his infantry into a large mango orchard with embanked sides about 200 yards to the north of the road, on the righthand side for anyone coming from Conjeeveram. He placed his horse lines out of sight on the other side of the road.

At six o'clock in the evening, with darkness drawing on, Clive's advance-guard, without any cavalry to scout the way ahead, came panting up the road. At a range of 250 yards nine French guns opened a sudden and devastating fire, sweeping away the head of Clive's column. For a few moments there was a danger of panic. Then Clive noticed that on the left side of the road, the far side from the French guns, a wide nullah yawned invitingly. He led his men in a wild dive into it and set about restoring order. Through the gloom long lines of cavalry could be discerned away to the left; he engaged them with two guns and two platoons of infantry; another platoon and a gun he sent back to shepherd his baggage to a safe place down the road. Then he took breath to consider the situation. His remaining guns further down the column had come into action against the French in the orchard, while the enemy cavalry, possibly fearing the onset of darkness, made no attempt to charge. In front of him, however, sudden stabbing flashes of light and the dull clangour of musketry indicated the French were trying to work their way down the nulla. It was an extremely unpleasant situation. As he afterwards observed, 'Hitherto we had effected nothing but what was to our disadvantage'. The three British guns engaging the French in the orchard were clearly overmatched and must eventually be silenced.

Retreat, however, was not to be thought of. He considered two alternatives. He could launch a frontal attack on the orchard, or he might try to find a way round it, come back onto the Arcot road and resume the battle next morning from a direction which screened Arcot from an enemy advance. An attack into the French guns would be a bloody and desperate affair, and before attempting it he resolved to look for a route round them. He sent out a reconnaissance patrol of a Portuguese sergeant and a few sepoys. The patrol reported back that there was a path round the enemy in the orchard, but that they had also discovered that the enemy there had put out neither piquets nor sentries to guard against an attack from their rear.

Clive leapt at the chance. He ordered Lieutenant Keane with 200 Europeans and four or five companies of sepoys to take the patrol commander as a guide, stalk round the orchard and attack it from behind. He himself accompanied Keane's party for a short distance and may have contemplated commanding it. But behind him the British fire in the nulla had begun to falter. He hurried back to find that the men, believing themselves deserted, despite the entreaties of their officers, had begun to filter back and some had already vanished into the night. Exerting himself to the utmost, Clive managed to rally them; by now the moon was up and it was with considerable anxiety that he listened to the musketry fire at the head of the nulla and the artillery duel across the road, waiting for Keane to attack. At about 11 p.m., when he must have been wondering if that officer had lost his way, two crashing volleys rang out in the darkness beyond the dim outlines of the mango trees.

Keane, any noise he made blanketed by the artillery duel still in progress, arrived behind the orchard undetected, formed his men up, delivered a couple of volleys at a range of fifty yards and then charged into the trees. This sudden attack coming out of the darkness behind them unnerved the French. In complete disorder they took refuge in a resthouse in the middle of the orchard, while their sepoys rushed across to the road, infecting all they met with their panic.

Raja Sahib's army disintegrated. The Prince with the remnants retired on Pondicherry, while the French surrounded in the resthouse laid down their arms. The French lost all their guns, fifty Europeans killed and sixty captured; the British forty Europeans and thirty sepoys killed and many wounded. The disaster ended all prospect of further French operations in the Carnatic. When the wretched Raja Sahib put in an appearance, a furious Dupleix for some days refused to speak to him, then he packed him off to join his father at Trichinopoly. Clive returned to Fort St David. On his way he came across a monument Dupleix had erected to commemorate the French victory over Nazir Jang. He knocked it down, not as an idle act of vandalism but to demonstrate that the French days of power were numbered; in this he was perhaps a little premature.

At Fort St David Saunders was busy organising a force to reinforce the troops about Trichinopoly and strike a decisive blow against Chunda Sahib and the French. He was, however, puzzled whom he should put in command. Clive was the junior captain in the Company's army. To give him the command would antagonise all the senior officers in the Company's service; on the other hand, little could be expected from de Gingins. Fortunately a welcome if stout figure shortly afterwards stepped ashore. The directors of the Company in London had met all Stringer Lawrence's demands and shipped him straight back to India. In March he set out for Trichinopoly with Clive and a reinforcement of 400 Europeans, 1,100 sepoys and an enormous convoy carrying supplies and munitions of war.

Law's former difficulties bulked small compared with those that now beset him. The army of Mohammed Ali and his allies now outnumbered that of Chunda Sahib. Law dared not venture into open country for he knew that Morari Rao and his veteran Mahratta horsemen would harass every step he took. He resolved to remain in his camp and engage Lawrence when, hampered by his vast convoy, he drew near to Trichinopoly. His decision found little favour with Dupleix who wrote, 'It will be difficult to persuade those in France that 30,000 men let pass 2,000 escorting an unimaginably large baggage train', a taunt that totally ignored Mohammed Ali's army, which grew in numbers almost daily. Splendid in his concepts and his diplomacy, the great Frenchman lacked the detailed military knowledge to conduct a campaign and had sent Bussy, his most brilliant subordinate, chasing a will o' the wisp of imperial power in the far north of the Deccan.

As Stringer Lawrence approached Law perfected his plans. He anticipated the Englishman would come up from the northeast, following the main road from the coast. His first hope was that Lawrence would be checked at Coiladdy fort, which dominated that route, and settle down to a time-consuming siege. The English commander, however, was far too wily to fall into the trap which caught Boscawen outside Pondicherry four years before. He took by-roads and swung wide to the south. His guides failed him and his column came within cannon-shot of the fort, but Lawrence deployed some guns to mask it and continued his advance without suffering any serious loss. That evening, 26 March 1752, he camped ten miles from Trichinopoly.

Now Law pinned his hopes on Lawrence coming back to the coast road which ran westwards close to the Cauvery. He posted troops and guns on the little pagoda that crowned Elmiseram Rock and garrisoned French Rock, intending to use them as strongpoints on which he could pivot. He ordered his French troops to extend from Chuckleypollam to French Rock to check the British advance up the river bank, while Chunda Sahib lined up his cavalry eastwards from French Rock towards Elmiseram; here Law hoped he would outflank the left of Lawrence's column and attack him in the flank and rear while the French engaged him in front.

In the early morning sunlight of a day that promised to be scorchingly hot, the French and their allies took up their positions. But Law had reckoned without his adversary. Lawrence had guessed the Frenchman's strategy; he had no intention of fighting a battle until he had joined up with all the British and allied troops near Trichinopoly. As the long British column neared Elmiseram it looped away to the south, bypassing the French, and at midday halted by Golden Rock about three miles south of the city; at the same time Dalton, with the grenadier company of the Europeans and one other, 400 sepoys and four field guns, marched out to join him, while Morari Rao and his Mahrattas and Mohammed Ali's army skirmished with Chunda Sahib's troops between Elmiseram and French Rock to prevent them interfering.

Law turned his troops about so that the French were now on the right of the battle line and Chunda Sahib's on the left, then brought up his French battalion in a long and exhausting march to interpose between Lawrence and the city.

The Mahrattas, who had experienced little trouble in holding Chunda Sahib's cavalry in check, fell back before the French advance, supported as it was, so Orme asserts, by twenty-two field guns. Then the British and French faced each other. A fierce artillery duel broke out; the British guns, ten in number, under the skilful direction of Clive, had taken up a position under cover while the advancing French were compelled to fight in the open. Gradually the British manned guns gained the mastery. Chunda Sahib's cavalry with some gallantry came within grapeshot range, but Allum Khan, commanding them, was cut down by a cannon ball and his men, suffering casualties, became unsteady. Law hesitated to press home his attack against the deadly British guns, and perhaps the oppressive heat of the afternoon drained his men of energy. He retired to his camp at Chuckleypollam and Lawrence contented himself with continuing on his way to Trichinopoly. Dalton considered that Mohammed Ali's cavalry missed a great opportunity for a charge, but the Mahrattas refused to move, and the rest would not charge unless the Mahrattas led. British casualties were insignificant, only fourteen killed or wounded but seven men died of heat-stroke.

That evening in Trichinopoly Lawrence and Clive debated their next step. Lawrence wished to attack the French camp, but his allies thought the omens unpropitious. Lawrence stifled his anger and waited. On 1 April he sent Dalton to make a night raid on the camp at Chuckleypollam. Dalton lost his way and abandoned the attempt as dawn broke, but the mere threat was sufficient. On 3 April Law with his allies retreated onto Sriringham Island. Here their position was strong. The two rivers provided them with a natural moat and the two pagodas with formidable strongpoints; further their position safeguarded their communications with Pondicherry and the north. Law confidently expected to be able to hold out until Dupleix arranged for his relief. Reinforcements might come from France, and it was rumoured that Salabat Jung with the faithful Bussy might soon march south to reassert his authority over the Carnatic, particularly as he had come to terms with the Mahrattas.

Lawrence was well aware of these dangers, but deemed the French and their allies too strong to attack across a water obstacle such as the Cauvery. He now adopted an extremely bold plan. He decided to split his force and place a large detachment north of the Coleroon to cut the French off from Pondicherry. The risk was obvious. Law might concentrate all his army against the detachment and overwhelm it before the rest of the British troops could cross the two rivers and come to its assistance. Robert Clive was probably the only man who could be trusted to command so dangerous an operation; but he was the junior captain, and the Company's army was wedded to allotting tasks and promotions strictly in accordance with seniority. Morari Rao solved Lawrence's dilemma. He stated the Mahrattas would serve under no other leader. That settled the matter.

On 6 April Clive with 400 Europeans, 1,200 sepoys and 4,000 horse made a detour well to the east, crossed the river about seven miles below Coiladdy fort, then swung westwards and occupied a position by the village of Samiaveram, about ten miles north of the Sriringham pagoda on the main road leading to Arcot and Pondicherry; it was within sight of sentries posted on the pagoda walls. The road here ran between two pagodas. Clive fortified them and linked them with a redoubt. Having thus barred the road to Pondicherry and made his camp secure, he suddenly struck against the Lalgoody Pagoda on the north bank of the Cauvery and captured it together with a large and valuable quantity of grain.

Meanwhile Dupleix, deeply perturbed by all that had happened, resolved to reinforce the troops on the island and supersede Law. He mustered every soldier he could find and despatched a convoy under d'Auteuil escorted by 100 Europeans, 500 sepoys and 500 horse bearing a message to Law, tactfully explaining that his wife in Pondicherry felt lonely and that he was to return and console her. Clive had his first inkling that something impended when mysterious moves by the French troops on the island were reported; then on 15 April 1752 he heard that a French convoy had arrived at Utatoor twelve miles away down the Arcot road. He decided he must engage the French as far from the island as possible to avoid the danger of being caught between two fires. Leaving his camp standing to deceive Law's lookouts on the island, he marched that night for Utatoor. Three miles from that town he received positive information that no Frenchmen had entered it. Convinced he had been tricked out of his fortified camp by false information originated by Law, he turned round and raced back to Samiaverum, arriving exhausted after an eighteen mile night march early on the morning of the 16th.

Law heard of Clive's departure – the information on which Clive acted had been substantially correct and was not part of a deep laid plot; but now the French commander determined to take advantage of his absence to seize his camp at Samiaverum. On the evening of the 16th he sent a detachment of 80 Europeans and 500 sepoys to occupy the empty camp, as he supposed, by night. The Europeans included a number of British deserters under an Irish deserter from Boscawen's free companies called Kelsall and, it would seem, one from Clive's forces at Samiaverum, who offered to guide the party. Unaware that Clive had returned, at about eleven o'clock that night they entered the camp, Kelsall bluffing the sepoy guard by asserting they were reinforcements sent by Lawrence. They threaded their way through the Mahrattas, who were no great believers in the virtues of sentry duty, and penetrated unnoticed into the centre of the camp. They came to the smaller of the two pagodas which Clive had turned into a strongpoint; this one at night was only occupied by a small sepoy guard. Here they loosed a volley that riddled the bed Clive was sleeping on in a resthouse a few yards away, then the French charged in and occupied the pagoda from which it must be assumed the guard had fled.

Clive, unaware of his lucky escape – the volley killed his servant sleeping near him – leapt out of bed in his shirt tails to find out what was happening. He felt almost certain it was a false alarm occasioned by some sepoy sentries shooting at shadows. He went over to the other pagoda which housed his Europeans, found them standing-to, fell them in outside it, and went to investigate. He found a line of sepoys firing apparently at random in the general direction of the Mahratta camp and Sriringham Island. Mistaking them for his own, he strode furiously among them telling them to cease firing and knocking up their muskets; the sepoys were astounded by this extraordinary and enraged apparition appearing out of the night. Then one of their officers recognised he was dealing with an Englishman and slashed at Clive with his sword, wounding him across the head. Clive, under the impression he confronted a mutineer, turned on him with such fury that the officer ran off to take refuse in the small pagoda, with Clive in hot pursuit. When he came to the pagoda Clive was flabbergasted to find it swarming with French soldiers; recovering himself before the equally astonished Frenchmen realised who he was, he ran back to his Europeans, taking with him two French prisoners that he had encountered and induced to surrender by telling them they were surrounded.

He found his Europeans standing steadily where he had left them, but the French sepoys had vanished into the night. In the darkness it was impossible to tell what was happening; Clive decided on an immediate counter-attack to retake the pagoda, before any other French attack could develop. The entrance to it, however, was narrow, the French defence obstinate, and the British attack foundered. Outside all was now quiet. Clive ringed the pagoda and waited for dawn. As the light came up it was apparent that there was no other enemy in the camp. He brought guns up to the pagoda. The French made a desperate and fruitless attempt to break out. To save a useless loss of life Clive, under a flag of truce, summoned the French to surrender. Kelsall, knowing that if he was captured his life was forfeit, shot at Clive, missing him but mortally wounding a sergeant supporting him, for he was faint from his wound. The French soldiers in the pagoda, horrified by the outrage, and apprehensive of what vengeance might be exacted if they continued to resist, laid down. their arms, forcing the British deserters to do the same. Now the Mahrattas, at last aware of what had been happening, saddled up, rode after the French sepoys, caught up with the demoralised band and butchered them to a man.

Law had lost his complete detachment, and d'Auteuil, hearing of the disaster, retreated to consider how he could find a safe route into the Island. Kelsall and two of his companions, including the treacherous guide, were hanged. Clive's wound does not appear to have troubled him, as he remained at duty and Stringer Lawrence, writing to congratulate him on the action, contented himself with facetiously hoping it would not spoil his manly good looks.

Despite Stringer Lawrence's assurances that from his lookout on the Pagoda Rock he could see any move made by Law, Clive had been uneasy about his situation and on several occasions had asked Lawrence for men. Now the 'old gentleman' allowed himself to be convinced that Law had no intention of attacking across the Cauvery and he detached Dalton with 150 Europeans, 400 sepoys and 1,000 horse to Utatoor, to chase d'Auteuil away; at the same time he ordered Clive to close in on the island and besiege the Pitchunda Pagoda. Dalton failed to bring d'Auteuil fully to action, but after a skirmish the Frenchman beat a hasty retreat to Volconda, leaving most of his stores behind him. Lawrence pulled back Dalton to reinforce Clive; the gallant ex-marine, to avoid any complications over rank, agreed to serve under him as a volunteer.

The ring round Chunda Sahib and Law tightened. On 21 April Manoji, commanding the Tanjore army, captured Coiladdy fort. Then Lawrence secured a lodgement on the island close to the dam and himself re-occupied the empty French camp at Chuckleypollam. The Mahrattas and the Mysore army firmly barred all the roads from the west, while Clive, patrolling the northern bank of the Coleroon, constructed a redoubt from which to breach the walls of the Pitchunda Pagoda. The river that protected Law had become a barrier that fenced him in.

While his men built the redoubt, Clive deployed his guns along the river bank and bombarded a large camp where followers, shopkeepers, dancing girls and all the other

impediments of an Indian army were lodged. They hastily fled
to the shelter of the Jumbakistna Pagoda. On 10 May his siege
guns were run up onto their platforms in the redoubt and
after a few hours bombardment the garrison of the pagoda
surrendered. On the island supplies were nearly exhausted.
Law refused to contemplate breaking out and Chunda Sahib
recognised the end was near. With his usual magnanimity he
summoned his chiefs, regretted he had not sufficient money to
reward them for their services, but announced he would
distribute all he had; then he released them from their
allegiance.

On 14 May his chiefs asked for a free passage through the
British lines, so that they could return to their estates. To the
fury of the Mahrattas who saw chances of plunder and rich
prizes in the shape of ransom money slipping through their
hands, Lawrence insisted that the requests should be granted.
That day most of Chunda Sahib's followers left him, and with
some 2,000 horse and 3,000 foot who still remained faithful he
retired to the Sriringham Pagoda, while the French, as infidels,
occupied the less holy Jumbakistna.

On 18 May, Lawrence crossed onto the island to deal the
coup de grâce. He paused for heavy guns to reach him from
Devicotta so he could breach the pagoda walls. Still Law did
nothing, hoping desperately that d'Auteuil would achieve a
miracle and relieve him. D'Auteuil indeed started to advance
towards his doomed compatriot. On 27 May Clive, hearing that
the French were coming down the Arcot road, once again night
marched to Utatoor, hoping to ambush them in the streets of
that town. During the 28th he waited; then on the 29th he was
told that d'Auteuil, learning he was in Utatoor, had stopped
seven miles short and was now returning to Volconda. Clive's
Mahratta horsemen, riding in hot pursuit, caught the French
up and harried their retreat, while Clive with 100 Europeans,
1,000 sepoys and six guns hurried after. That evening the
harassed d'Auteuil arrived at Volconda to find the gates of the
town barred against him. The Governor was now quite certain
where his allegiance ought to lie. The Frenchman forced an
entrance and stormed the lower fort; then Clive came up
behind him. Sandwiched between Clive threatening to blast
the lower fort with his guns and the Governor securely perched

on his high citadel above, d'Auteuil surrendered. On 30 May Clive retraced his steps to the Pitchunda Pagoda bringing with him 100 French prisoners; the French sepoys he merely told to return to their homes.

Law still refused to surrender, and talked grandly of holding the Jumbakistna Pagoda to the end unless he was allowed to march back to Pondicherry with his troops. Stringer Lawrence, unimpressed, pulled the noose closer about him. On 31 May Chunda Sahib made a despairing effort to escape. He bribed a Mahratta officer to let him through the lines of the Tanjore army so he could escape to the French port of Karikal, some eighty miles to the east. The officer accepted the bribe, met Chunda Sahib, took him prisoner and led him to Manoji.

Lawrence wrote:

'Next day June 1st, the Nabob, the Mysore and Mahratta Generals, Manoji and myself, being assembled, debated how to dispose of him. The Nabob and Manoji judged it very dangerous to let out of their hands a man who had already given so much trouble. The Mysore General and Morari Rao were for keeping him in their possession. Finding they could not agree I proposed that we should have care of him and keep him confined in one of our settlements; this was by no means approved and we parted without coming to any resolution; but some of Manoji's people put an end to the dispute by cutting off his head, which was done the 3rd of June.'

The same day, despite all his brave talk, Law capitulated with more than 600 Europeans and 300 French trained sepoys, all of whom became prisoners of war.* Four 13-inch mortars and thirty-one cannon fell into the hands of the victors. The remnants of Chunda Sahib's army were allowed to disperse. To all appearances the war was over. Nothing remained to Mohammed Ali but to take possession of his kingdom. By risking nothing Law had lost everything.

* The figures quoted are those given by Stringer Lawrence in his account of the war. Orme gives higher figures, but for this part of his history he took much of his information from Robert Clive, who had a tendency to exaggerate.

Chapter 8

The Alliance Breaks Up

Early in June 1752, Saunders, sitting in his palatial residence in Fort St George, Madras, once again the centre of British power on the Coromandel coast, considered the objections made to his plans by his irate and, in his view, obstructive Commander-in-Chief. After all he was nothing more than a passed-over captain who had joined the Company on being told he had no hope of promotion to major in the regular army. He had come back to India after he, Saunders, with the assistance of Clive, had already frustrated Dupleix's designs; he had done little more than push a favourable situation to its logical conclusion. With his limited grasp of affairs he seemed unable to understand that the real enemy was the French. Moreover, he was suffering from an attack of fever and plainly incapable of forming a balanced view.

True, a difficult situation had arisen. Towards the end of June Stringer Lawrence had written to say that he had gone to Volconda expecting Mohammed Ali and his allies to follow. But to his astonishment he learned no one had left Trichinopoly, where a violent argument had broken out between the Nawab and Nanj Raj of Mysore. Lawrence was now staggered to find that, although Trichinopoly was mortgaged to the British, Mohammed Ali, without bothering to tell anyone, had promised the city to Nanj Raj in return for his assistance. Now Nanj Raj demanded payment. Mohammed Ali, however, refused to contemplate yielding his one sure possession until he was securely installed in Arcot. To complicate the issue, Monaji made it plain that his master, Partap Singh of Tanjore, would never tolerate such an addition to the territory of Mysore.

The dispute was beyond Lawrence to settle, and indeed,

except for its very dangerous implications, it was not one that directly concerned the British. In disgust, he left Captain John Dalton with 200 Europeans, 500 sepoys and an unidentified number of the Nawab's largely useless army in Trichinopoly, and marched northwards to Tiruvadi about fourteen miles inland from Fort St David.

Short of actually handing over Trichinopoly, Mohammed Ali did all he could to meet Nanj Raj's demands. He ceded him Sriringham Island and the district that went with it and, as an earnest of good faith, allowed 700 infantry from the Mysore army under Gopal Raj, Nanj Raj's brother-in-law, to enter the city. For a period Nanj Raj appeared ready to accept this not unreasonable offer. If the British had guaranteed it he might have done so and Dupleix's ambitious plans been thwarted, but the British had no desire to see Nanj Raj installed in Trichinopoly. Morari Rao had all along schemed to recover his lost governorship and obtain the city for himself. Now he innocently suggested that, as an impartial arbitrator, he should hold the city himself, a suggestion that appealed to no one. Then he persuaded Nanj Raj to insist that before he gave any more help Mohammed Ali should reimburse him for all his expenses during the campaign just ended.

Even if Mohammed Ali wished to meet this demand he was utterly unable to do so. None of the minor chieftains of the Carnatic was so foolish as to pay tribute to a Nawab who did not come among them sword in hand. Dalton wrote to Fort St George on 13 July that 'Morari Rao's only intention is to protract the war and to this end instils suspicions into the minds of the Nabob and the Raja [Nanj Raj] promising friendship to both. . . . He has also offered his services to the French if they will advance him three lacks of rupees.'

Here lay the essence of the dispute between the Council led by Saunders and Lawrence. Lawrence supported the view put forward by Mohammed Ali, that it was essential to come to terms with the French. Deprived of a reliable paymaster, Morari Rao would return to his estate of Gooty and Nanj Raj have no alternative but to negotiate. Lawrence therefore proposed to blockade Pondicherry. Dupleix was furious that British soldiers were detaining Frenchmen and declared he would not negotiate until their illegal detention, as he phrased it, was ended. The prisoners could be a useful bargaining card, but the legal implications of British soldiers holding Frenchmen captive caused Saunders some uneasiness, and he was careful to maintain that in this matter the British merely acted as the agents of the Nawab.

He disagreed strongly with Lawrence's and Mohammed Ali's proposals. The legal consequences of risking an action on French soil worried him. He preferred to eliminate the strongholds the French had acquired in the Carnatic while supporting Chunda Sahib, and to which their title in consequence was suspect. In particular, he wished to capture the key fortress of Gingee. Lawrence in his irritating and dogmatic fashion held such an aim to be misguided and militarily unrealistic. The two men almost inevitably clashed. Both were strong characters but with limited vision. Now Saunders overruled Lawrence, as with the concurrence of the Council he was entitled to do, and the soldier retired to his sickbed in high dudgeon, no doubt his temperature dangerously increased.

Clive was seriously ill as well, but there was a young major recently out from England, Major Kinnear, who had taken over command when Saunders had been forced by illness to leave the army. He, unlike his crusty and aged superior, saw the wisdom of the Governor's proposals.

Meanwhile a large convoy from France had arrived at Pondicherry. Dupleix removed most of the French sailors, drafting them into his European companies to fill their depleted ranks and replacing them with Indian sailors who could be paid off when the convoy returned from China, its final destination. By this means he replaced much of his losses.

On 23 July 1752, Kinnear with 200 Europeans, 1,500 sepoys and 1,500 of the Nawab's horse, all taken from the troops camped at Tiruvadi, set out to capture Gingee. The fort was garrisoned by 120 French soldiers and a large number of sepoys. Apart from the natural strength of its fortifications, it was situated in a hilly tract of country, through which the few roads wound tortuously along hillsides and through defiles where a handful of men could defy an army.

On 26 July Kinnear approached the fortress and summoned it to surrender. The French governor politely declined. Kinnear looked at the strong walls crowning rugged hills and saw he could do nothing short of a formal siege. Two siege cannon, which by some curious lack of foresight he had omitted to bring, were en route to join him, when he learned that Dupleix had despatched a force of 200 Europeans and 1,500 sepoys to reinforce his garrison. Kinnear realised he must defeat this force before it entered the hills, or else it could seal the main road to the coastal plain, and caught between a blocked pass and the fortress he would either have to attack some naturally strong position or be starved into surrender.

Temporarily abandoning the siege he took the road to Fort St David. He successfully negotiated ten miles of mountain road and emerged into the coastal plain to find the French detachment holding a strong defensive position in the village of Vikravandi, about five miles further on. Despite his fifteen-mile march, he at once launched a frontal attack. The French guns behind cover opened a deadly fire; his sepoys panicked; Kinnear himself was shot in the leg; his Europeans gave back, losing forty men killed and wounded in the process. Now he had no alternative but to withdraw. The victorious French pursued him; the British abandoned Tiruvadi and took refuge in Fort St David. Kinnear died shortly afterwards more from vexation than his wound. At a single stroke much of what the British had gained at Trichinopoly was lost; the dispute with Nanj Raj suddenly assumed a very menacing aspect.

At Madras consternation reigned. Lawrence left his sickbed and got ready to return to Fort St David with two newly arrived companies of Swiss infantry. Saunders, against his advice, immediately embarked one of the companies in open boats with orders to make their way to Fort St David. As they were passing Pondicherry, Dupleix sent out a warship and scooped in the helpless soldiers, to the immense indignation of Saunders, who fulminated bitterly, and with a delightful inconsistency, at the perfidy of the French in attacking the soldiers of a friendly power.

Lawrence embarked on a ship already in the harbour, the *Bombay Castle*, with the other company and sailed safely to Fort St David. He took the field on 17 August 1752 with 400 Europeans, 1,700 sepoys, 4,000 troops from the Nawab's army and nine guns. The French under de Kerjean, Dupleix's nephew, promptly withdrew within the bounds of Pondicherry. To the annoyance of the 'old gentleman' Saunders forbade him to violate French territory. He now repeated his stratagem at Cuddalore and feigned a hurried retreat. De Kerjean had no desire to follow, but his uncle chided him for irresolution and pointed out that a senior French officer was likely to arrive soon and supersede him.

Lawrence had camped at the village of Bahur, about five miles northwest of Fort St David, and de Kerjean, reluctantly complying with his uncle's instructions, camped about two miles to the north. Lawrence joyfully seized his chance. He employed his favourite tactic, a night approach, followed by an attack at dawn or just before it. That he successfully employed this difficult manoeuvre on more than one occasion demonstrated how skilled his troops had become.

At two o'clock on the morning of 26 August 1752, he moved off with his sepoys leading, his Europeans formed as a separate battalion behind them and the Nawab's horse riding on the left. As dawn was breaking a French sepoy piquet challenged the column they could dimly see approaching. The British sepoys shattered them with a volley. The piquet had, however, been well placed, and as the advance continued a long pearl grey line of French soldiers came into view, steadily waiting for the British, their guns deployed in their intervals, the gunners with their slow-matches burning.

The British infantry passed through the ranks of the sepoys and closed with their enemy. The French guns belched grape, but the steady red line never wavered. Then the musketry rolled out. The British fired by platoons as they advanced; the French returned fire for fire; the British refused to halt, the French to give way; with a crash the two lines crossed bayonets. For a few moments there was a grim hand-to-hand struggle; then the British grenadiers fighting in the centre and by a curious chance opposed by the French grenadiers, broke through. At once the French line collapsed and the men ran away, many throwing away their arms to speed their flight. Lawrence turned to order the Nawab's cavalry to charge to complete the victory, but they had already disappeared to plunder the French camp; nevertheless the French losses were heavy. De Kerjean, gallantly trying to stem the flight, was captured with a hundred of his men, and as many more were killed or wounded;

all the French cannon fell into the hands of the victors. British losses were not light, four or five officers and seventy-eight men out of the 400 strong European battalion were either killed or wounded.

British prestige had been restored and in Fort St David a delighted Mohammed Ali heaped congratulations on Stringer Lawrence. Yunas Khan, Morari Rao's deputy (Innis Cawn in contemporary spelling), and 3,000 Mahrattas had been wandering northwards in a rather uncertain fashion; now they rode in to join Lawrence at Tiruvadi which he had re-occupied. However, Nanj Raj with the Mysore army, 16,000 strong, lingered at Trichinopoly and Manoji, reluctant to adventure deep into the Carnatic when matters were so uncertain, had returned to Tanjore. In September Clive, with a party of raw recruits just come from England and some freshly enlisted sepoys, sallied out from Madras to attack two French-held forts, Covelong, eighteen miles south of Madras, and Chingleput thirty-six miles to the southwest on the banks of the Palar river, from which the French had been harassing those loyal to Mohammed Ali. By an extraordinary feat of leadership Clive moulded his unpromising mob into soldiers and captured both strongholds before the onset of the monsoon put an end to active campaigning.

The British appeared to have retrieved their reverse at Gingee, but diplomatically the initiative was rapidly passing to Dupleix. He had, however, to find another claimant to the Carnatic to give a specious air of legality to his ambitions.

For a brief period he swallowed his dislike and proclaimed Chunda Sahib's son, Raja Khan, as the rightful Nawab. But Raja Sahib lacked any real support in the province and Dupleix soon discarded him in favour of a happier solution. Muzaffar Jang, in the moment of triumph over Nazir Jang, had conferred on him authority over the whole of the Indian Peninsula south of the River Kistna. Dupleix determined to revive this authority and now pretended to receive sanads, or letters patent, from the Emperor himself confirming him in this appointment. A supposed envoy from Delhi, gorgeously apparelled and with a suitable escort, arrived at Pondicherry. Dupleix, mounted on an elephant, met him at the bounds of the French territory and ceremoniously conducted him to his palace, while bands played and guns boomed out in salute. The British sourly dismissed the whole affair as a French farce and declined to recognise their new overlord.

The French Governor now possessed the troops and a legal basis for action, but one vital ingredient was missing: he had no money. He had already paid into the French Company's treasury much of his own considerable fortune; in the end he was to ruin himself financially, but it was not enough and the Compagnie des Indes, who viewed his schemes with some alarm, refused to remit more money than was needed for the everyday running of his settlement. Armed with the Imperial mandate, he looked around for some wealthy candidate for the Nawabship who could help finance the war. His eye lighted on Murtaza Ali Khan, the cowardly, treacherous, but indubitably rich, Governor of Vellore. Murtaza eagerly accepted Dupleix's offer to instal him as Nawab and advanced him three lakhs of rupees. As time went on, however, he realised Dupleix was using him merely as a catspaw and withdrew from the contest. Stringer Lawrence caustically noted that Dupleix left 'him where he found him, only something the poorer'.

At this time events in the north took an unfavourable turn for the British. Ghazi-ud-din, Nizam-ul-mulk's eldest son, holding the second most important post in the Empire, that of Bakshi or Paymaster-General, had bitterly resented Salabat Jang arrogating to himself the viceroyalty of the Deccan; that autumn he resolved to uproot the upstart and his insolent French supporters. He advanced southwards with an enormous army, and Balaji Rao, anxious to avenge the humiliations inflicted on him by Bussy, took an army to join him. Ghazi-ud-din occupied Aurangabad without opposition but then, for an Indian prince of that era, displayed an astonishing lack of prudence. He accepted an invitation to dine with one of his numerous stepmothers, the mother of his half-brother, Nizam Ali. Nizam Ali had carefully veiled pretensions to rule the Deccan himself; his mother loyally furthered her son's ambitions by bringing to Ghazi-ud-din a dish which she proudly and accurately described as prepared by her own two hands. The unfortunate Prince ate the dish and died in agony that night. His army, lacking a paymaster, at once dispersed and his son, who adopted his name, or more accurately his title, of

Ghazi-ud-din, went back to Delhi, where he aimed even higher than the viceroyalty of the Deccan. Salabat Jang's position was now assured and Balaji Rao thought it advisable to reconcile himself with the Viceroy and his powerful French allies.

Possibly because the Mahratta Confederacy had become officially friendly with the French, possibly because he knew that if the British were victorious they would never concede him Trichinopoly, Morari Rao in late November threw in his lot with the French and went with his army to Pondicherry.

Previous to that, all through the hot summer months the wrangle over Trichinopoly had continued with ever increasing rancour. Dalton walked in daily peril of assassination and at night swung the cannon on the ramparts to point at the barracks of the Mysore contingent, as a delicate hint that it would be unwise to start an insurrection. Some French prisoners lodged in the city were a constant embarrassment, and on one occasion Captain Poverio, a Neapolitan in the Nawab's army, was bribed to open the city gates to the Mysore army at night and arm them while six stout men were to murder Dalton.

Poverio revealed the plot immediately to Dalton, who planned to lure the Mysore army to its destruction by admitting them into the city and then ambushing them in the dark. Mohammed Ali had left his brother-in-law, Kirud-din, as official Governor of the city. Dalton, perforce, informed him of his plan and that worthy, scared that it might miscarry, thought fit to tell Nanj Raj that his plot had been discovered. The Mysore Prince at once disclaimed all knowledge of such an infamous intrigue, but offered a large reward to anyone who would bring him Poverio, dead or alive. The Neapolitan, however, survived and later Lawrence saw to it that he was granted a pension by the Company.

Dalton had frequent ceremonious meetings both with Nanj Raj and Morari at which profuse expressions of friendship were exchanged; Dalton suspected that the main purpose of these was to see whether or not he was still alive. Lawrence actually suggested that in view of the proven treachery of the Princes, Dalton should take the opportunity at one of the meetings to capture the two and solve the problem of Trichinopoly at a blow. Saunders vetoed a proposal that must have gravely damaged the British reputation for good faith. It is one difficult to reconcile with the old soldier's generally scrupulous honesty; it was probably the fruit of a moment of acute exasperation.

On 8 December 1752, Dalton wrote that Morari Rao had departed 'to have a lakh and a half of rupees to join the French'. At the same time Nanj Raj, still professing friendship, turned to overt hostility, sending armed bands of horsemen to roam the plains to the south of Trichinopoly; these seized anyone bringing grain into the city, cut off their noses and confiscated the grain. The movement of grain ceased and Saunders authorised Dalton to treat Nanj Raj as hostile. At ten o'clock on the night of 23 December Dalton secretly crossed the Cauvery with most of his men to raid the Mysore camp, lying to the north of the Sriringham Pagoda. His men broke into the camp undetected and marched through it in a four deep column, two ranks firing to the right and two to the left. Orme recorded of the action: 'the enemy, according to their senseless custom, raised a number of blue lights in the air . . . but these lights served much better to direct the fire against themselves'.

As dawn came up, Dalton recrossed the river, having escaped virtually unscathed. He had caused consternation in the Mysore camp, but many of their men were in the Sriringham Pagoda and these he had not been able to touch. He accordingly planned the following night, 24 December, to push a 12-pounder cannon and some smaller guns into a well-built choultry on the far bank of the Cauveri and about 600 yards away from the Pagoda and to bombard it. He hoped to cause such panic that the Mysore army would not dare camp within a night march of the city.

That night seventy Europeans and 300 sepoys with the guns established themselves in the choultry under cover of darkness. Dalton lined the rest of his men along the south bank of the river, here about 400 yards wide, to cover their flanks by fire. In a letter to the Council at Madras he revealed what happened next morning:

'The enemy appeared out of the Pagoda and made a push with their sepoys at the choultry, but were repulsed. . . . They came again at about 12 o'clock with their whole force and foot all round. The bloodiest action ensued that I believe has ever been seen in this part of the world, for they had intoxicated their people with bang [an alcoholic drink] and rode on very surprisingly. . . . They made a third charge and our rascally sepoys gave way which so discouraged the Europeans they quitted their officers and ran out of the post, the natural consequence of which was that the horse instantly charged them and killed or wounded almost the whole.'

Dalton, having lost more than a third of his Europeans, retired within the city walls. He at once expelled the 700 men from Nanj Raj's army, keeping their commander, Gopal Raj, as a hostage. By attacking an army 16,000 strong with so small a body of men the optimistic marine had over-reached himself. After two such actions, culminating in a British defeat, no hope of negotiating a settlement with Nanj Raj remained. As 1752 ended Dalton braced himself to stand a siege, and all that had been won in the spring appeared lost. The indomitable Dupleix once more was in the ascendant.

Chapter 9

The Second Battle for Trichinopoly

Stringer Lawrence in his rain-lashed camp glowered at his latest missive from Fort St George. It was November. In the harsh monsoon weather his army was melting away from sickness, yet Saunders and his Council refused to allow him to retire to cantonments and wait for the monsoon to end. No doubt, having delivered their verdict, the councillors had returned to their well-found houses and consumed a glass or so of Madeira while cursing the weather. Lawrence had already complained that he was treated 'like a cypher' in military matters, and had forwarded a letter detailing his grievances, which the Council thought it judicious to ignore. Now he wrote, 'As I can be of no further service I propose leaving the army.' In Madras Saunders, by now fully alive to the sterling qualities of his military commander, wrote a soothing reply, dwelling on his duties to the Company and his country and reversing the foolish letter that forbade him moving into monsoon quarters. Lawrence reluctantly withdrew his resignation, but after this, the last of the many ill-considered rebuffs he had been made to suffer, he found it difficult to conceal his distaste when writing to the Council.

It was an extremely unfortunate situation. A dangerous political crisis confronted the British and there was no one with any political acumen to deal with it. Clive had gone home. Saunders and his Council, steadfast and determined though they might be, were merchants not statesmen. But a short time ago the Company had paid obsequious tribute to the Nawab. La Bourdonnais' attack on Madras, followed by Dupleix's repudiation of his treaty, had generated an intense distrust of everything French and in particular of Dupleix. In endeavouring to frustrate his designs the Company, almost unawares, had drifted into becoming an important military power, a largely accidental event with implications as yet little comprehended. Stringer Lawrence, when ordered by the Council to negotiate with Nanj Raj, on one occasion wrote with the exasperation now habitual to him when corresponding with that body: 'I have neither the leisure nor the inclination to enumerate the many times I have represented my incapacity to transact business that does not immediately relate to the command of troops.' Saunders on the other hand displayed little capacity to transact business that did not relate immediately to trade; the vacuum thus created cost the Company dear.

In Pondicherry, however, was a man who relished transacting political business and far-reaching strategy. Dupleix planned to hold Lawrence in check in the area of Tiruvadi while Nanj Raj, as he hoped, seized Trichinopoly. He instructed his new military commander, Astruc, an experienced soldier, to avoid battle but to keep Lawrence occupied. Astruc fortified a camp a few miles from Tiruvadi, while Morari Rao's Mahrattas harassed British convoys, traversing the fourteen miles from Fort St David to that town, with such success that on occasion Lawrence was compelled to take his whole army to escort them in. In April 1753 he felt strong enough to attack the French. He advanced a few miles to a village from which he planned to strike at Astruc, only to meet with an unpleasant surprise. The French camp was surrounded with a ditch, glacis, ravelins and ramparts. He could not hope to attack it successfully, nor, in view of the depredations of the Mahrattas, bypass it. He wrote somewhat naïvely to the Council, 'Who would have imagined it?' Baffled he returned to Tiruvadi to receive a very disquieting letter from Dalton at Trichinopoly.

Here, Nanj Raj, encouraged by his success in December, had sent his brother-in-law, Viranda, with 5,000 horse and 3,000 foot early in January 1754 into the plain south of the city. For the next two years, much as the Greeks and Trojans contended on the plain about Troy, so the French and British fought bitterly for supremacy on the plain surrounding Trichinopoly. Its geography vitally affected the pattern of that conflict. The Cauvery River, running half a mile north of the city, bounded it to the north and northwest, while to the south and southeast it was bordered by a belt of jungle which, beginning about three miles to the south of the city, curved in a shallow arc eastwards and northwards to meet the river beyond the village of Cootapara, and about eight miles to the east.

The main supply routes ran: north across Sriringham Island to Arcot and Pondicherry; east along the south bank of the Cauvery to Tanjore and the coast; south through the jungle to the Tondiman District, a considerable territory, the Poligar, or chief, of which remained faithful to the Nawab throughout the war. The routes to the west led to Karur and the State of Mysore and consequently were of no interest to the British. During the war Nanj Raj and his allies remained securely installed in the two pagodas on Sriringham Island, barring the road to the north; most of the actions were fought to decide who would control the routes to the east and south.

As became apparent during the campaign of 1752, French Rock about a mile east of the city and the pagoda-crowned Elmiseram Rock some three and a half miles to the east dominated the routes leading to Tanjore. To the south two more lone rocks were of critical importance, Sugarloaf about two and a half miles south of the city and Golden Rock about a mile and three quarters to the west of Sugarloaf. These two commanded the routes to the Tondeman district; but nearly two miles southwest of Golden Rock a group of low hills called Five Rocks afforded a suitable base from which a force could operate against them. Just northwest of Golden Rock a small wood named Fakirs' Tope, or Beggars' Copse, offered a useful site for a camp. To the west of the city the two hamlets of Weyconda and Warrior each contained a pagoda and a choultry and could be turned into strongpoints; these on one or two occasions furnished the French with a useful refuge but had little influence on the fighting.

When Viranda with his army entered the plain he camped at Beggars' Copse and his cavalry, patrolling up to the gates of the city, severed it from all its sources of supplies. The Nawab's governor of Trichinopoly, Nirud-din, assured Dalton that the city was amply provisioned, but when the genial ex-marine checked the stores for himself he found to his horror that they contained only sufficient food for twenty more days. He wrote immediately to Lawrence, telling him the appalling news. The 'old gentleman' received the letter at Tiruvadi on 20 April and realised at once the gravity of the situation. If Trichinopoly fell Mohammed Ali, at present with him at Tiruvadi, would become a homeless fugitive and the French the dominant power in the Carnatic.

He left Captain Chase with 150 Europeans and 500 sepoys to hold the town and on 22 April 1753 marched to succour Dalton, accompanied by Starke as the member of Council to advise him on Company affairs. Astruc, in accordance with his instruction to avoid battle, did nothing to prevent him. Lawrence first made up the coast to Tanjore, hoping to enlist the support of Partap Singh. The weather was blisteringly hot and scorching winds raked the marching column, but he dared not dally. Meanwhile the cheerful Dalton was far from idle. He knew Viranda from the previous year and despised him as nervous and incompetent. He resolved to play on his fears. Each night under cover of darkness he ran some guns within 200 yards of the Mysore camp and lacerated it with grape, withdrawing before dawn. The Mysore cavalry were helpless in the dark and their infantry feared to leave the protection of their camp. Eventually, Viranda, worn down by a bombardment to which he could make no effective reply, abandoned the copse and returned to the quiet safety of the island, leaving the plain to the British.

By now Lawrence had reached Tanjore. Here Partap Singh staged a magnificent reception for him. 'After a refreshment of fruits, a shower of rosewater and being anointed with attar of roses, we were dismissed with presents of elephants, horses and seerpaws [ceremonial dresses].' A fine contingent of horse and foot joined the British, but disappeared during the night. The wily Raja, that expert in procrastination, as ever was lavish in words but niggardly in deeds. Lawrence, resigned to obtaining no significant help, left Palk, who replaced Starke as the member of Council accompanying him, to represent British interests at the Raja's court, and on 6 May resumed his march for Trichinopoly. He arrived there a couple of days later with a hundred of his men sick from the atrocious weather they had experienced. Next day, however, Astruc with 200 Europeans and 500 sepoys quietly joined Nanj Raj on the island.

Lawrence, his force seriously depleted by illness and the desertion of many of his Swiss to the French, yet resolved to attack immediately, drive Nanj Raj away from Sriringham Island, re-open communications with the north, and return to Tiruvadi before Morari Rao and the French took advantage of his absence. Deducting the irreducible minimum to guard the fortress, he mustered 500 European infantry, 80 European gunners, 2,000 sepoys and 3,000 of the Nawab's horse; these last, long unpaid, refused to fight, but with the remainder, on 10 May, he crossed the Cauveri before dawn onto Sriringham Island, using the main ford just north of the city. He drove in a Mysore piquet posted to guard it, but they gave the alarm. Astruc took in the situation at a glance. He ordered the Mysore cavalry under a gallant Rajput named Hari Singh to charge the British while he deployed his men. Hari Singh led his undisciplined hordes forward in a series of charges which slowed down the speed of the British advance, while Astruc formed his men in a nulla a short distance away and skilfully positioned his guns behind cover. Then he drew his cavalry back to protect both his flanks and loosed a hail of musket balls and grape at the British. Although the British outnumbered the French, standing in the open they were being shot down by an enemy behind cover; if they advanced the Mysore cavalry, who had already shown considerable determination, could come sweeping down on their flanks and Lawrence had no cavalry of his own with which to oppose them. He pulled his men back to the cover of a bank a short distance in the rear.

Astruc riposted by infiltrating some sepoys into a building overlooking the British left. Lawrence ordered Captain Polier with his company of Swiss and the grenadier company to throw them out. With a roar the grenadiers leapt forward, chased the sepoys away from the building and followed close on their heels towards the nulla held by the French. Astruc in some alarm began to pull his men back from the nulla. But Polier had only been told to take the building and he recalled the grenadiers, when Astruc at once re-occupied his old position. Possibly an opportunity was missed, but Lawrence could see plainly enough what was happening and could have ordered a general advance if he had thought the moment propitious. He made no move, and the action degenerated into a harmless cannonade in which

neither side gained the advantage. At nightfall Lawrence withdrew to the south bank of the river. Once again an attempt to
take the island had failed. The British never attempted it again.

British losses were not severe but Lawrence, however he
might try to disguise it, had suffered an undeniable repulse.
Recognising that he could not expel his enemy from the island,
he began feverishly to stock up supplies in the city. Away to
the north the Company suffered two more damaging defeats.
Chase in Tiruvadi, after a mediocre defence, surrendered to a
French besieging force, while near Arcot Ensign Joseph Smith,
with a detachment from the garrison of the fort, valiantly but
rashly gave battle to a large army from Vellore, where Murtaza
Ali Khan still cherished illusions that the French were going to
make him the Nawab. Largely owing to the misconduct of
Mohammed Ali's troops, Smith's little force was routed and
all the Europeans either killed or captured.

The future looked bleak indeed. Saunders on 11 May wrote
to Lawrence urging him to come to terms with Nanj Raj, even
if it meant surrendering Trichinopoly for a period as a surety
for the money Mohammed Ali owed him; he suggested
Lawrence might get Partap Singh to mediate. At the same time
he wrote personally to Nanj Raj pointing out he was deluding
himself if he thought that either the French or Morari Rao had
any intention of allowing him to keep Trichinopoly.

Lawrence, however, had more pressing problems than
engaging in a long drawn out negotiation with Nanj Raj, for
which he deemed himself unsuited and which would depend
for its success on the ready co-operation of Mohammed Ali.
Stocks of food had to be replenished or else the need for a
negotiated settlement would not even arise. On one thing he
was determined; he would never allow his field army to be
trapped inside the fortress. He camped at Beggars' Copse to the
south and sent 700 sepoys under Yusuf Khan to obtain supplies
from Tondeman.

Yusuf Khan (known as Issaf Cawn in contemporary
chronicles) was a remarkable character. Born a low caste Hindu,
he turned Mussulman to escape from the handicaps of caste.
Through sheer ability he rose to command a band of foot-
soldiers in Chunda Sahib's army. It was said that he took part
in Raja Sahib's vain assault on Arcot Fort. He subsequently

left Chunda Sahib's service and with his little band went to Nellore. Clive, looking for more soldiers before the battle of Kauveripauk, recruited him with his followers, appointing him as subedar to command them; he was often known as the 'Nellore Subedar' after the place where he was recruited. Lawrence, recognising his superlative worth, promoted him to command all his sepoys. He wrote of him: 'he is brave and resolute, but cool and wary in action . . . he is a born soldier and better of his colour I never saw in the country'.

But while Yusuf Khan and his sepoys were away collecting provisions, Dupleix sent Astruc a formidable reinforcement: 300 Europeans, 1,000 sepoys and 3,000 Mahratta horse under Yunas Khan, Morari Rao's deputy. With such an addition to his strength Astruc resolved to take the offensive, establish himself on the plain and starve Trichinopoly into surrendering. Leaving a garrison on the island, he crossed the Cauveri, swung round the city to the west and camped at Five Rocks to the south of the British. Lawrence backed away nearer to the cannon on the fortress ramparts, but left a garrison of 200 sepoys on Golden Rock to keep in touch with Yusuf Khan still gathering supplies in Tondeman district. He himself, wracked with fever, retired to a bed in the fortress.

On 26 June 1753 – for some reason he noted it as the 27th – Palk in Tanjore awoke to the mutter of heavy gunfire sounding from far away in the west. He wrote to the Council that it continued unabated until half-past ten and that from its weight he judged British forces were in action. Astruc had struck. With Tanjore neutral all he needed to complete the blockade was to seize Golden Rock. In the early hours of 26 June he advanced to attack it. Lawrence, on his sickbed, heard the sound of distant firing and learning that the French were threatening Golden Rock, despite his weakness left his bed, dressed and rode out to the British camp. Leaving 100 men as camp guard and caring nothing for the enemy who outnumbered him by ten to one, he led the remainder to aid his garrison on the rock. As the small British column marched forward, the firing by the rock intensified; then his sepoys could be seen tumbling down its slopes. Shortly afterwards the Lilies of France floated over its summit.

Now Golden Rock was lost, it seemed madness to continue

the advance against the host flooding into the plain: on the other hand, if Yusuf Khan and his sepoys were cut off in Tondeman, lack of supplies must soon force the British to abandon the city. Lawrence turned to his men and demanded, were they prepared to go on? With a great shout they replied they wished for nothing better. Ahead of them they could see the pearl grey coats of the French extending in a well drilled line across the plain, with the captured rock on their left and masses of sepoys on either flank. Bands of Mahratta horsemen swooped menacingly around while nearly a mile behind the French a vast mass of Mysore cavalry milled about uncertainly. Perhaps Astruc never anticipated so bold a counter-stroke, for he allowed the British to advance unmolested by his cavalry. The 'old gentleman' sent his grenadier company and two other platoons of Europeans straight at Golden Rock, while with the remainder he closed with the French on the plain. With superb gallantry the grenadiers scaled the rock and rushed the summit. The French, staggered by the fury of the charge, did not wait to receive it.

In the plain the two lines came to grips; but the triumphant grenadiers lined the top of the rock and poured down a devastating series of volleys on the French below them. The pearl grey line broke. Leaving three guns behind them the French fled towards Five Rocks. Mahratta horsemen came forward to shield them, but they refused to reform. However, the battle was by no means over. A host of Mahratta and Mysore cavalry had moved round behind Lawrence's little force to cut it off from its camp and the city.

Unperturbed, the 'old gentleman' spent some three hours securing the French guns and resting and organising his men, then, forming a hollow square, he thrust towards the serried ranks of horsemen barring his way. His guns thundered grape, tearing a pathway through them while his men marched steadily forward, their muskets ready, but reserving their fire for the last few yards of a charge. Balapa, a nephew of Morari Rao, galloped down on the bayonet tipped square, but only a handful of men followed him. He fell, shot dead by a grenadier, and his surviving followers swerved away. Had the rest of the Mahrattas shown a similar spirit to Balapa's matters might have gone hard for the British; but their ranks thinned by grape they feared to charge down on that resolute infantry, and striding purposefully forward the British regained their camp almost unharmed. Stringer Lawrence had known and admired the young Balapa in happier days when the Mahrattas were his friends, and he sent his corpse to the Mahratta camp in his own palanquin, 'a respect I felt justly due to so gallant an officer'.

This amazing victory gave Lawrence a much needed respite and restored British prestige, but as he observed, 'the numbers of the enemy were so great that a victory or two more would have left all my men on the plains of Trichinopoly'. While the French recovered from their defeat and their allies sulked over their failure, Yusuf Khan slipped into the city from the south with supplies sufficient to last for another fifty days. In the city the Nawab's army, still without pay and with no likelihood of obtaining any, mutinied and only 200 British bayonets saved the Nawab from their wrath. They deserted to Nanj Raj, adding to the numbers of his army but not to its strength.

The first crisis was over and Trichinopoly safe for some weeks. Lawrence, hamstrung by lack of cavalry and aware that only the first round had been fought, now considered how he might add to his strength. Madras had promised him a reinforcement which would have to come up by Tanjore, and even before the battle he had decided that he must persuade Partap Singh to take up arms. Confident that only a comparatively small garrison was needed to hold Trichinopoly, he took most of his army to Tanjore, going by jungle trails to avoid the enemy cavalry. He tactfully halted short of the capital and here Palk told him that Partap Singh, impressed by his victory, had agreed to provide the British with troops. Some time later his old friend Manoji arrived with 3,000 horse and 2,000 infantry; this time they did not disappear into the night shortly after their arrival. On 3 August Lieutenant Repington marched in with 170 Europeans newly arrived from England. Rested and refreshed, Lawrence thought it time to return to the plain. He tarried long enough, however, to write a biting letter to the Council complaining about the condition of the draft.

The weather was very wet. He took advantage of a dry afternoon on Monday 7 August to 'march to a Collery [Kallan] fort within four miles of Sugarloaf', so he reported to the Council. All the 8th the rain teemed down. He remained in camp; he dared not risk meeting the Mahrattas with his powder damp. On the 9th the weather cleared and he set out for the city, keeping well to the south. Brenier, who had replaced Astruc after the fiasco at Golden Rock, awaited him, having garrisoned Sugarloaf, French Rock and Elmiseram. Lawrence was embarrassed by having to escort an enormous convoy amounting to some 4,000 bullocks – later to his intense chagrin he discovered that many of them carried baggage for the Nawab. He deployed his British troops forward and placed his convoy on his left, escorted by the Tanjore cavalry under Monaji. The old fox was not to be caught venturing across the plain which was swarming with enemy cavalry. He skirted the edge of the jungle, keeping just out of cannon-shot of Sugarloaf.

As he swung to the southwest of that rock where Brenier had concentrated all his French infantry, he noted that Golden Rock was garrisoned by only a few French sepoys. Lawrence wrote to the Council on 10 August: 'I ordered Mr Repington with two platoons and the front division of our sepoys to run and get possession of it, which they luckily effected though the enemy, too, ran as hard as they could and the Morattoes [*sic*] made some desperate pushes'. The outdistanced French detachment halted a short distance from Golden Rock. They were now at a considerable distance from their comrades at Sugarloaf. During this time his army had closed up on the rock and Lawrence had tucked his convoy away, well clear of danger. The advanced French detachment was dangerously isolated and the 'old gentleman' did not believe in missing such a chance.

He called down the advance guard and grenadier company from the top of Golden Rock and reinforced them with four more platoons; then he ordered the whole to attack the French, while at the same time he disposed his guns to cover their flanks from the cavalry in the plain. The scarlet line moved off, then jerked to a halt. The officer he had placed in charge rode back to say nervously that he must have some guns before he went forward. Lawrence, furious at the delay, contemptuously told him to remain with the main body and himself rode forward to take command. He related: 'Captain Kirk at the head of the grenadiers, Captain Killpatrick with the piquet [advance guard] and myself at the head of the four platoons marched on, the line keeping admirable order.'

Too late Brenier recognised the peril and hurried forward to Golden Rock with the rest of his men. Two French guns with their advanced detachment spouted flame. Captain Kirk at the head of the grenadiers fell dead and the grenadier company, dismayed by the loss of a revered commander, stopped in their tracks. Killpatrick at once spurred his horse over and, placing himself at their head, demanded did they intend to let their commander die unavenged? With a cheer the grenadiers surged irresistibly forward. The French detachment ran back in a disordered mob, breaking up the line of their comrades advancing to aid them, while the British followed close on their heels. Lawrence noted, 'the panic spreading through the whole, the battalion did not stay to give or receive fire but ran off in a great confusion round Golden Rock and away to Five Rocks'.

The way to Trichinopoly lay open and Lawrence piloted his convoy securely into the city. He urged Manoji to pursue the French with his cavalry, but he refused for fear he might imperil the safety of the convoy. Lawrence was disappointed at this failure to exploit his success, but nevertheless wrote, 'I must do the Tanjorean Horse justice . . . they protected the convoy and kept at a distance the Mahrattas which confirms my former opinion that they are the best horse in the country'.

In the action Lawrence lost forty Europeans, he estimated the French lost one hundred. They drew back westwards to Weyconda, but on 26 August Morari Rao, himself, with 3,000 horsemen marched in accompanied by Astruc with 400 Frenchmen, 2,000 sepoys and six guns. Once again the advantage in numbers had tilted to the French, and Lawrence knew he could take no liberties with Astruc. However, before Astruc arrived Manoji on 11 August had retaken Elmiseram, and now that his communications east to Tanjore were the more important, Lawrence retired to fortify a camp by French Rock east of the city.

Astruc followed him into the plain and camped between Sugarloaf and Golden Rock, linking the two by an entrenchment. Deadlock ensued. Lawrence was too weak to attack the French while Astruc, for his part, preferred to use his superiority in cavalry to harass the British lines of communication rather than to come to grips with his fiery old adversary. The Mahrattas harried every convoy bound for Trichinopoly with no little success. Lawrence grimly waited for reinforcements. The two camps were barely two miles apart, and Orme related that through glasses the soldiers of both sides could see their adversaries settling down to dinner of an evening.

On 19 September 1753 Captains Ridgeway and Caillaud with 230 Europeans and 300 sepoys marched into the British camp. Now Lawrence planned to strike. He began to edge his way closer to the French, taking an 18-pounder siege gun from the ramparts of the fortress to create the impression that he only intended to come within gun range of their lines.

Although the French entrenchment between Sugarloaf and Golden Rock looked formidable enough they had not fortified their left, relying on a detachment on Golden Rock to protect it. Lawrence planned to carry out his favourite tactic, to assault Golden Rock under cover of darkness, swing round behind the entrenchment and roll the French up from their left. The main attack was to be made by his 600 European soldiers advancing in three divisions each 200 strong and moving one behind the other. His sepoys were to follow behind as a second line, while Manoji and his troops were to feign a frontal assault.

At four o'clock on the morning of 21 September 1753 the grenadiers stole away into the darkness, leading the British column. Knowing every nook and cranny of the rock, they stealthily climbed up it, then in the deep darkness preceding the dawn hurled themselves down on the garrison. The surprise was complete. Barely firing a shot and leaving behind them undischarged two loaded cannon, the garrison scrambled down the steep slopes and into their open camp. Below the rock, Lawrence formed his Europeans into line, brought the sepoys up on their right, then drove forward. The French sepoys, seeing the formidable scarlet line looming out of the half-light, made no attempt to resist. The French battalion, the men snatched from sleep and facing an assault from a totally un-expected direction, hastily formed their ranks; four of their guns loosed an ill-aimed salvo, then the British were on them. The ranks of the French crumbled, while the British sepoys swept round their flank and captured Sugarloaf behind them. Astruc and nine French officers, 100 men and 11 guns were captured and 100 more men were either killed or wounded.

During the attack Killpatrick received a shot through the body. 'Concluding that it was mortal, he would not permit any of his people to stay with him, but sent them on with their company in the pursuit of the enemy. Some straggling Mahratta horsemen came up in the meantime and according to their custom, cut at him with their sabres as they passed, but the surgeon, by accident, seeing he was in danger, stayed and protected him.' Killpatrick was yet to render the Company much valuable service. The Tanjore cavalry were too occupied in plundering the French camp to pursue the vanquished.

Staggered by this defeat the allies withdrew to the island. Lawrence confidently but inaccurately predicted 'the Dalloway certainly must give up the cause'. The monsoon broke putting an end to operations. Saunders sought desperately to profit by the enforced pause to bring the war to an end. Mohammed Ali was bankrupt and unlikely to be able to repay the Company for their vast expenditure, ostensibly made on his behalf, and Saunders feared he would not have enough money for the 'Investment', the yearly purchase of Indian goods for export to England on which the Company depended for its existence. Financially speaking the prolonged conflict was bleeding the Company to death. Nanj Raj offered to make peace in exchange for 130 lakhs of rupees – equivalent to a little more than one and one-third million pounds at a time when the whole National budget in Britain often did not exceed 12 million pounds. He wanted the districts round Trichinopoly as security until the money was paid. Mohammed Ali had no money and the Company could not possibly raise such an enormous sum. There was no alternative to continuing the battle or accepting defeat. The latter was unthinkable.

To ease the pressure on the foodstocks in Trichinopoly and in the hope of finding a healthier camp for his men, Lawrence went into monsoon quarters with most of his army by Coiladdy fort, confidently expecting the French to cease hostilities until the weather moderated. But the French had by no means finished for the year. They had received a reinforcement and now planned a masterstroke, nothing less than to repeat Bussy's feat at Gingee and storm the fortress by a night assault. They selected Dalton's battery on its western face as the point for their attack. Here the twin ramparts surrounding the city

protruded outwards to shield an old entrance at this time
disused. To protect it Dalton had constructed a battery on the
outer rampart above the old gateway, now bricked up. The
corresponding gate on the inner rampart was still in use; it
was guarded by two arms from the inner rampart, which projected in front of it and nearly interlocked, leaving only a small
tortuous passageway for anyone entering by the gate.

Killpatrick, still recovering from his wound, had relieved
Dalton in command, for Dalton, on grounds of ill-health when
the fighting appeared to have finished for the season, had been
permitted to return to Madras to take ship for England. Just
before midnight on 27 November 1753 the Duty Officer on his
rounds checked Dalton's battery. He found the piquet there
of fifty men alert and at their post. He passed on. Three hours
later a party of 600 Frenchmen supported by 200 more under
Maissin, their new commander, stole silently out of the black
overcast night, crossed the nearly dry ditch, leant their ladders
up against the 18-foot high rampart towering above them and
noiselessly clambered onto the top, to find the battery, save for
one or two sleepy men, empty and deserted. No doubt the

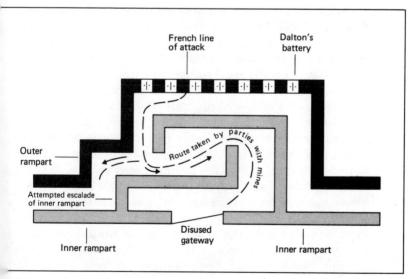

Diagram of the French Escalade at Trichinopoly, 27/28 November
1753

monsoon night was wet, and having satisfied their officer, the piquet, confident that after eleven months of inactivity nothing impended that particular night, had gone elsewhere to seek shelter.

Two or three shots were fired, possibly one by a somnolent sentry. The French, knowing that the alarm had been given, perhaps to confuse the garrison, perhaps to relieve the tension of that silent night advance, swung two 12-pounder guns from the battery round and fired them at the town. They also loosed off a volley of musketry, and to the accompaniment of a roll on their drums gave a great cry of *'vive le roi'*. The delay was fatal to their chances of success.

Killpatrick, owing to his half-healed wound unable to leave his bed, at once stood the garrison to, and despatched his reserve of Europeans, who always slept nearby, to that part of the ramparts where the firing and shouting had occurred. Meanwhile the French pressed on. A large party, hauling the ladders onto the city side of the outer rampart, descended into the 8-yard gap between the inner and outer ones, while the remainder stayed on Dalton's battery to cover them with fire. Once inside the gap between the two towering ramparts, the French divided; two small parties with mines, led by a British deserter, groped their way forward in the darkness towards the inner gate to blow it in, while the others reared ladders up against the 30-foot inner rampart, intending to scale it.

Too late. Lieutenant Hanson, commanding the British reserve, instantly realised that the inner gate was the danger point; he led his men on to the inner rampart above it and on to the two projecting arms that guarded the approach to it and ordered them to keep up a steady fire in the general direction of the gate, whether they could see an enemy or not. At the same time cannon on flanking towers opened up with grape on the French ladders, smashing them all. Only a single French officer and his drummer managed to climb on to the top of the inner rampart. The drummer was killed at once, the officer cut down and captured. The heavy curtain of fire the defenders brought down in the area of the gate killed both the parties carrying mines, although one managed to come within ten yards of their objective.

Now the plight of the French was terrible. The men in the

gap between the two ramparts were trapped without any hope of escape, while those on Dalton's battery, overlooked by the inner rampart at short range, were raked by a deadly fire and had no means of descending the 18-foot wall on which they stood. Some jumped and were injured or killed, while most cowered hopelessly behind whatever cover they could find and longed for a dawn that never seemed to be coming. The British, not at all clear what had happened, waited for daylight with equal impatience. As the light came up the desperate situation of the French was revealed. The British ceased firing and permitted the survivors to surrender: 360 French laid down their arms, including sixty-seven who were wounded, and thirty-seven bodies were discovered in the space between the ramparts.

The French had suffered a disaster; but they still maintained their grip on Sriringham Island and Lawrence distrusted his ability to drive them out. With the new year Saunders and Dupleix appointed commissioners to negotiate an end to the interminable war that was ruining both companies. Dupleix, however, declined to waive his claim to rule all India south of the Kistna, and this the British could not concede. The negotiations collapsed in mutual recriminations.

Although 1753 ended well, by May 1754 the British were once more on the brink of disaster. The allies on the island, as a first step to resuming the siege, determined to detach Partap Singh from his alliance with the British, and, for a paradoxical reason, partially succeeded. Morari Rao sent a large body of his Mahrattas to ravage Tanjore. They carried out their task with their habitual thoroughness, and Lawrence was forced to allow Manoji to take his troops to repel them. By a mixture of skill and good fortune, Manoji succeeded in cornering them and destroying them. Lawrence's jubilation over this success was short-lived. Partap Singh, partly as a result of a palace intrigue fomented by Dupleix, partly because he feared that Manoji was becoming overmighty, dismissed his Commander-in-Chief and dispersed his army on the grounds that it was no longer needed. Lawrence at Trichinopoly was once again deprived of all cavalry; Partap Singh, as a small concession, still allowed supply convoys to be run from his realm to the city.

Lacking cavalry to bring him information and reconnoitre

the routes for his convoys, Lawrence resembled a short-sighted man who had lost his glasses; he knew nothing for certain; everything was blurred and out of focus. After their experiences of the previous year the French did not venture to leave their camp on the island, but now, quite unopposed, their cavalry ceaselessly swept over the plain. Every British convoy had to be furnished with a heavy escort and in February Lawrence suffered a catastrophe. A convoy escorted by 180 European infantry, including his incomparable grenadier company, 700 sepoys and four guns, was ambushed as it emerged from the jungle just to the east of Cootapara and cut to pieces; scarcely a man escaped. By this action Lawrence lost a third of his European soldiers, including his choicest.

He switched his convoys to the south, to the Tondeman District, where they could approach within three or four miles of the city protected by jungle. Here Yusuf Khan, his lion-hearted commander of sepoys, rendered him magnificent service; he organised convoy after convoy, varying their routes through the jungle and running them across the plain after dark or escorted by a powerful party of Europeans. Nanj Raj, appreciating his services to the British, embarked on an infamous conspiracy to discredit him. Lawrence used as his interpreter a Brahmin named Poniappa who had become jealous of Yusuf Khan's pre-eminence and loathed him as a renegade, low-caste Hindu. By arrangement Nanj Raj supplied Poniappa with a letter addressed to Yusuf Khan, purporting to finalise arrangements with him for betraying the fortress. Poniappa showed the letter to Killpatrick, who immediately arrested and imprisoned Yusuf Khan. Fortunately, investigations revealed the plot, Yusuf Khan was reinstated and Poniappa blown from the mouth of a cannon. 'The common punishment for traitors', Stringer Lawrence observed.

As the days passed, the attacks by the Mahratta and Mysore cavalry on the British convoys took an increasingly heavy toll and stocks in Trichinopoly began to run low. Lawrence's health collapsed and he took to his bed. Early in May a large convoy was assembled in Tondeman, carrying supplies vital to the continued defence of the city. Spies revealed its timing and route to the French and they resolved to exert all their strength to intercept it. The stage was set for the last and decisive major action of the war. If the convoy failed to reach its destination, Trichinopoly must fall.

At four o'clock on the morning of 12 May Captain Caillaud with Yusuf Khan, 120 Europeans, 500 sepoys and two guns left the British camp just outside Trichinopoly to bring in the convoy. They had, of course, no cavalry, but Yusuf Khan with his customary fearlessness rode on by himself to scout the way ahead. As he walked his horse through the darkness he came to a slight rise beyond which lay the rendezvous with the convoy. Suddenly his horse threw up its head and neighed; answering neighs sounded from the darkness ahead. Yusuf Khan rode cautiously up the slope; as he topped the rise an ill-aimed volley rang out and he could see the shadowy figures of a number of French troopers. He turned his horse and raced back to warn Caillaud, who had halted the column as soon as he heard the shots.

Caillaud was a cool and able young man. He discussed the matter with Yusuf Khan; they concluded that the French, thinking they had fired at a stray local inhabitant, would not suspect that the British were near. They decided to ambush the ambushers. Keeping clear of the road itself, they advanced up it, Caillaud on one side with the Europeans and Yusuf Khan on the other with the sepoys.

As the first bars of dawn lightened the sky, they charged through the trees and into the French position. Taken utterly by surprise, the French disappeared into the jungle. Caillaud disposed his men to defend the rendezvous and waited for the convoy. As the sun came up he realised that the jungle around him was still alive with Frenchmen; then across the plain to the northward he saw long columns of infantry and cavalry which already cut him off from Trichinopoly. The British had stumbled into a trap; the spring had been released and now the moment of execution had arrived. As Caillaud contemplated a desperate situation, Captain Polier put in an appearance with the rest of the field force. Hearing the firing, Lawrence had ordered him out to investigate, although he himself was too ill to leave his bed.

The total British force now amounted to 360 Europeans, 1,500 sepoys and some newly recruited peons serving Mohammed Ali. The French, according to Lawrence in his account, totalled 500 French, two companies of European deserters, 50 French troopers and 5,000 sepoys, with a mass of Mysore cavalry; of the Mahrattas there was no sign. It was a very ugly situation. The two captains conferred and agreed that they must fight their way back to their camp; the convoy would have to come in after dark.

They set out, their rear harassed by the French who had laid the original ambush, and uneasily prepared for the inevitable collision with those who were coming from the island. Ahead of them they saw a low roll in the ground. Marching fast they gained it before the French. The Europeans lined the crest while the sepoys, echelonned back, covered the right flank and rear.

The French deployed; as the pearl grey line advanced, two short 6-pounder guns with the British poured on them a deadly hail of grape. The French hesitated; Caillaud at once led forward his men. A single volley was enough; the French ran back towards the island and the road to Trichinopoly lay open. The British resumed their march. The French sepoys, without closing, hung about them directing at them a steady long range musketry that took an ever increasing toll of lives. Six out of the nine British officers present were killed or wounded, fifty-six Europeans and 200 sepoys, but the column reached camp still intact. To Stringer Lawrence's joyful surprise, the French, discouraged by their reverse, did not camp on the plain, an act which, by cutting off the convoy, must have put Trichinopoly in the greatest peril, for the British were in no condition to renew the struggle; however, the French and their allies returned to the island and the convoy came in safely after dark. Trichinopoly was saved.

The Mahrattas, fortunately, had taken no part in the action. Morari Rao had become disenchanted with a war that offered so little profit; like any experienced financier he had resolved to cut his losses and be quit of an investment which paid so poorly. He demanded an enormous sum of money from Nanj Raj as the price of his further assistance; when that affronted prince refused, he withdrew to the north bank of the Coleroon while he opened a negotiation with the Nawab to inquire what he would pay him to leave the Carnatic. Mohammed Ali, unworried by an empty treasury, started to treat. Meanwhile a new force appeared in the field. A little time before, Mafuz Khan, Mohammed Ali's brother, released from captivity had entered the Carnatic with an army, ostensibly to aid his brother, in reality to extort as much money as possible from the British for the least possible service. As he wrangled with Saunders he drifted slowly southwards towards Tanjore.

Nanj Raj, blind to any consideration save the conquest of Trichinopoly, now plunged into folly. Despairing of imposing a military blockade, he decided to destroy the sources of the British supplies. He made a fruitless incursion to ravage the Tondeman district, where the peasants after three years of war knew how to conceal their possessions from plundering soldiers, then turned east, took Coiladdy fort and began to demolish the dam near it on which Tanjore depended for its water. Lawrence, certain that Partap Singh would be stung into action, on 23 May left half his troops with Killpatrick in the fortress and with the remainder retook Coiladdy fort and began to repair the damage.

Morari Rao during this time prepared to take his departure; but first he intended to avenge the defeat his troops had suffered at Manoji's hands. He swept down on Tanjore, surprised Manoji's successor and destroyed his army. Partap Singh, in great alarm, asked Lawrence urgently for help and recalled Manoji. Lawrence at once marched to his assistance, but Morari Rao's stroke probably owed as much to shrewd financial calculations as to a desire for revenge. He now told the Nawab he would leave the Carnatic for ever in exchange for three lakhs of rupees. Mohammed Ali would have been hard put to find three rupees, but Partap Singh, delighted at the chance to see the last of his fellow-countryman, accepted for him, stipulating the first instalment, half a lakh, would be paid to him at Volconda. Morari saddled up and left; pausing but to extract one more lakh of rupees from Nanj Raj, he disappeared towards his estate of Gooty, 200 miles to the north.

On 17 August Lawrence, with a European battalion now 1,200 strong and 3,000 sepoys, and accompanied by Manoji with 5,000 horse and foot, for the last time took the road to the devastated plain that he could by now navigate blindfold. The French and Nanj Raj had reinvested the city and on his approach put up a pretence of offering battle. The French were to draw Lawrence on by a feigned retreat, while a new Mysore commander, Hyder Ali, circled round the British column and captured its baggage train. In the event the feigned retreat of the French became a real one, Hyder Ali mistimed his stroke and the allies scuttled back successively to Beggars' Copse, to Weyconda, and finally on 1 September 1754 to the island.

Lawrence was moving his army into monsoon quarters in the Weyconda and Warrior pagodas when tremendous news arrived. A new French Governor, Godeheu, had landed at Pondicherry and Dupleix was returning to France. The French and British Governments had ordered their Companies to cease hostilities and a British fleet under Admiral Watson carrying a complete British infantry battalion of the regular army, the 39th Foot, was expected shortly in Madras. Then he received orders instructing him that all hostilities were to be suspended from 11 October 1754 until 11 January 1755, while commissioners from the two Companies met to reconcile their differences.

Nanj Raj, nearly insane with rage over what he considered the treachery of his allies, asserted he would fight on, if necessary alone. He remained on the island until April 1755, when he heard that Balaji Rao, in search of the Mahratta chauth, and Salabat Jang, looking for the unpaid tribute due to the Emperor, were converging on Mysore. He sullenly departed. He himself did not long survive his humiliation, but the angry sentiment that he had been disgracefully cheated by Mohammed Ali and the British lived on in Mysore and was to have its effect in the future.

The Directors of the *Compagnie des Indes* in Paris had wanted to end the war immediately after they heard of Law's capitulation on Sriringham Island; they left Godeheu in no doubt that his first duty was to achieve a settlement. On 1 January 1755 a provisional treaty was signed in Pondicherry and sent home to Europe for ratification. It preserved the status quo between the two Companies; prisoners were to be exchanged, initially on a one for one basis; Mohammed Ali was to be recognised as the rightful Nawab of the Carnatic, Salabat Jang as the Viceroy of the Deccan. Neither Company was to meddle any more in the affairs of Indian princes.

On the surface it might appear that the long and ruinously

expensive war had altered nothing. The son of Anwar-ud-din ruled the Carnatic, the son of Nizam-ul-mulk the Deccan, the British and French Companies had made some minor gains in territory but had bound themselves to interfere no more in Indian internal affairs. In the Deccan Bussy had made some significant acquisitions; if these were taken into account the French might seem to have emerged the better placed.

But in fact everything had changed. The European soldier had proved himself unquestionably supreme on the Indian battlefield. With such a weapon at its disposal, neither Company was likely for long to restrict its activities solely to trade, and the quarrel between the two had yet to be settled. A British-supported Nawab of the Carnatic, owing a nominal allegiance to a French puppet Viceroy, could not long be tolerated by either side. But as the arrival of a British regular infantry battalion foreshadowed, when the contest was resumed it would be not between rival Companies, but between rival nations.

Chapter 10

Peace and a Catastrophe in Bengal

The war was over. The European battalion dissolved into its original independent companies and returned to barracks. By now it was a finely tempered fighting force, very different from the low grade militia that failed to hold Madras in 1746. It had been noticeable that in the battles the issue had almost invariably been decided by the European troops on either side. The sepoys, organised in separate companies under their own commanders, had yet to achieve a corporate spirit, a sense of identity with their own particular army. They carried company flags and were commanded by subedars who paid them, looked after them, and were the only officers they really knew.

Occasionally British sergeants were posted into their companies to drill them, and these no doubt cuffed the sepoys soundly when their musketry was slow or their line ragged. But they wore no uniform; they were still no more than bands of semi-trained mercenaries following their own particular leader and seeing no dishonour in changing sides when this seemed profitable. In 1756, however, they took a decided step forward, when for the usual fortuitous reasons they began to wear uniform. Pigot, who had succeeded Saunders as governor shortly after the war ended, found himself with a large quantity of unsaleable broadcloth on his hands. He solved his problem with characteristic ingenuity; he issued the broadcloth to the sepoys as uniform, making a suitable deduction from their pay. No doubt it was a shrewd financial move; but much more important, with their new red coats the sepoys could feel themselves to be fully fledged members of the Company's army.

In Madras there were some changes in command. George II, having been graciously pleased to send the Company a battalion of his infantry to protect their settlement, made it plain that the Lieutenant-Colonel commanding it should be Commander-in-Chief. Stringer Lawrence, with what grace he could muster, found himself relegated to command the Company's army under his new chief, a somewhat galling reward for his services. However, the Directors, on the insistence of Clive, at that time in England, voted him a ceremonial sword. Yusuf Khan was promoted to command all the sepoys and given a gold medal as a reward for his services.

The Directors also recruited a new Lieutenant-Colonel, Heron, and sent him out to Madras. Heron's date of joining the Company's forces as a Lieutenant-Colonel was later than that on which Stringer Lawrence was promoted, so he ranked junior to the 'old gentleman'. He was placed in charge of the Madras field forces. No doubt Lawrence, after his exertions and ill-health, was happy enough to devote himself to the quieter tasks of administration. As with Major Kinnear, the dangers of appointing a newly arrived officer to command in the field were soon to become apparent.

After hostilities had ended, the Council at Madras, who were no economists, pressed on Mohammed Ali the need to reimburse the Company for the large sums of money they had spent on his behalf, a somewhat casuistical argument which conveniently ignored that they had supported him almost entirely to further their own ends. How a prince who had just begun to rule a province impoverished by war could find such sums of money they considered no concern of theirs. The supple mind of Mohammed Ali was equal to the occasion. He suggested that if the Company would re-establish his authority over the two southern provinces of Madura and Tinnevelly, they could take the revenue from them to pay off his debts.

Unmindful of their agreement with the French not to meddle in the affairs of the Indian princes, the Council fitted out an expedition under Heron. The two provinces at this time were in a state of anarchy, different regions being ruled by Poligars who were little better than robber barons, preying on the towns and their neighbours and only rendering tribute when confronted by a force they feared to resist. They maintained fierce bands of retainers, called Kallans, who recognised no law save that of fidelity to their masters. They were noted horse thieves.

In 1752 some Poligars assisted the British outside Trichinopoly, and in due course Lawrence and Clive lost all their horses.
The culprits were two Kallan brothers who, when accused of
the crime, did not deny it but said they could get the horses
back in two days. One accordingly was allowed to go to retrieve
the horses while the other was held prisoner as a surety. When
after two days the other brother had not reappeared, Lawrence
had the captive hauled before him. He demanded to know
what had happened to his brother, and sternly warned him
that he would hang if his brother did not return. The captive
Kallan coolly replied that surely the English were not so
innocent as to suppose that his brother intended to come back
with so valuable a booty, which would make the fortunes of
their family, merely for the price of his miserable life that he
had often risked to obtain a single meal. Caught between com-
passion and an amused admiration for his coolness, Lawrence
and Clive let the man go free. Such were the Kallans.

In February 1755 Colonel Heron with Yusuf Khan and his
sepoys and Mohammed Ali set out to reconquer Madura and
Tinnevelly. Mohammed Ali soon found campaigning too
arduous and returned to Trichinopoly. Heron blundered at
the outset; on his own authority he made an alliance with the
Poligar of Marava, to the enormous indignation of the Poligar
of Tondeman and the Raja of Tanjore, deadly enemies of the
Poligar whose land bordered on theirs.

Heron occupied Madura without difficulty; the Governor
attempted no resistance but took refuge in a nearby pagoda.
Without heavy guns Heron marched against it and found its
walls too thick for him to breach with his field guns. Deficient
though he might be in scruple, Heron lacked nothing in courage.
He refused to retreat and proposed to burn down the gate.
His officers turned down his proposal as ridiculous, whereat he
replied that if necessary he would do it himself. At this Yusuf
Khan volunteered to go with him. So the two went forward
alone with their bundles of straw to burn down the gate. To
the amazement of the army, they succeeded in firing it and the
garrison of the pagoda surrendered. Heron plundered it
remorselessly, seizing a number of brass images held in peculiar
veneration by the citizens of Madura. He offered to sell them
back to the Brahmins at a price which they either could not

or would not pay. He then kept them, saying he would melt them down for their metal; the Madurans were horrified at the prospect of such sacrilege. In due course, the Council at Madras, ever careful to avoid giving offence over matters of religion, censured his action, but by then it was too late.

He continued his conquering way to Tinnevelly, antagonising all as he went. Here he received a curt note from the Council instructing him to terminate his alliance with the Poligar of Marava. He promptly told the Marava contingent with him to be gone and when they hesitated proceeded to attack them.

Heron remained at Tinnevelly until May when the Council at Madras, hearing Salabat Jang was marching south, recalled him. On 29 May 1755, as he was marching through a jungle defile near Nattam, the Kallans ambushed his rearguard and recovered the brass images. Heron, well ahead with his senior officers, left his rearguard to its fate. Joseph Smith, commanding it, eventually managed to extricate his men but with heavy loss. He subsequently described the expedition with more passion than grammar, as 'the most infamous I ever wish to be witness of'.

The Council at Madras, discovering that however much his personal fortune might have benefited Heron had failed to raise sufficient money even to cover the costs of his expedition, concurred with this view. Heron was court-martialled but escaped to Pondicherry. At this time Salabat Jang with Bussy was at the gates of Mysore and the Council thought the situation too menacing for them to indulge in any further adventures in the south. When the peril in the Deccan receded, it was succeeded by a disaster in Bengal. As a result the Council dared not spare any European troops to operate south of Trichinopoly.

Mohammed Ali, meanwhile, appointed his incompetent and indolent elder brother, Mafuz Khan, to rule the two provinces, an appointment that rapidly reduced them to even greater chaos than before. In the end, the Company, still without any money from Mohammed Ali, coerced him into allowing them to administer the two until his debt was paid off. They adopted a Moghul type organisation by appointing a dewan to collect the revenue and Yusuf Khan with 1,000 sepoys as military governor to enforce his demands. Yusuf Khan and the Dewan quarrelled incessantly over their respective responsibilities, while Mohammed Ali affected bitterly to resent the supersession of his brother; the hatred that sprang up between the Nawab and the Commander of Sepoys was in due course to bear tragic fruit.

In June 1756 Admiral Watson with his fleet sailed into Madras Roads, carrying Robert Clive as a passenger. Clive, with a commission as a Lieutenant-Colonel in the East Indies, had been appointed Second-in-Council and Deputy Governor to his old friend George Pigot, who had just replaced Saunders as Governor of the Madras Presidency. Before Clive took up his new post, however, he had gone first to Bombay as Commander-in-Chief of an expedition designed to help the Mahrattas overthrow Salabat Jang, or at least compel the Viceroy to dismiss his French allies.

Bussy's relationship with the Viceroy had not always been easy and only his remarkable diplomatic gifts had prevented an open break, the main source of discord being payment for the French troops. The great nobles of the Deccan, having little veneration for a ruler who, Orme observed, lacked both sagacity and courage, recognised the French as the main obstacle to dispossessing him, and schemed to encompass the downfall of Bussy whenever an opportunity offered. Bussy successfully frustrated their designs, until in January 1753 he fell sick and went to the French settlement at Masulipatam to recuperate.

Said Lafkar Khan, Salabat Jang's dewan, took advantage of his absence to persuade the Viceroy that French help was not only far too expensive but also unnecessary. He suggested that if the Viceroy removed himself from Hyderabad, the onetime capital of Golconda, and went 300 miles to the northwest to reside in Nizam-ul-mulk's old capital, Aurangabad, he could terminate his agreement with the French in safety.

Lafkar Khan had miscalculated. As soon as he was fit enough, Bussy concentrated his troops and boldly marched on Aurangabad. To Salabat Jang's nervous protestations about the exorbitant cost of French aid, Bussy had a ready answer; further discord on the vexed question of money could be avoided if the Viceroy would cede him the rents of the northeastern coastal provinces of Mustafnagar, Elore, Rajamundrum and Cicacole in addition to that of Gondavir, which had already been ceded to the French with the port of Masulipatam. These provinces were collectively entitled the Northern Circars. Salabat Jang agreed and, although the chief nobles of the provinces staged a brief rebellion, Bussy successfully took possession of his new territories. Now except for the British factories at Vizagapatam and Ingeram, the French ruled 450 miles of the eastern coastal plain from the mouth of the River Kistna to the pagoda of Juggarnaut.

They seemed to have gained a dominating position in the Indian Peninsula, and as Britain and France drifted steadily towards war the British shared the apprehensions of the Mahratta Peshwar, Balaji Rao, about such massive encroachments. After his previous experiences Balaji Rao feared to engage Salabat Jang and Bussy unless he himself could rely on the support of European infantry. He asked the British for assistance; to the directors it seemed an opportunity far too good to miss. Early in 1755 they sent Clive with three companies of the Royal Artillery out from England to Bombay to organise an expedition into the Deccan in conjunction with the Mahrattas. After Salabat Jang had been humbled or unseated Clive would go on to the Carnatic.

Clive was only to command if, as seemed likely, Stringer Lawrence could not be spared from the Carnatic. The Duke of Cumberland sponsored a move to appoint Colonel Scott, at that time inspecting the defences of the Company's forts, to take charge of the expedition, but that officer died in Madras in May 1754. When Clive landed at Bombay in November 1755 he found the Council there far from enamoured of the enterprise. The punishment inflicted on the port by Aurangzib was not forgotten and the fate that overtook the Portuguese on Salsette Island was a grim warning against indulging in adventures on the mainland. The French were no obvious threat on the west coast and Bombay was far more concerned about the depredations of Tulaji Angria on their shipping: he appeared a worthy successor to his piratical father and harassed their convoys unmercifully.

However, Tulaji, grown over-confident, had disowned his allegiance to the Mahratta confederacy and refused to pay

tribute. Balaji Rao was as anxious as the British to teach him
a lesson. In April 1755 Commodore James, with the Company's
ships *Protector*, 40 guns, *Swallow*, 16, and two bomb vessels,
together with a Mahratta fleet, sailed to attack Tulaji's fleet,
at that time anchored off his stronghold, Severndroog. In light
airs the pirate fleet escaped and took refuge in his second
stronghold, that of Gheria. James, however, on 2 April attacked
Severndroog and captured it.

Now the Council at Bombay wanted to exploit this success
and finally extirpate the pirates. Just before Clive arrived,
Admiral Watson with a Royal Naval squadron consisting of
four ships of the line, *Kent*, 64 guns, *Cumberland*, 66, *Tyger*,
60, and *Salisbury*, 50, accompanied by the *Bridgewater*, 20 guns,
and the sloop, *Kingfisher*, 14, had sailed into Bombay harbour.
With such a fleet to hand it seemed folly to miss so excellent
a chance to destroy Gheria. The Council pointed out to Clive
that the provisional treaty just concluded with the French at
Pondicherry expressly prohibited the British from interfering
in quarrels between Indian princes. The treaty had yet to be
ratified in London and Paris, but once it became binding on
the Company as a whole it might be necessary to withdraw a
contingent operating with the Mahrattas, an act that Balaji
Rao would inevitably look upon as a betrayal and resent
accordingly. On the other hand an expedition against Gheria
would be welcomed by all the European settlements along the
west coast and would please the Mahrattas.

Clive and Watson agreed, and on 11 February 1756 Watson
with his fleet, carrying Clive as Commander-in-Chief of the
land forces together with a contingent from Bombay, anchored
off Gheria. Tulaji Angria panicked at the sight of so formidable
an array and fled to a Mahratta army that was advancing against
Gheria on land, hoping to come to some arrangement with
them whereby he could ransom his stronghold. Gheria, however, fell to Watson after a negligible resistance; its fortifications were dismantled and the pirate fleet burnt.

The operation was chiefly notable for a dispute between
Clive and the naval officers over the division of the prize money.
Clive maintained that as land forces commander he ranked
with Rear-Admiral Pocock, Watson's second-in-command. The
naval officers objected that he should rank as a post-captain

and Watson upheld them. Clive refused an offer from the Admiral to make good his share out of his own pocket, saying that he had put forward his claim only as a matter of principle. Clive was to fight hard before Watson grudgingly conceded to him his rights.

He came with Watson to Madras in June 1756, where he renewed his friendship with George Pigot and went to take up his appointment at Fort St David. The news from the Deccan was interesting. Bussy and Salabat Jang were again at odds and the Viceroy now appealed to the British to help him get rid of the French. The development sounded promising, and with a complete disregard for the treaty so recently concluded at Pondicherry, the Madras Council began to organise an expeditionary force. Then came strange and disturbing news from Bengal.

The Viceroy there, Alivardi Khan, although prolific in daughters, never had a son. On 10 April 1756 he died. His brother, Haji Ahmad, had three sons whom Alivardi Khan, the Nawab of Bengal as he was normally styled, married to three of his daughters. The eldest son of Haji Ahmad he made Governor of Dacca, the middle one, Governor of Patna, and the youngest, Governor of Purnea. Haji Ahmad and his three sons died while Alivardi Khan was still alive and the succession now lay between their offspring. The Begum Ghasiti, the wife of the eldest son, after the death of her husband continued to rule in Dacca; she had no son of her own but had adopted Murad-ud-daula, the younger son of the Governor of Patna. She now proclaimed her adopted son the new Nawab on the grounds that hers was the eldest branch. Siraj-ud-daula, the elder son of the Governor of Patna, maintained that as the elder he had a better right to succeed than his brother Murad, and indeed Alivardi Khan had nominated him as his heir. Shaukat Jang, who had succeeded his father as Governor of Purnea, advanced his claim on general principle.

Everything seemed to presage a complicated civil war, but in the event Siraj-ud-daula, with the assistance of the Commander-in-Chief, Mir Jafar Ali Khan, was proclaimed Nawab in Murshidabad: his title, however, had yet to be confirmed by Delhi. He was an extremely handsome youth, but foolish, vain and capricious. He had already offended many prominent men and few Europeans in the settlements along the Hooghly expected him to reign for any length of time. However, Begum Ghasiti submitted almost at once and Shaukat Jang, too, pretended to come to terms.

The Calcutta Council under their Governor, Roger Drake, regarded the new Nawab with contempt and they omitted to send the customary present on his accession; then largely by accident they became embroiled in a dispute that emphasised their discourtesy. A few weeks before he died Alivardi Khan had appointed Raj Ballabh, Begum Ghasiti's chief minister at Dacca, to become his own chief minister in Murshidabad. Raj Ballabh distrusted Siraj-ud-daula and, knowing the old Nawab was on his deathbed, sent his son Krishan Dass, his wives and, it was believed, a large amount of treasure he had accumulated in Dacca by various means to Calcutta for safekeeping.

Siraj-ud-daula duly disgraced Raj Ballabh and, learning to his chagrin that all his treasure was in Calcutta, despatched an emissary to demand the surrender of Krishan Dass, the wives and the treasure. The emissary, when he came to Calcutta, first visited a prominent Hindu merchant, Omichand, who had represented the British at the Nawab's court at Murshidabad, but had been removed for abusing his position. The emissary came direct from Omichand's house to see the Governor; Drake, suspecting, according to his own account, that the emissary was nothing more than a member of Omichand's staff sent to further some intrigue, refused to accept the Nawab's letter and ordered the emissary out of Calcutta.

Siraj-ud-daula, furious at the treatment meted out to his representative, now made three demands on the British. Krishan Dass and his treasure and the wives were to be surrendered, the fortifications at Calcutta, which he had heard were being strengthened, were to be dismantled, and the practice of issuing *dustucks* to British merchants was to be discontinued. The system of *dustucks*, whereby the Governor by signing a document could exempt goods in passage from all local taxes and dues, had been negotiated with the Emperor Farrukhsiyar in 1717. The system had long been a source of friction on the grounds that it was not intended to cover anything more than bonafide imports and exports of the Company's goods while in transit between factories, and did not apply to the inland trade carried on by merchants in their private capacity. The system had undoubtedly been abused.

The Council at Calcutta was now in a quandary. Apart from the propriety of delivering Krishan Dass into the hands of his enemy and almost certain death, the position of the new Nawab was still insecure; by surrendering Krishan Dass and the treasure the Council might be fatally antagonising a future ruler of Bengal. To dismantle the fortifications of Fort William, when it was common knowledge that war with France would break out at any moment and a civil war in Bengal could not be discounted, seemed inexcusably rash, while as for the *dustucks*, their sale produced a handsome private income for the Governor, but here something might be negotiated.

Diplomacy was clearly necessary, but Drake replied to the Nawab rejecting his demands in terms that left him speechless with rage. In retaliation he began to blockade the British factory at Cossimbazar about six miles down the river from Murshidabad. By 2 June 1756 its chief, William Watts, reported that the factory was surrounded and an attack imminent. Drake hastily wrote to Madras to ask for help. Governor Pigot viewed the request with disfavour but could not ignore it. He sent Killpatrick with 200 soldiers as a reinforcement. They arrived too late. On 3 June Watts surrendered the factory and on 5 June the Nawab set out to enforce his demands on Calcutta.

Drake and his Council heard the news with stupefaction. It was unbelievable that an Indian prince proposed to attack a European fort. Even the Mahrattas had refrained from attacking Governor Dumas in Pondicherry when he refused their demands. The Council still had no conception of the peril in which they stood.

Fort William had been built in the customary pre-Vauban style of a rectangle with its long sides, about 200 yards in extent, running parallel to the river and with a bastion in each corner. No ditch had been dug, warehouses had been constructed against the southern face of the ramparts; the ramparts themselves were only eighteen feet high and overlooked by houses nearby; they were so shaky in construction that it was doubtful if they would support the weight of heavy guns. The garrison consisted of about 260 European soldiers of whom perhaps only 160 were English, and two companies of militia made up of Company servants, Portuguese, Armenians, Topasses and others, giving a grand total of about 500 so-called Europeans. In addition there were 1,500 Buxerries armed with matchlocks, the Bengal equivalent of peons. Captain Minchin commanded the soldiers, two members of Council, Holwell and William Mackett, the companies of the militia.

Drake conferred with his Council and Captain Minchin his garrison commander about what should be done. The obvious solution, to strengthen the ramparts of the fort, demolish the houses overlooking them and hold Fort William until Admiral Watson could relieve them, was unpalatable, for the Europeans would inevitably lose many of their possessions and have to live uncomfortably if securely in an antiquated fort. With a garrison of 500 Europeans, properly organised Fort William should have been impregnable against an Indian army without a siege train.

Neither Minchin nor Drake were capable of imposing such unpopular measures. Instead they decided to construct batteries commanding the three main approaches to the fort, each to be garrisoned by about 100 men. One was built 200 yards to the north of the fort, one about 300 yards to the east, by the Court House, and a third commanding a ditch about 400 yards to the south. The batteries, of course, could not support each other and houses on either side of them offered any attacker a good covered way between them; in street fighting the European infantry lost almost all the advantages conferred on them by their superior arms and training; only one battery had to fall to make it necessary to abandon the other two. Worse dispositions it would be difficult to imagine.

On 16 June Siraj-ud-daula's advance-guard, coming down the river from the north, struck against Perrin's redoubt constructed to command the crossing over the Mahratta ditch about 1,500 yards to the north of Fort William. The East Indiaman, *St George*, was anchored close by so that she could sweep with her guns the approaches to the ditch and redoubt. It was held by Ensign Piccard with fifty men and about forty Buxerries. Piccard had served for a short time in the Carnatic, possibly with the Bengal company that joined Clive just before the battle of Kauveripauk. Aided by fire from the ship, Piccard beat off all attacks, probably giving the defenders a false sense of security.

As the Prince's main army came up, it sheered away from the northern route. All 17 June a host of men, horses, elephants and vast trains of bullocks dragging heavy guns, poured into the plain to the east of the city. Piccard withdrew his men to North Battery. By that evening it was clear that the Nawab intended to attack next day and during the night the north-east bazar went up in flames.

At eight o'clock on the morning of 18 June 1756 a large body of enemy advanced down the road towards South Battery; a few rounds cleared the street; the enemy vanished into nearby houses, kept up a desultory fire on the battery and infiltrated round it to the east. Lieutenant Blagg with a party of twenty-two men occupied two houses on the east flank of the battery and prevented it being attacked from the rear. Protected on one side by the Hooghly and on the other by Blagg's party, the Battery maintained its position without difficulty.

In the north events followed a similar pattern and again the enemy infiltrated round to the east. It was at East Battery with both flanks exposed that, as might have been expected, the decisive action occurred. Captain Clayton commanded here with Holwell and a Lieutenant Le Baume. Despite his vulnerable flanks Clayton made his situation worse by dividing his little force and sending an advance party with two guns 500 yards up the road to occupy an isolated position by the city gaol. The enemy attacked at nine o'clock; they were checked in front, but matchlock men worked their way through the houses and shot up the advanced detachment commanded by Le Baume from the flanks and rear. His men seem to have put up a stout resistance, but fired on from all sides eventually Le Baume had to withdraw leaving his guns behind.

At noon, as was customary in Indian armies at that time, the firing ceased so that the soldiers could eat their morning meal. At two o'clock the battle was resumed. Now the matchlock men ignored North and South Batteries and concentrated their attention on East. From houses overlooking it they poured in a plunging fire on the defenders to which no effective reply was possible. About four o'clock Clayton spiked his heavy 18-pounder and withdrew with his field guns. The Nawab's men thrust forward towards the fort. Both North and South Batteries had to be evacuated before they were cut off. Orders to retire never reached Blagg and his party, but they hacked their way back, losing only two men in the process.

Now Drake formed a new line holding the church just to the east of the fort and two houses that overlooked its ramparts. Thus, after less than a full day's fighting, the main British defences had been breached. The troops were discouraged, and it is probable that a number of the topasses deserted. That night the European women were evacuated to an East Indiaman, the *Dodaly*, anchored in the river and, for reasons never satisfactorily explained, two members of Council, Manningham and Frankland, thought it desirable to accompany them.

At a Council meeting held at two o'clock next morning the decision was taken to give up the fort, but no details were agreed as to how this should be done. During the night an attempt at an escalade was reported and Drake had the great drum beaten to summon the garrison to stand-to; the garrison disregarded the call, but the attackers paid it rather more attention and withdrew. The same night the lascars and buxerries all deserted.

During the 19th the enemy closed in on the outlying strongpoints and by ten o'clock had penned the garrison within the fort. That night the Portuguese and other women were ordered to embark. The embarkation became a scene of appalling confusion, during which it is believed that 150 soldiers and merchants managed to scramble aboard the ships; Minchin and Drake, who up until then had displayed courage and coolness, jumped into the last boat to pull away from the shore. For Minchin there can be no excuse, but Drake had good reason to dread what would happen if he fell into the hands of the Nawab, and the fort by now was doomed.

Holwell took command of a distracted and by now largely drunk garrison. He proposed to hold the fort during the next day, bring down the *St George* from its station by Perrin's redoubt and embark the garrison during the night. That day the enemy kept up a heavy fire from houses overlooking the ramparts but were held in check. In the evening, however, the *St George*, sailing down to the fort, went aground and had to be abandoned.

The night passed quietly and early next morning unavailing efforts were made to persuade the other vessels in the river, which had by now dropped some three miles downstream, to return to take off the garrison. Their refusal to move remains an enigma – possibly they feared the fate of the *St George* which had been boarded and burnt. During the morning the Nawab's army, according to Orme, made some determined efforts to scale the ramparts, but were beaten off; attempts at an escalade in broad daylight argue a reckless courage that the Nawab's army never subsequently displayed, and it must be surmised that the number of the garrison prepared to man the defences was small. When at noon the firing died away, it was evident that such of the garrison as had remained loyal were both exhausted and utterly disheartened.

Owing to some extraordinary negligence, little dry powder remained and Holwell now sent a letter to the Nawab offering to surrender on terms. At four o'clock an Indian officer appeared bearing a flag of truce. While Holwell parleyed with him a crowd of the Nawab's troops gathered in the roadway outside the walls of the fort. Suddenly they burst through the gates unresisted, and the garrison, swamped by numbers, threw down their arms. That night 145 of them, including Holwell, were confined in a narrow room from which only twenty-three emerged alive next morning; Holwell was among the survivors.

The defence of Calcutta had been disgracefully mismanaged. For the fort to be surrendered after only three days of siege and with its walls unbreached excited the derision and contempt of the other European communities. As for Siraj-ud-daula, he said he did not rate the Europeans as worth above a slipper.

Chapter 11

The Recovery of Calcutta

On 15 December 1756 Clive stepped ashore at Fulta, a small village not far from the mouth of the Hooghly, to be greeted warmly by Roger Drake. Clive, as Commander-in-Chief of the Land Forces, had sailed with Admiral Watson and his fleet from Madras to reconquer Calcutta. His troops' consisted of five companies of the Madras Europeans and some gunners and train, totalling about 570 Europeans, 1,000 sepoys and 300 lascars; these last were not fighting troops, but employed mainly on servicing the guns and equipment. In addition three companies of the 39th Foot, numbering in all 270 men, served on the ships as marines. That they were not under Clive arose from a dispute over who should command on land.

When on 16 August the appalling news came to Madras that Calcutta had fallen, adventures into the northern Deccan were forgotten and the Council concentrated on organising and equipping an expedition to Bengal to the exclusion of all else. But although the immediate objective was clear enough, the future of Madras itself was perilous and obscure. Rumours perpetually circulated that Britain and France were at war. A letter received from the Directors on 14 May 1756 reported that in France 3,000 regular troops destined for Pondicherry were being embarked on six ships of the line.

The information had not been confirmed, but it would be rash entirely to discount it. Watson was prepared to take his complete fleet to Calcutta, but in the light of the possible French naval strength dared not weaken it by detaching ships for particular tasks. Adlercron announced that he was willing to take the 39th to Calcutta, provided that he commanded on land. The Council, after its experiences with Kinnear and Heron, felt

186

reluctant to entrust so important an operation to an officer who had no practical experience of Indian warfare; moreover Adlercron, as an officer serving the King, had refused on several occasions to carry out its instructions. If the French threat materialised the Council might need to recall its expeditionary force at short notice. Adlercron declined to guarantee he would return if so required by the Council; the Council thereupon declined in its turn to appoint him to command the land forces.

Adlercron, highly incensed, replied he would permit no forces of the Crown to go to Bengal. He could scarcely agree to serve under Clive, whom he probably regarded as something of a military adventurer, or send his regiment and remain behind himself. But his refusal to allow any regular troops to go – he ordered a detachment of the Royal Artillery already on board ship to disembark, – brands him as petty and small-minded, however much allowance is made for wounded vanity. Admiral Watson, however, who had no doubts about his duty when the interests of his country were at stake, demanded three companies of the 39th to serve on board his ships as marines. Defying the Admiral was altogether another matter, and Adlercron assented, stipulating his men should serve only as marines. The quarrel emphasised the undefined relationship between the Company and the officers of the Crown, one that was to cause endless friction. It is the more remarkable that two such masterful men as Clive and Watson managed to co-operate so well; it sheds an interesting light on the characters of both.

The refugees from Calcutta had landed at Fulta to reprovision their crowded ships for the voyage to Madras. But once ashore, there came a reluctance to depart. Siraj-ud-daula had returned to Murshidabad, leaving them unmolested, the Company brought in much valuable revenue to his viceroyalty and he had no wish to expel them now that they had learned who ruled in Bengal. Drake had no desire to leave; once he quitted the province his authority as Governor must lapse. Then Killpatrick arrived with his reinforcement of 200 men. Drake, buoyed up by the hope that further reinforcements from Madras might enable him to recapture Calcutta before the news of its fall reached his masters in England, decided to stay on. After some discussion about its legality outside Calcutta, he reconstituted his Council and resumed his authority as President. Manik-chund, appointed by Siraj-ud-daula to be Governor of Calcutta, left them unmolested, but it was to be two months before the ships from Madras arrived. Watson delayed sailing until 16 October to avoid the worst heats of the year for his over-crowded ships, but in consequence ran straight into the northeast monsoon.

By the time Clive arrived, the Directors in London had instructed their three presidencies to form secret select com-mittees, so that important decisions might be taken more quickly and not be broadcast to an enemy. Drake accordingly formed such a committee which, when Clive landed, consisted of himself, Watts who had been freed by the Nawab, Becher and Holwell. Clive joined it, but the Council at Madras, distrust-ful of that in Bengal, not without reason, and apprehensive about future developments in the Carnatic, insisted that he remained under their authority. Clive, who had seen how Saunders' inept meddling in military affairs had played no small part in prolonging the war in the Carnatic, shrewdly exploited his instructions to give himself, in effect, a free hand in Bengal. To the helpless indignation of Drake and his truncated Council, he blandly explained that in view of his orders from Madras he must reserve to himself the right to act independently of the Council, if he thought fit to do so. But for this lip service to the authority of Madras, which he ignored whenever it suited him, Clive might have accomplished nothing of note in Bengal other than aiding in the recovery of Calcutta. Watson, of course, acknowledged no authority except his own and was quite clear that the planning and execution of the mission was his affair, an assumption no one cared to question.

At this time Clive faced great difficulties. Killpatrick's little force had nearly all succumbed to fever; even with the volun-teers from Calcutta and a few surviving members of the Bengal Europeans, his force amounted to little more than a hundred fit men. Clive himself suffered from a feverish cold and, worst of all, two ships carrying troops and stores, storm-beaten by the monsoon, had disappeared into the Bay of Bengal, depriving him of about 250 Europeans, 400 sepoys and most of his artillery.

It was reported that the Nawab, having reinforced his troops

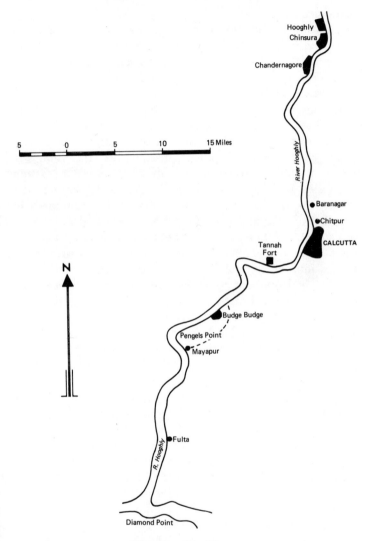

The Hooghly River

south of Calcutta, proposed to sink blockships where the Hooghly channel narrowed by Tannah fort. At a council of war convened by Watson it was agreed that the expedition must proceed without waiting for the missing men and equipment.

The first obstacle to be overcome was the mud-walled fort at Budge Budge, some fifteen miles up the river. On 27 December 1756 the advance began. Watson had three ships of the line, *Kent, Tyger* and *Salisbury*, and the two smaller warships, *Bridgewater* and *Kingfisher*; the land forces consisted of two companies of the 39th, numbering about 120 men, 300 Madras Europeans, the Bengal volunteer company of about 100, 500 sepoys, two small field guns and a cart for ammunition.

On 28 December the fleet disembarked the Company's European soldiers, the two field guns and the cart at Mayapur, five miles downstream of Budge Budge. They were joined by the sepoys who had marched overland. This force under Clive was to skirt Budge Budge to the east by a night march and block the Calcutta road upstream of the fort; early next morning the fleet would bombard the fort, driving the garrison, it was hoped, into the arms of Clive's soldiers.

Clive had objected to a night march over unreconnoitred country, and asked that his men should be taken to their position by boats; he was however overruled, a novel and unpleasant experience. The march fulfilled his worst fears. There were no draught animals to drag the guns or the cart, but Clive dared not risk an engagement without artillery, and he had to detail men to haul them. Man-handling the guns and cart in the dark along narrow paths intersected by ditches was an exhausting and time-consuming business; the guides took a circuitous route which they insisted was necessary if the march was to go undetected, and it was not until eight o'clock next morning, some fourteen hours after they started, that Clive with his men wearily reached their position astride the Calcutta road. Here they could see the upperworks of the ships, and hear the distant thudding of the cannon as they bombarded the fort about a mile and a half lower down the river.

Clive placed his company of Calcutta volunteers to bar the road to any enemy coming from the direction of Calcutta and sent Captain Pye with the grenadier company and the sepoys to occupy the northern edge of Budge Budge village. He held the remainder of his Madras Europeans, about 230 in number, in reserve, allowing them to rest in an open plain without posting piquets in the jungle bordering it to the east, from which they had just emerged.

To block a British advance on Calcutta, Manikchund with an army about 2,000 strong had camped some two miles inland from the fort. Clive's guides the previous night probably took great care to prevent him discovering the camp and then revealed the British position to Manikchund, for the Indian general resolved to surprise him. He approached quietly and unobserved, then his matchlock men gathered on the edge of the jungle and in a hamlet close to where Clive had posted his two field guns. A sudden blast of fire woke the Europeans, while a wave of matchlock men overran the two field guns before the gunners could reach them. For a moment all was confusion; then the veteran Madras Europeans snatched up their weapons, formed line and opened fire, but in places the enemy came within twenty yards of their ranks.

Hearing the sounds of battle, the Calcutta volunteers rushed up to help their comrades. Clive scrawled a hasty message asking Pye to send him his sepoys; then he directed the volunteers to recover the guns while he led three platoons into the hamlet with the bayonet. The surprise had failed, and the matchlock men quailed before the gleaming bayonets and devastating volleys; they ran back towards the jungle; the gunners at once swung their recaptured guns into action. Large numbers of cavalry could be seen forming up on the edge of the trees and a general on an elephant, whom Clive identified as Manikchund, was apparently urging them to charge. The cavalry viewed with distaste the steady scarlet line opposed to them, the British guns began to belch grape and in the distance sepoys and more red-coated soldiers came into view. Then Manikchund received a ball through his turban and drew back his elephant; at this his army took flight into the jungle with the British in hot pursuit. They suffered some forty casualties struggling across a creek, after which Clive called off the chase. It had been a sharp affair, and the bold initial charge of Manikchund's infantry had come as an unpleasant surprise. In the action the Madras Europeans lost some eighteen men; Manikchund, Clive estimated, about 200.

Earlier Watson had ordered the two companies of the 39th to land. The first was under Captain Eyre Coote. Coote, seeing

Pye and his men by the village, took them under command, and was preparing to storm the fort, its walls already badly shattered by the guns of the fleet, when Clive's messenger arrived. Coote was reluctant to abandon his assault but Captain Weller, his senior, by now had come ashore with the second company; to Coote's annoyance Weller ordered all the troops to go to Clive's assistance. They came up just as Manikchund's men had begun to flee.

Now that Manikchund had been routed Clive took the whole force back to Coote's former position by the fort. It was well on into the afternoon and Watson sent ashore 150 seamen to lead an assault. Weller, feeling unwell, returned to his ship and Coote urged on Clive an immediate attack; but Clive, knowing his men were tired out, decided to defer it until next morning. Coote petulantly returned to Watson's flagship, *Kent*, to arrange for his men to be re-embarked for the night. But that evening a somewhat inebriated seaman, named Strahan, strolled over to the fort to have a look at its defences. All appeared quiet, so he clambered up a ruined part of the wall onto the platform at the top, then called on his fellows to follow him. The seamen swarmed up into the fort and in the darkness a chaotic mélée broke out; four were wounded, by whom is uncertain, and the fort was captured. The only serious casualty was Captain Dugald Campbell, accidentally shot dead by a sailor when posting a sepoy guard over the fort's magazine. The exploit by the sailors made the soldiers look over-cautious and not a little foolish.

This scrambling action sufficed. Manikchund, shocked by the stern British reaction to his attack, abandoned Calcutta and withdrew to the north. On 2 January 1757 the fleet, having found Tannah fort empty, sailed on to Calcutta; after exchanging a few shots, Fort William surrendered. Clive and his men were still some distance away, marching up the Calcutta road, and Watson landed Eyre Coote with the detachment of the 39th, instructing him to hold it until he came ashore in the evening.

Now occurred a ridiculous incident that illustrated the difficulties with which Clive had to contend. When he came up to the fort, Coote, interpreting his orders with a wooden and aggressive literalness, barred the fort to the Company's troops, only grudgingly admitting them when Clive threatened him with arrest. He then wrote to the Admiral reporting Clive had flouted his authority. Watson, in a passion, threatened he would bombard the fort unless Clive gave it up. Clive, conscious that his supremacy as Commander-in-Chief on land was challenged, refused to budge. Eventually cooler councils prevailed and as a compromise Clive agreed to hand over the fort to the Admiral, but to no one else. Watson was duly rowed ashore, took over the fort and ceremoniously handed it over to Drake as the Company's representative. Well might Clive write bitterly to Pigot, 'The mortifications I have received from Mr [sic] Watson and the gentlemen of the squadron in point of pre-rogative are such that nothing but the good of the service would induce me to submit to them'. Perhaps one of the most unusual features of this curious incident was that Clive and Watson, instead of becoming mortal enemies, contrived to remain on good terms. The fiery Admiral probably respected a man who stood up for his rights, and where the good of his country was concerned, in his cooler moments, never allowed his personal feelings to influence his actions. Clive never appealed to him for help in vain.

Calcutta had been recaptured, but the city had been plun-dered and much of it lay in ruins. The Company had crippling losses to recoup, and it was too much to hope that the skirmish with Manikchund would induce the Nawab to agree to terms sufficiently generous to compensate the Company for its losses. The problem was, what to do next? The Admiral and Drake made a formal declaration of war on the Nawab; this enabled the British to claim the rights of a belligerent on the Hooghly. An attack on Dacca, the capital of eastern Bengal, was mooted, but for Clive with his handful of men to go adventuring into the depths of Bengal, leaving Calcutta virtually unguarded, was plainly unwise and the plan was discarded; it was the sort of hare-brained scheme that had brought the Company to disaster in the war against Aurangzib. Instead it was resolved to send a force under Killpatrick up the river to raid the port of Hooghly.

On 10 January 1757 Killpatrick, with Coote and a force of 700 Europeans and sepoys, escorted by *Bridgewater* and *King-fisher*, successfully attacked the port, inflicted considerable damage and burnt a quantity of grain. Siraj-ud-daula, furious at the insult, assembled his army and went down the river to trounce once again the insolent Europeans. Before his advance Killpatrick prudently withdrew to Calcutta.

But definite news now arrived that Britain and France were at war. The British peril was great. If Renault, the French Governor of Chandernagore, joined the Nawab with his French troops, the little British force would be hard put to survive. Clive ordered all his money invested in India to be transmitted back to England. Watson was sure that the British fleet would overawe the French. In this he probably erred. Renault explained his views in a letter to his directors in Paris on 18 January 1757, as translated by S. C. Hill, 'We have much more to fear from the Nawab than from the English . . . the defeat of the English and their second expulsion from that country would be a much more desperate position for us. For one cannot say how far the Nawab would push his violence and whether he would not be inclined to revenge upon us this last irruption of the English.' He did not rule out an eventual alliance with the Nawab, once he had been humbled, but for the present preferred to rely on the traditional neutrality observed by the European settlements along the Hooghly. He had no presentiment of what that momentous year would bring forth.

Clive fortified a position for his little army by the Chitpur tank, a large embanked artificial pond just to the north of Calcutta, and waited. Siraj-ud-daula drifting along the Hooghly with an army of perhaps 25,000* fighting men, seemed inclined to treat, but nevertheless still came on.

In Calcutta the clash of authority between Clive and the Council came to a head. The Council ordered him to act in accordance with their instructions, otherwise, they said, they would have to report his conduct to the Directors and absolve themselves from all blame for any reverses that might occur. It was their last attempt to bring their great commander to heel, one, it is believed, largely inspired by John Zephania Holwell, who not long afterwards left for England. Clive solemnly replied that as the servant of the Madras Council he had no

---

* Estimates varied from 20,000 to 75,000. Clive put his army at 40,000, but he almost certainly exaggerated.

right to disregard the express instructions they had given him when he left for Bengal. He added, 'I do not intend to make use of my power for acting separately from you without you reduce me to the necessity of so doing'.

His European troops, chiefly through sickness, had dwindled to only 300 fit men. He asked the Admiral to put the companies of the 39th under his command, a request that stalwart sailor at once granted. Then on 20 January the missing *Marlborough* sailed up the Hooghly to disembark his artillery and 400 sepoys. The entrenchments at Chitpur had been completed and the walls of Fort William strengthened. Clive felt confident he could defend Calcutta, but he had no wish to be compelled to do so.

With Bussy supreme in the Northern Circars and a large French fleet due to arrive in the autumn, it was vitally important to negotiate a peace with the Nawab that was likely to endure and permit the Madras troops to return to the Carnatic. At the same time the Company had to be compensated for the ruinous losses it had suffered or face possible bankruptcy; he could not pitch his demands too low. Yet he could recall that after the French defeated Mafuz Khan at St Thomé, Dupleix could never again depend on the goodwill of Anwar-ud-din. If Siraj-ud-daula was humiliated in battle, Calcutta would always be at risk while he remained Nawab.

Siraj-ud-daula, always professing his readiness to treat, drew ever nearer. On 2 February, Edward Ives, surgeon on *Kent*, recorded that Watson dined with Clive at Chitpur. While they were still at table the

'Nawab's army came into view. The Admiral returned in his boat to Calcutta to give the enemy a proper reception should they attempt to recover the fort. The same evening the Colonel [Clive] marched out of the camp with a detachment of men and six field guns two miles towards the enemy and drew up opposite their line of march. A cannonade presently began between them and the Nawab who fired from ten pieces of cannon some of them 32-pounders and which continued until it was dark, when the Colonel, perceiving nothing of importance could be gained by it, ordered his men to desist and return to camp. In this little affair we had a few men killed and among

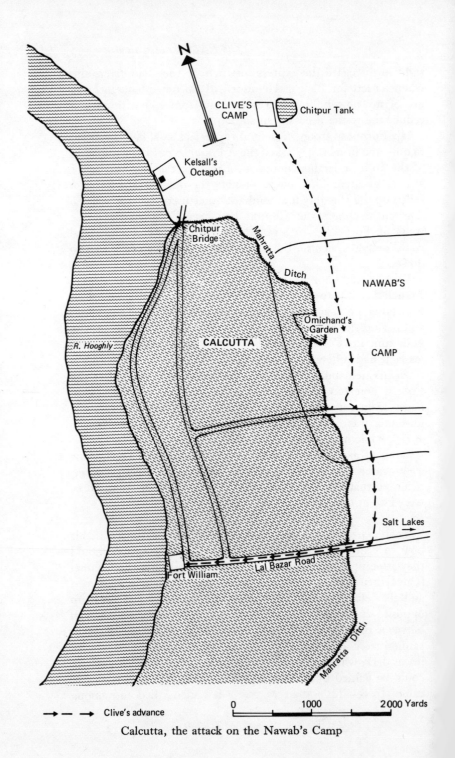

N

CLIVE'S
CAMP

Chitpur Tank

Kelsall's
Octagon

Chitpur
Bridge

Mahratta

Ditch

NAWAB'S

Omichand's
Garden

CALCUTTA

CAMP

R. Hooghly

Salt Lakes

Fort William

Lal Bazar Road

Mahratta Ditch

→ - → → Clive's advance

0   1000   2 000 Yards

Calcutta, the attack on the Nawab's Camp

the wounded were Nicholas Weller of the King's Regiment, and Captain Fraser of the Company's troops.'

Clive's six little 6-pounder guns, outranged by the Nawab's artillery and lacking proper transport to move them, had proved ineffective.

During 3 February a host of men, guns, horsemen, elephants and bullocks streamed into the plain to the north and east of the city, but the Nawab, saying he was at Nawabgunge, about six miles to the north, still proclaimed his desire to treat. Next morning, 4 February, Clive despatched two envoys, Scrafton and Walsh, to discuss terms. They spent most of the day searching for the Nawab, only to find him that evening installed in Omichand's garden inside the Mahratta ditch. They had an unsatisfactory interview, and escaped under cover of darkness to bring Clive the ominous news that part of the Nawab's army was camped within the city around Omichand's garden and that they were convinced that his offers to treat were only a blind to keep the British inactive while he massed his troops in Calcutta.

It was clear that by next evening most of the Nawab's army would be inside the city and Clive had seen at Arcot how in street fighting the well-trained European lost most of his advantages. He had to strike at once. Already most of the Indian workmen and servants had disappeared, the bazaars were empty, and food supplies running out. With his small, heterogeneous army, without cavalry, or draught animals to haul his guns, to attempt a pitched battle would be to court a disaster.

The Nawab's army included a powerful force of cavalry and about fifty guns; it had just experienced a year of victories, the men were well trained, by Indian standards, and confident. To oppose them Clive had about 600 European soldiers, composed of his Madras Europeans, some Bengal Europeans and two companies of the 39th, 800 sepoys, six field guns – 6-pounders – and a howitzer. He had no means of moving his guns, other than by detailing some of his scanty force to drag them.

It was already too late to launch a night attack, but he dared not delay. He went aboard *Kent* to confer with the Admiral, and Watson agreed to furnish him with 600 seamen. Early in the morning a heavy mist rolled in from the river, generally clearing at about eight o'clock in the morning. He estimated that two-thirds of the Nawab's host lay encamped on the far side of the Mahratta ditch and one-third on the near side. It was only possible to cross the ditch in any numbers at the crossing points where the roads came in from outside. Clive planned to drive down the far side of the ditch under cover of the morning fog and spread confusion among the Nawab's troops camped outside the city. Then at about half-past eight in the morning, when the fog cleared, he would cross the ditch by a causeway about a mile beyond Omichand's garden, beat back towards the garden, and destroy that portion of Siraj-ud-daula's host which had already penetrated into the city; those outside would be still disorganised by his sudden and unexpected attack, and, owing to the ditch, isolated from the garden. By this means he could go some way to off-setting the disparity in numbers.

Captain Warrick with 569 seamen reported to the Chitpur camp at two o'clock in the morning of 5 February 1757 to find Clive's men formed up and waiting. To their fury, the seamen were detailed to haul the field guns and carry ammunition. At three o'clock the little army marched off into the darkness. At first all went well. As dawn broke a thick fog shrouded the countryside and at six o'clock the advance-guard broke into the enemy camp by some unguarded horse lines. Then matters started to go awry. The fog was unusually dense, visibility being reduced to ten yards, the guides lost their way, a confused action developed and the column itself fell into disorder. By eight o'clock the fog showed no signs of lifting. When at last it dispersed at about nine o'clock, Clive discovered his advance-guard was almost on the lip of the ditch opposite Omichand's garden and well short of the causeway he intended to use to re-enter the city.

A large number of enemy infantry and guns in the garden, securely protected by the ditch, opened fire, increasing the confusion in the already disordered ranks of the British. Nevertheless, Clive pressed on to his chosen crossing place. But the causeway over the ditch had been barricaded and was defended by more enemy infantry. Clive strove to form his men up for an assault, but their ranks were raked by enemy guns emplaced near the garden and to make matters worse, his own artillery accidentally fired on the sepoys leading the advance.

An assault was clearly impracticable. Clive abandoned his original plan and pressed on round the outer edge of the ditch to where the Lal Bazar road entered the city. Now the mass of enemy infantry, horsemen and guns in the plain had a clear view of the little British column painfully pushing forward round the perimeter of the ditch. They opened a destructive fire on them; the British fought back fiercely and their enemy feared to close, but two guns had to be left behind and a third was nearly captured. However, at last they came to the Lal Bazar crossing only to find the way barred by a line of enemy cavalry. After a few rounds of grapeshot, the cavalry galloped off and Clive's army successfully filed over the ditch. Here Clive halted and formed line of battle with the ditch in front. The enemy in the plain had suffered severely and except for some long range artillery fire showed no desire to continue the action. However, all prospect of driving back towards Omichand's garden had vanished. Clive marched his weary men down the Lal Bazar road and about noon arrived under the walls of Fort William. He rested them during the afternoon, then that evening returned to Chitpur camp. Out of his army, he subsequently reported to the Council at Madras, he had lost 157 men killed and wounded; he himself had had his secretary and ADC killed by his side. Only his superb leadership and the staunchness of his men had prevented a disaster. That night, reflecting on their losses and the confusion of the day, his men felt discouraged and some criticised the attack as ill-planned and rash.

In the action Siraj-ud-daula had lost about 1,000 men, by no means a crippling blow for an army 25,000 strong; but he himself had at one moment been in the forefront of the battle, a position he did not much relish, and the sheer audacity of the attack had shaken his nerve. Next day he withdrew from the neighbourhood of Calcutta; the same day he learned that Ahmad Shah Abdalli, King of the Afghans, had defeated the Moghul Emperor, entered Delhi and was reported to be on the move eastwards. He could no longer hope to capture Calcutta, and if Ahmad Shah Abdalli continued his conquering march Bihar and Bengal would soon be in deadly peril.

Moreover, if he had to fight the ferocious Afghans, the splendid British infantry, of whose prowess he had just received such unwelcome proof, might be invaluable allies. He determined to settle with the British and perhaps wait for a more propitious occasion to obtain his revenge.

When he heard of the Nawab's retreat, Watson at once wrote to Clive urging an immediate pursuit. For Clive to follow up the still formidable army of his foe with his small and unbalanced force would have been to jeopardise all he had gained to no purpose. He declined, holding a council of war to justify his decision. Even the cantankerous Coote for once appears to have agreed with his superior.

It can be argued that Clive's original plan miscarried and that his action outside Calcutta was little better than a failure. The safest way to judge an action is by its results; by that criterion Clive achieved all and more than he could have hoped for. The Indian princes and the Europeans in the settlements along the Hooghly were amazed at his audacity. Ghulam Hussain, the author of *Seir Mutakherim*, wrote that he had driven Siraj-ud-daula away without the loss of a man. The Indian historian's hyperbole is a measure of the impression Clive had made. Siraj-ud-daula thereafter had no desire to encounter Clive again on the field of battle; it was a wish he was not to have gratified.

Chapter 12

The Destruction of Siraj-ud-daula

On the sunny morning of 23 March 1757, Admiral Watson stood on the shattered quarterdeck of *Kent* and gazed across fifty yards of muddy Hooghly waters to where on the river bank the French fort at Chandernagore lay a smoking ruin, white flags fluttering from its broken bastions. The chief French settlement in Bengal had surrendered.

A curious chain of events culminated in the action that dealt French power in India its first near-mortal blow. After his defeat outside Calcutta, Siraj-ud-daula signed treaties with the Bengal Council and with Watson, who seemed to want one for himself. The Nawab restored to the British all their old privileges and agreed to compensate the Company for its losses from the sack of Calcutta. The Council for their part guaranteed not to harbour any disaffected subjects of the Nawab, and both sides entered into a treaty of friendship entitling either to call on the other for assistance. Little provision, however, had been made for the losses suffered by individual merchants and they protested angrily that the terms were far too lenient. But Clive, nervous that the French might bestir themselves, was anxious to conclude an early and moderate peace treaty, one which would not give rise to bitterness in the future.

Once matters had been settled with the Nawab, only the problem of Chandernagore remained. Clive could recall that in 1745, when Commodore Barnet with a British squadron was anchored off Madras, Governor Nicholas Morse, obeying the strict injunctions of Anwar-ud-din, refrained from attacking Pondicherry when it lay at his mercy and paid a heavy price for his forbearance. Clive did not intend to repeat this error and now planned to destroy the French settlement before French reinforcements could arrive in Indian waters.

Watson shared his views, but his big ships could only navigate the winding deep-water channel of the Hooghly when the tides ran high, and the expedition had to be delayed. Siraj-ud-daula, hearing of the British intentions, flatly forbade the attack. Neither Watson nor Clive were prepared to violate the treaty they had so recently concluded, and they abandoned the project.

Clive, aware that Pigot in Madras expected his return at the earliest opportunity, now considered how best to ensure the safety of Calcutta. If Chandernagore could not be destroyed, it had to be neutralised. Traditionally the Europeans engaged in no hostilities on the Hooghly; now the Council started to negotiate a treaty of neutrality with the French. Governor Renault for his part, conscious of his weakness, was eager to conclude one; the two councils were on the point of signing an agreement when Watson, up to this time a passive spectator, suddenly spoke up. He asked Renault if he had the power to bind all the French forces in India. Renault replied that only the French Governor-General at Pondicherry had such power. Watson then announced he would sign no treaty of neutrality unless it was countersigned by the Governor-General himself. This effectively brought the negotiation to an end. It would take three months at least to obtain such an authorisation from Pondicherry, and then there was no certainty it would be forthcoming.

The mortified Bengal Council, uneasily aware that they had misled the French and furious that the Admiral should presume to dictate to them, had to tell the French deputies of his decision. They then represented to Watson that if he would not neutralise Chandernagore he must destroy it. Watson curtly refused. Clive shared in the general exasperation and wrote wrathfully to Madras: 'If I am not misinformed he [Watson] runs counter to His Majesty's instructions which require that he should give attention to all representations made to him by the Company's agents in India for their service.'

Then the distant Afghans took a hand. It was rumoured that they were on the march eastward. Siraj-ud-daula called Watts, once more the Company's representative at Cossimbazar, to his presence and quoting the treaty asked for British assistance.

The Council viewed the request with some misgivings, but Clive overbore the timid and on 8 March started up the Hooghly with about 500 Europeans and a number of sepoys. He did not hurry, so that a reinforcement of Bombay Europeans, reported in transports at the mouth of the river, could join him. He halted near Chandernagore, writing to the Nawab that he could not continue to Murshidabad while a hostile French settlement lay between him and Calcutta; he added that he would not attack the French unless the Nawab gave him permission to do so.

Meanwhile the Bombay contingent, having reached Calcutta, were being ferried up the river to him in parties of about a hundred. When they heard of its fall, the Bombay Council had despatched two companies and some gunners, probably totalling about 450 men – the Bombay companies were exceptionally strong – to help retake Calcutta. The last party arrived at Clive's camp on 14 March, but on 10 March some vital decisions had been taken.

On that date Siraj-ud-daula heard that Afghan troops were approaching the state of Oudh which bordered on his province of Bihar. Panic-stricken he summoned Watts and verbally gave permission for a British attack on Chandernagore. At the same time he wrote to Admiral Watson, concluding his letter: 'if your enemy with an upright heart claims your protection you will give him his life; but then you must be well satisfied of the innocence of his intentions; if not, what ever you think right, that do'. The letter reached Watson on 12 March; the same day he received one from England enclosing an official copy of the Declaration of War on France, and directing him to harass the French in every way possible. Watson interpreted the Nawab's letter as giving him a free hand against Chandernagore and disregarded as frivolous a later one countermanding it. On 13 March he prepared his ships to sail up the river. On this Clive summoned Renault to surrender; being given the expected defiance, at three o'clock on the morning of 14 March he thrust into the outskirts of the town.

The French had a garrison of about 500 Europeans, a mixture of soldiers, sailors and French officials, and perhaps 300 sepoys. (Estimates of the number of sepoys varied, Clive said 700, but Jean Law in his journal gives the figure of 300.) Clive had with him no siege train and his Europeans probably now numbered about 1,000. Nand Kumar, the rascally Governor of the port of Hooghly, had lent 2,000 of his men to protect the French. Now, when they were needed, he withdrew them, ostensibly, as he told the Nawab, because he feared they might be defeated and so disgrace his prince; in reality in return for a bribe of 12,000 rupees Clive had arranged to give him. Their withdrawal uncovered the flanks of the French batteries sited round the perimeter of the town. Coote drove in one battery, and, as their outer defences had been breached, the French had no option but to retire to their stronghold, Fort D'Orléans, on the banks of the river. Here they offered a stubborn resistance. Clive, without either sufficient men or equipment to carry on a regular siege, did little more than blockade the fort and wait for the arrival of Watson.

On 18 March Watson, with three ships of the line, anchored off Prussian Gardens about two miles downstream of Fort D'Orléans. The French had barred the river with a boom and sunk blockships in the deep-water channel. It is said that a French deserter revealed that there was a navigable channel between the blockships; on the other hand the masts of the ships showed above the water, and the French subsequently asserted that they had shifted with the tide. It is unlikely that Watson owed his success to anything but the magnificent seamanship of his squadron.

During the night of the 18th a party of seamen cast adrift the boom, while another cut the moorings of three French ships anchored above the town, which, it was suspected, were intended for use as fireships. The three vessels, empty as their crews were serving on land, drifted firmly aground on a sandbank. Next night a party charted the position of the blockships and on the 20th, despite a heavy fire from the shore, another buoyed a channel between them.

Watson waited for the neap tides before attacking, for otherwise the lower-deck guns of his ships would not elevate sufficiently to bear on the walls of the fort. Then at six o'clock on the morning of 23 March, before a strong southerly wind, the three line-of-battle ships, *Tyger* flying the flag of Admiral Pocock leading, followed by Watson in *Kent*, and then *Salisbury*, sailed majestically up the river, threaded their way past the blockships and came to anchor opposite the fort and less than a hundred yards from its ramparts. Unfortunately *Kent*'s anchor dragged and the ship drifted a little way downstream, crowding out *Salisbury* which, in consequence, was unable to join effectively in the action.

At about seven o'clock Watson hoisted the red flag to commence firing. For two hours *Kent* and *Tyger* and the French batteries on the two river-side bastions fought it out almost gun muzzle to gun muzzle. Neither side could miss. *Kent* was hulled more than one hundred times, some shots penetrating through both sides of the ship; her quarter deck was reduced to a shambles. But at about nine o'clock the French guns fell silent, and when the gunsmoke cleared white flags could be seen flying from the rubble that had once been bastions. *Kent* was irretrievably wrecked, seventy members of her crew including most of the officers had been either killed or wounded, and it never proved possible to make her seaworthy again. *Tyger* suffered nearly as heavily. In the fort two hundred men lay dead or wounded.

The ferocity of the engagement shook even Watson's iron nerve. Without consulting Clive, he granted the French extremely generous terms. The officers were to be parolled, the European other ranks to remain prisoners of war, the sepoys to return to their homes, and the French officials to depart with all their possessions. In a moment of unusual pettiness he refused at first to allow Clive to sign the articles of the capitulation on the grounds that the army had contributed nothing to the victory. He finally relented, but on this occasion he did the soldiers less than justice; they had covered the ships up the river, so far as they were able, and with captured 18-pounder and 24-pounder guns had breached one of the landward bastions. Clive was preparing a storm when the French surrendered. Admittedly the army had lost only about forty men during the whole course of the siege.

Siraj-ud-daula watched the siege, wracked by indecision. The Afghan threat had receded and he now wanted to keep the French to counter-balance the dangerously growing power of the British. He sent Rai Durlabh with an army of 16,000 men to relieve Chandernagore; but his orders were vague and his general ill-disposed. Rai Durlabh made no serious attempt to intervene. The Nawab succeeded in angering the British without saving the French.

Chandernagore had fallen, but the southwest monsoon would break in two months time and Watson's ships were in no condition to put to sea. Clive and his army would have to remain in Bengal until the autumn when the monsoon would have blown itself out. He settled himself at Chandernagore, camping his troops some way out of the town to remove them from the temptations of the sellers of arrack. His problems were by no means over. Siraj-ud-daula had revealed himself to be unreliable; Jean Law still controlled the French factory at Cossimbazar, where a number of French deserters and sepoys from Chandernagore had gathered; Renault, allowed by Watson's misguided clemency to depart, was now reconstituting the Chandernagore Council at the Dutch settlement of Chinsura; Bussy was in the northern Circars and might strike against Bengal. The backbone of the French in Bengal might have been broken, but their limbs still writhed powerfully.

Clive instructed a party of sepoys to go to Chinsura, arrest Renault and conduct him to Calcutta, on the grounds, not unjustified at that time, that no distinction could be made between officers and officials, and that by reforming his Council the French Governor had violated his parole. The Dutch dared not resist and surrendered Renault, but there still remained Law and the ever-menacing figure of Bussy. Clive informed the Nawab he must expel all the French from his Viceroyalty.

The wretched Siraj-ud-daula wriggled and equivocated. He wrote to Clive congratulating him on his victory over the French and to Bussy: 'What can I write of the perfidy of the English; they have without ground picked a quarrel with M. Renault and taken by force his factory.' Clive relentlessly pursued his demand that the French should be expelled. Unwillingly Siraj-ud-daula acquiesced and ordered Jean Law to leave, but, characteristically, instead of directing him to go to the French settlement at Masulipatam, allowed him to go to Patna in his province of Bihar. Law had pleaded not to be sent to the Northern Circars, as he feared the British might intercept him en route, but once again the Nawab had given way to British wishes in a manner that gained him no credit but instead only increased their suspicions of his true intentions. Watts at Cossimbazar and Clive at Chandernagore both became con- vinced that in the Nawab they now had an enemy whose malevolence would only be restrained by fear.

Siraj-ud-daula's cruelty and exactions had made him feared and hated by most of the prominent men in his realm, notably by the great Hindu banking firm of the Jagat Seths, who had connections all over India. In moments of irritation the Nawab was apt to remark he would have them circumcised, and they believed that once he felt secure they and their possessions would be in mortal peril. They approached other disaffected nobles and began a conspiracy to overthrow him.

Initially they had difficulty in finding a suitable replacement, but eventually the Commander-in-Chief, Mir Jafar Ali Khan, who had been forced to submit to innumerable insults from his Prince agreed to lead them. The Seths, however, fearing they might only provoke another damaging civil war, insisted the conspirators should obtain the support of the British, and made overtures to the Council in Calcutta.

On 1 May the Council considered what attitude they should adopt. They concluded, 'The Nawab is so universally hated . . . and a revolution so generally wished for, that it is probable that the step will be taken, and successfully too, whether we give assistance or not. . . . In this case we think . . . by engaging as allies to the person designed to be set up we may benefit our employers . . . and do general good and effectually traverse the designs of the French'. The Council, of course, was only pre- pared to take such a dangerous step for a reasonable consider- ation, and there could be no question of the British acting as prime movers in the affair. Watson's ships could not sail above Chandernagore and Clive could not contemplate moving up the Hooghly without the assistance of a powerful ally.

Through the pre-monsoon heats of May the conspiracy waxed and waned. Nothing could be done until Mir Jafar had signed a treaty agreeing to the British conditions, but the Indian General procrastinated and became elusive. Watts had unwisely employed Omichund as a go-between. In the draft treaty with Mir Jafar Clive had suggested that Omichund should be offered five per cent of the Nawab's treasury as a reward for his services. Then Watts loosed a bombshell. He reported Omichund demanded 'five per cent on all the Nawab's treasure . . . besides a quarter of his wealth'. Watts added there was no hope of Mir Jafar acceding to such exorbitant demands, but that if they were rejected Omichund might be expected to betray the conspiracy to Siraj-ud-daula.

The news left the Council aghast. The monsoon would break some time before the end of June, after which campaigning, as the rivers rose and the roads dissolved into a sea of mud, would become almost impossible. There was no time to start a new negotiation. If Omichund betrayed the conspiracy, the lives of the conspirators and the British staff at Cossimbazar would almost certainly be forfeit and the Company fatally compromised; and in the autumn a formidable French armament was expected in India.

It was decided to draw up two treaties, a false one on red paper and the true one on white; in view of his conduct Omichund would receive nothing at all in the genuine treaty on white paper, but all his demands would be met in the spurious one on red. Admiral Watson, who doubted the wisdom of the whole enterprise, declined to sign the false treaty; his signature was added, with or without his consent; the matter was never satisfactorily settled. The morality of this transaction has been called in question and Clive was subsequently called on to justify it before a select committee of the House of Commons. It is, perhaps, enough to say here that deception to trap a blackmailer is not always looked on as immoral, and that after the incident the Indian princes and notables continued unhesitatingly to accept Clive's word. In principle the transaction is indefensible.

Clive, to reassure Siraj-ud-daula and in the hope that he might induce the Prince to withdraw his troops from his entrenched camp at Plassey, sent all but his Bengal troops back to Calcutta. Then he waited himself at French Gardens for Mir Jafar to reveal his intentions. But from Murshidabad nothing came. May gave way to June and Mir Jafar had yet to sign the treaty. The monsoon would break soon; time had become desperately short. Clive waited in a fever of impatience. At last Watts reported that Mir Jafar had signed the treaty, then on 9 June he wrote: 'Mir Jafar is turned out of the Nawab's service. Threatening messages continually pass between them.

Whether we interfere or not, it appears affairs will be decided in a few days by the destruction of one of the parties.'

If Clive did not move now he might be too late. He summoned Killpatrick with his troops from Calcutta – he left behind him only fifty fit men to hold the city – and on 13 June set out for Murshidabad. Watts and his staff left Cossimbazar on 12 June. Their departure indicated unmistakeably to Siraj-ud-daula that Clive intended war. He visited Mir Jafar, pleading abjectly for his support. Mir Jafar apparently agreed to join forces with him, so long as his troops were not called on to fight; but Clive knew nothing of this when he started up the river.

He left one hundred seamen he had begged off Watson to garrison Chandernagore and took another fifty with him to help man his guns. His army consisted of three companies of the 39th, and his European contingents from Madras, Bombay, and Bengal; these he organised into two battalions each about 400 strong; in addition he had with him eight 6-pounder field guns and a howitzer and 2,200 sepoys, more than half of whom he had recruited in Bengal earlier that year. Broome in his history of the Bengal Army asserts Clive formed his sepoys into battalions commanded by European officers taken from his Madras Europeans. Wilson in his history of the Madras army, however, queries Broome's statement on the grounds that in the order of battle for Clive's army the sepoys were only shown by companies.

In almost intolerable heat, the tiny army progressed slowly northwards, the Europeans being ferried forward in boats. On 14 June Watts and his party with Mirza Omar Beg, a confidant of Mir Jafar, rode in after an exciting journey down the river from Cossimbazar; he assured Clive all was going well with the conspiracy. By 17 June Clive reached Patli and on the morning of 19 June Coote with a detachment captured Cutwa fort about fourteen miles further on. Ominously the garrison commander, although a member of the conspiracy, made a token resistance and fired on Coote's men. Clive joined Coote at Cutwa on the evening of the 19th with the rest of his men. Then on 20 June he paused. To continue his advance he would have to cross the river into what was known as the Cossimbazar island, formed by two branches of the Ganges delta.

The Advance on Plassey

He faced an appalling dilemma. He had received no news of Mir Jafar's plans, been joined by none of the conspirators. It was not impossible that Mir Jafar had made his peace with the Nawab and been reinstated as the price for his assistance against the British. If this was so, without cavalry or an Indian ally, Clive could be marching to almost certain destruction.

On 21 June he convened a council of war, composed of all his officers of the rank of captain and above. He said that Siraj-ud-daula had 50,000 men and that Mir Jafar could be depended on for nothing more than remaining neutral. In these circumstances there appeared to be two alternatives, either to remain at Cutwa during the rains in the hope of bringing in the Mahrattas in the autumn, or an immediate attack. He then voted for remaining at Cutwa, and the majority of his officers followed his example. Coote differed. He argued it would be impossible to remain at Cutwa during the monsoon, the only real alternatives were to retreat or attack; a retreat would be disastrous and he voted for an immediate attack.

Clive pondered the issue. Coote's argument was nearly irrefutable. There was enough grain in Cutwa fort and the neighbourhood to sustain the army during the rains, but if the British halted it would be looked on as an admission of defeat, the conspiracy would break up, and the Nawab's cavalry cut the tenuous British line of communication to Calcutta. His situation would become even worse than that of de Gingins before Trichinopoly. Every petty noble, scenting a British reverse and anxious to appear loyal to his prince, would turn against him. However desperate it might seem, he had no real choice, he had to go forward. Years later he himself said as much, when he remarked that if he had abided by the decision of the council of war it would have been fatal for the Company. As it was, he might make a surprise attack on the Nawab's detachment he knew to be encamped at Plassey about fifteen miles away and perhaps gain a minor victory which, if Mir Jafar still refused to move, would enable him to withdraw from the contest without dishonour. Some time during the afternoon he resolved to advance at least as far as Plassey. Without cavalry he would have to move by night. He ordered Coote to take a detachment across the river at daybreak next day, presumably to secure the crossing and reconnoitre the routes forward, then the main body was to march at five o'clock in the evening to the Nawab's hunting lodge on the bank of the river a little more than a mile beyond the village of Plassey and about a mile short of the entrenched camp.

On the morning of 22 June he wrote to Mir Jafar to tell him that he would be crossing the river that evening and pleading for information about his plans. About three o'clock in the afternoon he received a curious missive from the Indian General which, while putting forward no plans for joining the British, suggested he still adhered to his treaty.

With this ambiguous information to content him, he set out for Plassey in pouring rain. He prudently ordered that his boats should accompany him, and left all his sick with a guard of a British platoon and one hundred sepoys at Cutwa. As the column plodded on with the rain sheeting down out of the darkness, it became strung out, and although the head arrived at the hunting lodge some time after midnight, it was not until three o'clock in the morning that soaked and weary the tail stumbled into a large mango orchard behind it. From the noise coming from the entrenched camp it appeared that it was still held, and information came in that Rai Durlabh, one of the conspirators, with an unspecified number of men was at Daudpore about six miles to the north.

In the early hours of 23 June Clive wrote a final message to Mir Jafar, which ended, 'if you will come to Daudpore I will march from Plassey to meet you, but if you won't comply with this, pardon me, I shall make it up with the Nawab'. He handed the letter to Mirza Omar Beg, who sent it off at seven o'clock that morning. The rain had stopped but the sky was still heavy and threatening when a little after six o'clock Clive climbed onto the flat roof of the hunting lodge to take a look at the entrenched camp. It was closer than expected, not much more than 1,200 yards from the lodge.

As he watched about three miles to the north a dark cloud appeared in the flat open plain that stretched away from the river bank to the east and north. Then before his appalled eyes an enormous mass of horse, foot, elephants, bullock trains and guns came into view; he was looking at the whole of Siraj-ud-daula's army, 50,000 strong with some fifty guns. Retreat by day was out of the question in the face of that host of horsemen; he would have to hold his position during daylight and slink back down the river after dark.

First he had to make the most of the few men he had with him. He drew up his army in one long, slender line of scarlet, three ranks deep. In the centre he placed his Europeans, divided up into four grand divisions each about 180 strong, the first under Killpatrick, the second under Archibald Grant, the third under Eyre Coote and the fourth under Gaupp. He divided his sepoys into two wings each of 1,000 men, which he placed on either flank, and deployed his cannon in the intervals between divisions and units. His line ran from the edge of the river by the hunting lodge to extend about 600 yards into the plain on the right, passing a few yards in front of the mango orchard. As his soldiers formed their ranks, they jested and laughed and seemed utterly unimpressed by the numbers of their enemy.

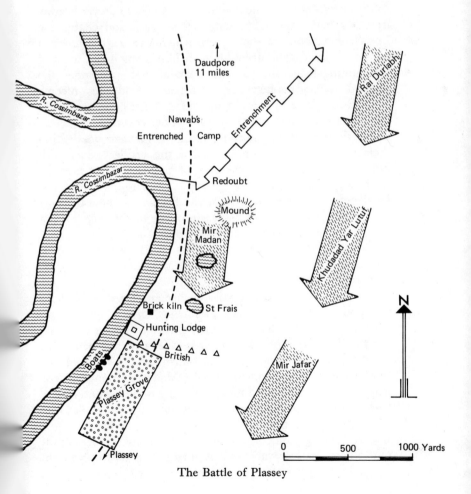

The Battle of Plassey

At about eight o'clock a gun spoke from the entrenched camp; the ball ricocheting along the ground struck a grenadier. Then a mass of horse, foot and guns issued out of the entrenched camp and guns deployed across his front. At the same time in the plain to the east massive columns began to encircle his right. Suddenly, behind the bank of an artificial pond about 300 yards in front, four field guns dropped smartly into action and opened a rapid and well-directed fire. Jean Law had sent his deputy, St Frais, with forty Frenchmen to be with the Nawab; they manned these guns. Still the unending columns continued to encircle his right about 1,000 yards away from his flank, and Clive dare not advance and charge the French guns, the grapeshot from which was tearing holes in his ranks. Instead he drew his men back behind the walls of the hunting lodge and the embankment that surrounded the orchard, leaving his howitzer and a pair of field guns in some brick kilns a little in front of the lodge. Then he judged these too exposed and brought them back under cover.

For the rest of the morning the guns boomed on. Behind their cover Clive's troops regarded the artillery duel with indifference. Occasionally the mass of men and horses near the river swayed forward as though about to charge, but then lost heart before the accurate fire of the British. By now the host in the plain had encircled the eastern face of the orchard, but remained a good 1,000 yards away, out of the effective range of the light British field guns, while their own heavy guns pounded away harmlessly at the embankment round the orchard.

Towards noon the heavy skies opened and for about an hour rain poured down in a steady, drenching torrent. During this time the enemy cavalry in front again formed up for a charge, but the British gunners kept their powder dry, and before the deadly grape the ragged line of Indian cavalry flinched and turned back; their commander, Mir Madan, the only general wholly loyal to Siraj-ud-din, was mortally wounded and carried back to the camp to the tent from which Siraj-ud-daula, with his customary caution, had chosen to direct the battle.

The enemy's gunners were not so successful in keeping the rain out of their powder and the firing died down. Now the troops by the river after their custom returned to the camp for their morning meal. A hush descended on the battlefield. Clive, confident he could hold his well-chosen position until nightfall, went into the hunting lodge to change his clothes and possibly have a short sleep; he had given up all thought of retreat and intended to attack the entrenched camp that night. He strictly enjoined on Killpatrick that no movement should be made without first obtaining his consent.

By the artificial pond the French gunners, seeing the Nawab's troops leaving them isolated, took their guns out of action and they too returned to the encampment. Killpatrick, noticing their position was empty, took forward his division with two guns and occupied it. Clive, hearing his orders had been dis-obeyed, rushed out of the hunting lodge in a rage and angrily expostulated with Killpatrick; but he realised it would be fatal to withdraw. He brought up Coote with his division, some companies of sepoys and two more guns to the pond and ordered Killpatrick back to command in the orchard.

He had scarcely adopted his new dispositions before masses of Indian horse, foot and guns sallied out from the camp. The battle flared up. Clive hesitated to advance before the silent threat of the multitude in the plain that still menaced his right. In front the enemy were checked, and the British artillery, maintaining a well-directed fire on the bullock teams drawing the enemy guns, prevented them from coming into action. At about four o'clock in the afternoon the enemy massed in front began to waver; they were unsupported by their own guns and the British artillery was taking a heavy toll of their numbers. Clive sensed that the battle was his. There was a second artificial pond some three or four hundred yards further on. He ordered his European and sepoy grenadier companies to storm it. Unhesitatingly they swept forward with levelled bayonets; their enemy did not wait, but ran back in confusion.

Now Clive thrust forward towards the entrenchment and a low mound overlooking the corner where it turned to run northeast. The enemy broke and fled. The Frenchmen aban-doned their guns and joined in the flight. Unknown to Clive, Siraj-ud-daula, sitting in his tent awaiting the outcome of the battle, had panicked and, mounting a swift camel, accompanied by 2,000 of his followers, had departed for Murshidabad. Deserted by their commander, his troops saw no reason to fight on. As the British burst into the camp, Clive, satisfied that the enemy troops over on his right must belong to the conspirators, called forward Killpatrick and the remainder of his army. He pursued the fleeing enemy, not halting until he reached Daudpore at about half-past six that evening. Without cavalry, the British, moving in ordered ranks, could not catch up with the fugitives, and most escaped.

Siraj-ud-daula's army had disintegrated, and all his guns and equipment fell into the arms of the victors. Clive had lost some eighty men, Siraj-ud-daula perhaps 500 killed. Although the numbers of the casualties on both sides were extraordinarily small, yet the effect of the victory was immense. A tiny British army, without any allies, had faced undismayed a vast Moghul host and overthrown it. Treachery had played its part, but the victory was above all else a triumph of British nerve and morale. The conspirators, nervously waiting in the wings, had contributed nothing but their neutrality. The battle has since been derided, but it is the effect of a battle, not the casualty list, that matters, and the Battle of Plassey transformed the East India Company from a rather aggressive set of traders into one of the sovereign powers in India.

As he advanced in triumph on Murshidabad to proclaim Mir Jafar the new Nawab, not even Clive realised the far-reaching effects of his victory.

Chapter 13

The French Strike in the Carnatic

At daybreak on 12 December 1758 the square figure of Stringer Lawrence could be discerned on the flat, green, grassy choultry plain to the south of Madras. He stared southwards to where his advanced piquets were running back before columns of pearl grey and white coated soldiers. Around him the two battalions of the Company's Madras Europeans and two companies of the 64th Foot, or Draper's Regiment (later re-numbered the 79th) formed their ranks. His gunners took post by their guns; first one then another crashed out. The distant French columns halted.

Bullock trains appeared in the distance dragging guns; these swung into action and a long range and largely harmless artillery duel developed. Lawrence studied the long columns deploying behind the enemy guns. Their strength was too great. A few brief orders and the red-coated ranks filed away to find shelter behind the ramparts of Fort St George. The second siege of Madras, that might well determine whether Britain or France would rule in India, was about to begin.

Clive and his men were still far away in Bengal. Shortly after the Battle of Plassey, Siraj-ud-daula, fleeing up the Ganges with a few companions, was recognised, seized, carried back to Murshidabad a prisoner and there assassinated. Too late, Jean Law had advanced from Patna to aid the Prince, and on 4 July 1757 Clive despatched Eyre Coote with about 200 Europeans and 500 sepoys to capture the Frenchman and disperse his followers.

In drenching monsoon rain and in appalling conditions Coote chased his adversary up the Ganges. Law, as soon as he heard of the disaster at Plassey, turned round and hastened back to

Patna. The fierce monsoon currents delayed Coote; storms sank his boats; his sorely tried Europeans mutinied and he flogged thirty to restore order; his sepoys, who behaved admirably at first, eventually quietly laid down their arms and said that they would go no further. Yet the dynamic spirit of their commander drove them onwards. Coote arrived at Patna to find Law gone, the Governor, Ram Narain, evasive and covertly hostile and a local population who made no attempt to hide their dislike. Nevertheless, he pressed on to the western border of Bihar. Law with his band of about 150 Europeans and 300 sepoys crossed the Karamnasa River and took refuge in Oudh. Coote dared not risk precipitating a conflict with Sujah-ud-daula, the powerful Nawab of that province. He ended the chase and returned to Patna. Clive soon after recalled him to Murshidabad.

In the autumn of 1757, however, it became clear that unaided the new Nawab, the ageing and indolent Mir Jafar, would never succeed in enforcing his authority. Clive first marched to Murshidabad and subdued the dissidents in Bengal; then in the New Year of 1758, accompanied by the Nawab, he went on to Bihar to compel Ram Narain either to fight or submit. Ram Narain thought it wise to submit, but as Clive disappeared up the Ganges there could be little hope that he would return to the Carnatic before the autumn of 1758.

Towards the end of 1756, when the news came to Madras that war had broken out with the French, it may have appeared providential that owing to the intransigence of Adlercron most of the 39th still remained in the province. That officer was still Commander-in-Chief, with Lawrence responsible for nothing more than the Company's attenuated army. The French Governor at Pondicherry, de Leyrit, had shown little enterprise, but clearly difficult days lay ahead for the British, and powerful French reinforcements were expected next autumn.

A difficult situation had already arisen in the Southern Provinces. Mafuz Khan, angered at his supersession, declared himself the independent sovereign of the region. Aided by disaffected poligars he captured Madura and intrigued for assistance with Hyder Ali, the Governor of the district of Dindigul in Mysore state, which adjoined Madura. Hyder Ali, a rising star in the political firmament of Mysore, saw in

Mafuz Khan's overtures an opportunity to add to his territory and increase his influence; he listened to the proposals with interest.

In Trichinopoly the cool and able Caillaud resolved to lance the boil before the infection spread. He took 150 Europeans and 500 sepoys, skirted Madura and linked forces with Yusuf Khan near Tinnevelly, on 17 March 1757, intending to re-assert British authority, on behalf of Mohammed Ali of course, and recapture Madura.

De Leyrit in Pondicherry snatched at what seemed a wonder-ful opportunity. Trichinopoly could only be thinly garrisoned now, and he ordered d'Auteuil to seize it. D'Auteuil, with some 900 Europeans and 3,000 sepoys and with who knows what memories to comfort him, after skilfully masking his intentions, suddenly turned southwards and blockaded the fortress. The Council in Madras, greatly alarmed, fitted out a force to relieve the threatened city, which Adlercron volun-teered to command. But Caillaud, hearing of the peril and his first attempt to storm Madura having been repulsed, left Yusuf Khan to continue the siege and moved back fast. Heavily outnumbered he could not hope to force a passage through the French forces camped around the city; but by using unfrequen-ted paths through paddy fields he slipped into Trichinopoly by an unguarded approach. D'Auteuil, not anxious to commence anew the siege of a fortress that had in the past proved so fatal to French ambitions, marched away northwards towards Wandewash, where a British force was reported to be threaten-ing a weak French garrison in the fort.

Early in April 1757 at Nellore, 100 miles north of Madras, the Governor, Najib Ullah, an illegitimate half-brother of Mohammed Ali, had refused to pay tribute to his ruler. At the Nawab's request the Council at Madras sent Major Forde of the 39th with 100 Europeans, 50 Africans and 400 sepoys to teach Najib Ullah a juster understanding of his obligations. Najib Ullah, no believer in running unnecessary risks, took refuge in Masulipatam, pretending to arrange for help from the French. The garrison of Nellore, however, displayed a bolder spirit. On 5 May Forde assaulted a breach in the city walls, but owing largely to the misbehaviour of his sepoys was repulsed, losing some forty out of his small number of Europeans.

The Council, by now far more anxious about the fate of Trichinopoly than collecting revenue from the wayward Governor of Nellore, directed him to desist and join Adlercron.

Adlercron, meanwhile, on his way to Trichinopoly took an inland route to avoid tangling with Pondicherry. About sixty miles from Madras he encountered the fort at Wandewash, an important strongpoint on the Pondicherry–Conjeeveram road, from which a small French garrison dominated the surrounding countryside and prevented Mohammed Ali's officials from collecting revenue. He paused here and the Council, hearing that Caillaud was back in Trichinopoly and the city safe, instructed him to capture the fort. Adlercron was organising a siege train when d'Auteuil appeared from the south.

The French now outnumbered the British and the Council, not too happy with their commander, recalled Adlercron to Madras, an order that officer was not loathe to obey. The rest of the summer passed in meaningless and inconclusive manoeuvring between Wandewash and Conjeeveram. Caillaud, seeing the French apparently fully occupied in the central Carnatic, resumed the siege of Madura. He launched an attack on 9 July 1757 and in his own words received 'a damnable drubbing'. Finally on 8 September the garrison, assuming, probably correctly, that Mafuz Khan lacked the means to reward their exertions, surrendered the town for a ransom of 170,000 rupees.

Thus during the first nine months of 1757, while Clive was away defeating Siraj-ud-daula, the British maintained their position in the Carnatic with an ease that surprised them. In the Northern Circars Bussy took Vizagapatam and eliminated all the British factories in the region. Madras was helpless to intervene. In July the 39th Foot were ordered home to England. A number of the officers and 350 of the men transferred to the Company's service; Adlercron, however, departed, a loss that few regretted. Lawrence reassumed his old post as Commander-in-Chief.

Then in September the Marquis de Soupire, with a regular French unit, the Lorraine Regiment, disembarked at Pondicherry; the first echelon of the formidable French armament had come. Caillaud returned to Trichinopoly, leaving Yusuf Khan to hold the Southern Provinces, a task which the sepoy commandant performed to admiration, thrashing both Mafuz Khan and Hyder Ali. Elsewhere in the Carnatic nothing of importance could be contemplated while the northeast monsoon still blew.

As the monsoon rains died away and the new year of 1758 was ushered in, Lawrence computed that with a total strength of 1,600 Europeans he faced some 3,000 French, and it had become painfully evident no troops could be expected from Bengal. However, de Soupire awaiting the arrival of the new French supreme commander in India, a Franco-Irishman, the Comte Lally de Tollendal, attempted nothing of note. On 24 March the welcome sight of British sails on the horizon marked the arrival of Admiral George Pocock with the Bengal squadron which he now commanded. Watson had died in Calcutta in August 1757 mourned by all, but Pocock was to prove himself a worthy successor to his fiery old chief. Shortly afterwards Commodore Stevens sailed in with four ships of the line, bringing the British total to seven; Prime Minister Pitt's decision to reinforce the British naval strength in Indian waters was to prove of vital importance.

On 7 April a French convoy was reported to the southward steering for Pondicherry. Pocock at once put to sea to intercept it. He came up with a French squadron of nine ships of the line off Pondicherry that was carrying the new Governor-General and his regiment. Lally in one of them went on to Pondicherry and disembarked; with the remaining eight Admiral d'Aché, with the Lally Regiment still on board, sailed to engage the British. An indecisive action followed. The French suffered the heavier casualties, and one of their ships, the *Bien Aimé*, ran aground and was lost. The spars and rigging of the British ships, however, had been extensively damaged, and Pocock, his ships temporarily disabled, put back to Madras to refit. He was dissatisfied with the conduct of one or two of his captains and he made some changes while his ships underwent repairs. For the time being the British fleet was out of action.

The new French commander, Lally, was an extremely brave, energetic and determined soldier who had achieved some re-nown on the battlefields of Europe. He possessed the boundless self-confidence of a headstrong, vain and obstinate man; impatient and mercurial in temperament, he lacked the intelligence to be aware of his own limitations. His portrait, showing him in the Bastille shortly before his execution, reveals the haughty, stubborn countenance of a man unable to understand any viewpoint but his own. Characteristically, before his death he wrote, '*Je meurs sans reproche*'. His remark, his self-satisfaction undimmed by imprisonment or the imminence of death, is that of a very brave man, but one unlikely to master the complex arts of the statesman, or know how to deal with the officials of the French Company whom he regarded with a contempt he was at no pains to conceal.

Immediately after he landed he wrote home bitterly complaining of the French Company's officials and their ignorance of affairs in the Carnatic. Nothing had been done to prepare for a French offensive, nothing was known of the British dispositions or strengths, so he claimed, and the Treasury was empty. If his allegations were true the blame would seem to lie with de Soupire rather than with the Company's officials. In spite of these difficulties he began his campaign to expel the British from India the day after he arrived in that country, and perhaps unfortunately for him in the long run he scored a notable success.

Without waiting for d'Aché to return and land the remainder of his troops, on 29 April 1758 he ordered d'Estaing, one of the distinguished Frenchmen who had accompanied him from France, to advance on Cuddalore with 700 Europeans and 700 sepoys. The sudden French incursion excited such alarm that many of the British sepoys and lascars deserted. On 3 May the garrison holding Cuddalore town surrendered on condition they were allowed to enter Fort St David. Now Lally concentrated all his forces, amounting to some 3,500 men, against that fort. Captain Polier de Bottens commanded here; he had demonstrated his courage clearly enough with Lawrence on the plains before Trichinopoly, but he was lacking in ability or the knowledge of how to handle men. He had with him about 300 of the Madras Europeans, 250 sailors who had landed from two frigates driven ashore by the French, and 1,600 lascars and sepoys.

Lawrence, writing of the siege, observed: 'The besieged lost the greater part of their black troops by desertion when they imprudently defended the outposts which, considering the weakness of the garrison, should have been abandoned and destroyed. Those who remained in the place, as well Europeans as others, were little disposed to the observance of discipline and regularity, for having too free an access to the several storehouses of arrack and other strong liquors, they were seldom in condition properly to do their duty.' The French troops outside the fort methodically built batteries and opened a destructive fire to which the response of the defenders was profuse, wild and ineffective.

On 10 May, although the rigging of his ships was only partially repaired, Pocock set out to bring succour to the fort. Adverse winds and the condition of his ships delayed him. It was not until 30 May that he came in sight of Pondicherry. D'Aché, reluctantly and only after some prodding by Lally, weighed anchor and stood out to sea. Once he made contact with Pocock he manoeuvred skilfully and easily outsailed his handicapped opponent. Then the wind dropped and the strong northerly current bore the British ships helplessly away in the direction of Madras.

The garrison at Fort St David, most of their cannon dismounted by the well-aimed fire of the French, saw with dismay the French fleet apparently in full control of the waters off shore. Water and ammunition had been expended prodigally; now both were in short supply. On 2 June, although the walls of his fort were still unbreached, Polier, after discussing matters with Alexander Wynch, who acted as Governor during Clive's absence, surrendered the fort, on condition that he and his men were exchanged against a similar number of French prisoners of war still held in Trichinopoly. Lally accepted and razed the fort to the ground; it was never subsequently rebuilt.

This early and unlooked for capitulation of the British stronghold in the Carnatic, second in importance only to Madras, stupefied the Council. They asked Pocock to return, evacuated Devicotta except for two companies of sepoys, and prepared Fort St George for a siege. But Lally could not hope to besiege Madras successfully while a British fleet mounting some 400 cannon and carrying more than 3,000 sailors lay anchored off its ramparts. He urged d'Aché to drive Pocock away. The French admiral, remembering the old adage that one ship at anchor was worth two under sail, firmly declined, and it was left to Nelson to disprove the axiom by his brilliant victory at the Battle of the Nile.

Unable to attack Madras and critically short of money, a condition that bedevilled almost all he attempted, Lally resolved to attack Trichinopoly, where a number of French prisoners of war were still incarcerated. On the way he proposed to revive the French right to the ransom of fifty-six lakhs promised by Partap Singh to Chunda Sahib and the French in 1750, but which, owing to the providential arrival of Nazir Jang, was never paid. He wrote to Partap Singh demanding payment of the money and a free passage to Trichinopoly. To Partap Singh the gambit was one that he now knew by heart. He replied in his usual evasive manner, and Lally marched on Tanjore to enforce his demands with some 1,500 Frenchmen and 3,000 sepoys. On the march, the French troops, ill-fed and unpaid, plundered every village they came across, arousing the bitter hatred of the inhabitants. In Tanjore State they perpetrated such outrages that even the supple Partap Singh felt a stiffening in his sinews. However, to gain time he offered the French four lakhs, as opposed to the fifty-six they demanded, and happily settled down to an interminable negotiation.

In Trichinopoly Caillaud viewed the situation with a dispassionate and experienced eye. He judged that Lally by the conduct of his troops and his own imperious manner had forfeited any real chance of bringing Partap Singh to terms, and that sooner or later the Frenchman would have to engage in open hostilities or withdraw. He left his trustworthy henchman Yusuf Khan with Captain Joseph Smith to hold Trichinopoly, pushed some experienced sepoy companies into Tanjore to give backbone to the garrison, and himself aided by troops furnished by his old friend, the Poligar of Tondeman, methodically harassed the French line of communications which ran eastwards to their port of Karikal. The local population, nursing a bitter hatred of the French, joined in with enthusiasm.

Eventually it dawned on Lally that Partap Singh had no serious intention of acceding to his demands. He brought up heavy guns and by 9 August had blown a practicable breach in the city walls. That afternoon the defenders unexpectedly interrupted the French siesta by a well-planned sally, catching most of them asleep. The French were too numerous and well-trained to be routed, but Lally himself was lucky to escape with nothing more than a kick in the belly from a horse. Next day he raised the siege and began the weary march back to Pondicherry.

Although showing that the garrison was far from down-hearted, the sally was not in itself sufficient to make Lally withdraw; it was Partap Singh's skill in procrastination that once again had saved his state. On 25 July Pocock, his ships at last repaired, sailed once more to settle matters with d'Aché. He came up with the French fleet off Karikal, and on 3 August in a day-long battle so battered the French ships that d'Aché made off towards Pondicherry while Pocock anchored near Karikal. With his base port blockaded and the whole country up in arms against him, Lally, almost destitute of supplies, had no alternative but to retreat.

In June Lally had recalled Bussy from the Deccan. Had he decided to withdraw all French troops from the Northern Circars and concentrate every man at his disposal against Madras, or if he proposed to be guided by Bussy in the policy he pursued, his decision might possibly have had some merit. Instead he replaced Bussy in the Northern Circars by the Marquis de Conflans, an officer without any noticeable ability who knew nothing of the intricate politics of the Deccan, and as for Bussy, Lally disregarded any advice he proffered.

Towards the end of August the arrogant Frenchman, his confidence unimpaired by a reverse he attributed to everyone's fault but his own, re-entered Pondicherry to find d'Aché preparing to depart. The French admiral stated categorically that in view of the totally inadequate dockyard facilities in Pondicherry he could not possibly risk another engagement with the British. Despite Lally's agitated appeals, in September he sailed away to Mauritius without fixing any date for his return. As a consolation he made Lally the useful present of £30,000 from prizes he had captured and left him 500 marines.

The same month Colonel Draper with a wing of his regiment numbering about 200 men disembarked at Madras. Unfortunately the transports carrying the remainder, about 600 men; owing to the imminence of the monsoon were diverted to Bombay. In October Pocock for similar reasons took his fleet to that port.

With the coast abandoned by both fleets the issue now lay
starkly between the hot-headed Lally in Pondicherry and the
wise, experienced but aged Stringer Lawrence in Madras.
Lawrence with his inferior numbers could not risk meeting his
foe in battle, and he may have had some qualms as to how his
polyglot European battalions would measure up to regular
French troops. Urgent appeals to Clive in Bengal to return
elicited nothing more than a bland assurance that he planned a
diversion in the Northern Circars. Lawrence could expect no
help until the northeast monsoon stopped blowing and Pocock
with the missing companies of Draper's Regiment could hazard
the voyage from Bombay to Madras. Abdul Wahab, Mohammed Ali's brother, went over to the French. The Nawab
reported, 'Abdul Bob [Wahab] Khan has raised disturbances
to the highest pitch'. To convince the French of his sincerity,
'he lately plundered Lalapetta and intends to attack Arcot'.
The Nawab's loyalty did not waver. On 19 June he wrote to
the Council, 'I am your friend and ally'. He tried to obtain
assistance from Morari Rao. That chieftain replied in terms
overflowing with honied sweetness, to end with the pith, 'How
can it be that the army march to you soon before a supply of
money is sent on account of expense?' That settled the issue
of help from the Mahrattas. Mohammed Ali harped on the
psychological importance of keeping possession of Arcot. On
1 October 1758 he wrote, 'You must know that whilst Arcot is
safe, all the country people, namely the killedars and jemadars
are yours, if not no one will be of our side'.

The clear-sighted 'old gentleman', nevertheless, decided he
must concentrate all his resources on holding Madras and
gathered in his out-lying garrisons, leaving only a scanty garrison at Chingleput which lay athwart the inland route from
Pondicherry. He left a sepoy garrison at Trichinopoly, but
withdrew Caillaud with the Europeans.

Towards the end of September, Lally, his men recovered
from their reverse outside Tanjore, marched on Arcot, hoping
to replenish his empty coffers from the treasury in Mohammed
Ali's capital. He met with little resistance; the British troops
were gone and the Nawab's had mostly deserted. On 4 October
he entered Arcot without opposition. Mohammed Ali, whatever his other failings, was seldom outmanoeuvred in matters

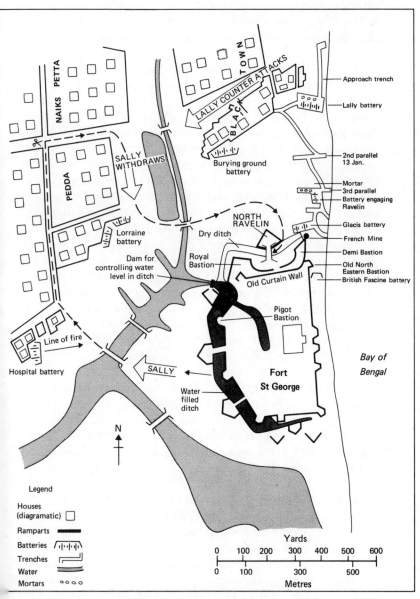

NAIKS PETTA

PEDDA

BLACK TOWN

LALLY COUNTER ATTACKS

Approach trench

Lally battery

2nd parallel
13 Jan.

Mortar
3rd parallel
Battery engaging
Ravelin

Glacis battery

French Mine

Demi Bastion

Old North
Eastern Bastion

British Fascine battery

SALLY
WITHDRAWS

Burying ground
battery

NORTH
RAVELIN

Dry ditch

Royal
Bastion

Old Curtain Wall

Lorraine
battery

Dam for
controlling water
level in ditch

Pigot
Bastion

Line of fire

Hospital battery

SALLY

Fort
St George

Water
filled
ditch

Bay of
Bengal

N

Legend

Houses
(diagramatic)

Ramparts

Batteries

Trenches

Water

Mortars

Yards

| 0 | 100 | 200 | 300 | 400 | 500 | 600 |

| 0 | 100 | 300 | 500 |

Metres

The Second Siege of Madras

of this sort; he had already taken refuge in Madras and the treasury was empty.

Lally was now virtually master of the Carnatic, but he was too ignorant to turn his success to account and too arrogant to accept any advice. Despite all Bussy's endeavours to dissuade him, he proclaimed Raja Sahib, the discredited son of Chunda Sahib, Nawab of the Carnatic, an appointment that gained him neither cash nor popular support. Then his unpaid army mutinied. He had to disperse his soldiers into billets while he cast about for money. If the French merchants had any money in Pondicherry, they kept it well hidden and no Indian merchant relished lending money to a man who boasted, accurately enough, that he knew nothing of politics or commerce. Eventually he pacified the mutineers by advancing them money out of his own purse, supplemented by contributions from the noblemen who had accompanied him from France.

Having settled the mutiny he discussed his next move. British power in the Carnatic was rooted in Madras; let the roots but be dug up and the tree would wither; and in Madras he would find all the wealth and resources he so sorely needed. De Leyrit doubted the wisdom of such an enterprise; yet after the monsoon Pocock no doubt would re-appear and the opportunity would be lost, perhaps forever. The gallant d'Estaing exclaimed, 'Better to die storming the glacis at Madras than to starve behind the walls of Pondicherry'.* Except for an indifferent defence of Fort St David, the British had shown a marked distaste for any form of fighting. La Bourdonnais with a motley crew of adventurers had compelled Madras to surrender in three days; could Lally with two regular regiments of French infantry fail? De Leyrit would be better employed in his counting house than presuming to offer his advice to the soldiers.

In late November Lally set out for Madras with 3,000 Europeans, including 300 light horse, and 3,000 sepoys. The British garrison numbered 1,800 Europeans and 2,000 sepoys. By the standards of European warfare the French superiority in numbers was insufficient for their purpose. Lally was unworried; after all, he was in command. The monsoon rains delayed him and it was not until 12 December that he arrived outside Fort

* Cambridge.

St George to see the British scuttle away behind its ramparts. But as the French were drawing near, Lawrence, satisfied that Lally aimed at Madras, reinforced the garrison at Chingleput fort, appointing Captain Achilles Preston, a well-tried officer who had served with Clive at Kauveripauk, to command it. At the same time Caillaud embarked on a perilous journey to Tanjore to try to organise help from Partap Singh. Lally, when he came to Chingleput, glanced at its fortification and saw they were too strong to storm out of hand. He could not spare the time for a regular siege or the men to mask it. He ignored it and went on to Madras; it was to prove a useful base from which the British could intercept his convoys from Pondicherry.

Fort St George now bore little resemblance to that which had fallen so easy a prey to La Bourdonnais. The houses of Blacktown within 500 yards of its glacis, the grassy slope the far side of the ditch, had all been cleared away. In front of the old fortifications new ones, after the approved style of Vauban, peered over the countryside, three-quarters hidden by the depth of the ditch. The eastward face of the fort, within twenty yards of the sea, was virtually unassailable from the land; the southern and western faces were protected by wide and deep waterfilled ditches. Only on the northern face, owing to the level of the ground, was the ditch dry, but even here a narrow inner ditch, known as a cuvette, was filled with water to a depth of seven feet. To guard this face, in the northwest corner of the walls an immense new bastion, called the Royal Bastion on account of its size, had recently been constructed, while in front of the old small northeastern bastion by the seashore, an extensive outwork, the Demi Bastion, had been erected. A rampart about 200 yards long linked the two bastions, and in front of the rampart lay the North Ravelin; this was a triangular mound of earth faced with masonry, its base running parallel to the rampart; its apex pointed outwards to the north, its two sides so aligned that they could be swept by fire from one or other of the bastions. It was against this face of the Fort that Lally was to launch his attack. Arrangements had been perfected for the storing of water, and there were plentiful supplies of food and ammunition. Madras would only be taken by assault.

13 December 1758 passed quietly; a few French reconnaissance parties appeared near the fort and a few random shots

were fired. The French troops, contemptuous of their foe, filed in careless disarray into the northwestern suburbs. Then at daybreak on 14 December French columns converged on Blacktown. Lawrence had left some piquets there and these beat a hasty and disorderly retreat, mingling with a large crowd of townspeople seeking refuge in the fort. Their lack of discipline and spirit boded ill for what was to come.

Command in the fort was exercised by a triumvirate of Governor Pigot, Colonel Draper and Colonel Stringer Lawrence. But both Pigot and Draper deferred willingly to the 'old gentleman', and all worked together with a harmony that gave direction and confidence to the garrison. Lawrence and Draper now were concerned by the unsoldierly conduct of the piquets and Draper suggested an immediate sortie to restore morale before the French had time to settle down. Lawrence, suspecting that his policy of withdrawal might have affected the spirits of his men, willingly concurred.

Draper was to lead the sortie. He planned to take 500 men and two field pieces and to attack the Pedda Naik's petta where, it was rumoured, the Lorraine regiment was at that moment scattered in search of plunder and liquor, while his second-in-command, Major Brereton, with 150 men, covered his right flank and rear by guarding the northern exits from Blacktown which the Lally Regiment had just entered.

Lawrence watched Draper's men march out; now that they were attacking, they seemed cheerful and confident. They thrust into the Pedda Naik's petta, where, coming on the Lorraine Regiment from an unexpected direction, they initially scored some success, over-ran some guns and captured d'Estaing. But the Lorraine Regiment soon rallied and, assisted by the French Company's European Regiment, the Battalion of India, pressed the British back and recovered the guns. A confused action developed in the streets and behind nearby houses and walls, making control very difficult. As the French pressure increased in front, Brereton reported that Lally's Regiment was forming up in Blacktown. All surprise had gone, the French were more concentrated and less drunk than expected and it was time to retire before the Lally Regiment from Blacktown cut the road back to the fort. Draper extricated most of his men, but there was difficulty in the passage of orders and his grenadier company, about seventy strong, never received any instructions to go back. They gallantly covered the withdrawal, but were then forced to surrender. In the sortie Draper lost about 120 men killed and wounded and 100 taken prisoner; Captain Polier, fighting with reckless gallantry, was mortally wounded. The French lost about the same number of men. The sortie had failed to achieve anything of note, but it established that the British intended to fight, and thereafter Lawrence had no reason to complain about the behaviour of his European troops.

Lally now laid his plans for the siege. He decided to cordon off the western and southern approaches to Madras by a series of posts while a frigate stood off shore and blocked those from the sea. He planned to attack the north face of the Fort and batter down the Northeastern and Demi Bastions close to the sea-shore. To do this he had to neutralise the fire of the Royal Bastion 200 yards to the northwest and any guns the British might have mounted on the North Ravelin.

He sited four batteries. Two, the Lorraine battery about 500 yards and the Hospital battery 700 yards west of the Royal Bastion, were designed to hammer that bastion in the flank, and enfilade the rampart and the Northeastern and Demi bastions beyond it. His great breaching battery, known as the Lally battery, he located close to the shore and about 500 yards away from the Demi Bastion; his fourth, the Burying Ground battery, he traced between the Lorraine and Lally batteries to silence any guns emplaced on the North Ravelin.

During the rest of December the French laboured to erect their batteries. The defenders shot at the working parties by day and by night loosed salvoes at ten minute intervals in their general direction. Sallies were frequent and minor combats occurred almost daily. But still the French pressed ahead. On 20 December, to break their stranglehold in the south, Jamal Khan, the sepoy commander, led 1,000 of his men to assault the French posts round St Thomé. The sepoys, however, refused to face the fire from a small French detachment and the sally fizzled out. The same day Pigot persuaded Mohammed Ali and his attendants to take boat for his old home at Trichinopoly, thereby ridding the garrison of some 400 useless mouths.

On 31 December Lally wrote Pigot a stiff note complaining

that the British had been shelling his headquarters. Pigot replied, 'In war mutual civilities and mutual severities may be expected. If the first has been wanting it has not been on my part. . . . If you do me the honour to inform me at what pagoda you fix your headquarters all due respect shall be paid to them.' A courtesy notably absent in more recent conflicts.

Then on 2 January 1759 the Lorraine battery opened fire and mortars started to shell the centre of the fort. Now battle was fully joined. Between 6 and 11 January the three remaining batteries came into action, and a storm of shot beat against the northern face of the fort. Here Captain John Call, the chief engineer, organised the defences; he kept a valuable diary of the siege.

By day the heavy crashing of gunfire never ceased. At night John Call with his working parties laboured feverishly to repair the day's damage, while the French with equal fury plied pick and shovel to dig trenches and parallels from the Lally battery towards the Demi Bastion. Call strengthened and heightened the left face of the Royal Bastion to counter the enfilade fire from the Lorraine and its associated battery, while during the hours of darkness, with mixed fortune, small parties raided the French at work on their trenches. On both sides the number of casualties steadily mounted, but the French obstinately stuck to their task and their trenches crept ever nearer.

Outside Madras the British commanders had been far from idle. Yusuf Khan left Trichinopoly for Chingleput on 21 November and spread terror and confusion along the inland road from Pondicherry as he went. On Christmas Day he joined Preston with 700 good sepoys, an equal number of semi-trained ones and 2,000 horsemen, skilled in plundering and scouting, but in little else. Yusuf Khan and Preston then mercilessly harried the French supply convoys using the inland routes. Lally responded by seizing the Dutch port of Sadras, forty-two miles south of Madras, to use as a base. He explained to the Dutch that he was protecting them from the British. A number of British wives, evacuated to Sadras for their safety, found to their horror they had fallen into the hands of the enemy they had hoped to escape.

Pigot, still hoping to break through the southern flank of the French cordon, ordered Preston to take St Thomé. Preston and

Yusuf Khan managed to reach St Thomas's Mount, but here were surprised by de Soupire and had to pull back eleven miles to Vendalur. They reorganised and towards the end of the month moved round to the west raiding up to the outskirts of Madras. Lally, infuriated by their successes, took the field against them himself; he described them as like flies 'no sooner beat from one part but they came from another'. Preston and Yusuf Khan – the latter acted in conjunction with Preston but does not seem to have been under his orders – checked Lally by taking up a strong defensive position, then looped round him, re-established themselves at the Mount and resumed their activities.

As January ended the siege reached its climax. Most of the buildings in Fort St George lay in ruins. The Northeastern and Demi Bastions, their masonry shattered, depended on the unceasing ministrations of Call and his working parties to avoid collapse. The French with indomitable resolution pushed their trenches up the glacis in front of the Demi Bastion almost onto the outer lip of the ditch. The British manning the banquette, or firestep, on the inside of the lip, nightly fought with bullet, grenade and bayonet, the French entrenched a few yards down the glacis. But still the French came on. They dug round to the seaward side of the glacis from which they shot along the inside of the ditch in front of the Demi Bastion, and the British had to retire into the Northeastern Bastion itself. Now the French started to construct batteries almost under the ramparts of the Fort. One, about ninety yards away, was sited to bear on the North Ravelin, while mortars emplaced in it showered the Demi and Northeastern Bastions with bombs. Then they built a battery on the top of the glacis itself. Despite the stubborn resistance of the garrison the French seemed set to blast their way into the Fort. From their seaward trench they mined towards the face of the Demi Bastion, intending to blow in part of its wall to afford them entry and to use its debris as a causeway with which to cross the ditch. Call started a counter mine under the French battery on the glacis. As they dug the miners in both galleries could hear the picks and shovels of their adversaries.

On 31 January the French battery on the glacis opened its casemates and blasted the Demi Bastion at point-blank range, but the hastily constructed gun platforms sloped upwards and the shot flew high. A torrent of fire from the Northeastern and the right-hand side of the Royal Bastion overwhelmed it and in an hour the battery fell silent. The siege had reached its crisis. While their outer batteries vainly endeavoured to subdue the guns of the defenders, the French strove unavailingly to bring their glacis battery into action. On 3 February they exploded their mine near the left-hand face of the Demi Bastion; but their gallery was short. Only about twenty-five feet of the Demi Bastion collapsed and the breach was too narrow for an assault.

Nevertheless the French persevered and for three more days tried to bring their glacis battery into action. The northern face of the Fort became an inferno of fire, but the British gunners stayed with their guns and from the Royal and Northeastern Bastions came such a tempest of roundshot and grape that on each occasion that the casemates were opened the cannon were almost immediately dismounted and the gunners killed or wounded. The French infantry tried to work their way round the seaward side of the fort but a fierce British counter-attack drove them back. By 7 February the French gave up; they evacuated their trenches and retired to the Lally battery; it was clear that the initial attempt to storm Madras had failed. For Lally time was running out; British ships had been reported near Ceylon. Yet he refused to contemplate raising the siege.

On 7 February Caillaud, now a Major, appeared at St Thomas's Mount and took command over Yusuf Khan and Preston. He had brought with him three companies of good sepoys and 300 indifferent horse, all he could obtain from Tanjore. As the result of a palace intrigue, Britain's stalwart friend, Monaji, was once more in disgrace and Partap Singh, in his usual fashion, promising everything performed nothing. On 8 February Caillaud learned the French intended an attack on the Mount. Lally, his siege operations at a standstill, had resolved to smoke out the nest of 'flies' – he was to find they more resembled hornets – that infested the Mount. It was the site of the garden houses, as they called them, of the richer citizens of Madras. Caillaud posted his sepoys in the houses and behind garden walls and awaited the arrival of the French. At daybreak on 9 February de Soupire attacked him with 300 European cavalry, 600 European infantry and 1,500 sepoys. Caillaud's cavalry soon galloped away, but his sepoys stood their ground with such steadiness that by nightfall de Soupire broke off the action. Caillaud withdrew to Chingleput to replenish his ammunition, which was nearly exhausted, and to try to gather his scattered cavalry together again.

Now little remained to Lally. On 14 February he poured out his frustrations and despair in a letter to the Council at Pondicherry which showed he was now contemplating abandoning the siege.

'I reckon we shall, at our arrival in Pondicherry, endeavour to learn some other trade, for this one of war requires too much patience . . . I had rather go and command the Coffres of Madagascar than remain in this Sodom. . . .
PS de Soupire has refused . . . the command of this army which I have offered him. For my part I undertake only to bring it back either to Arcot or Sadras. Send therefore your orders, or come and command it, for I shall quit it upon my arrival there.'

Curious sentiments for the French supreme commander in India.

On 16 February at five o'clock in the evening the sails of six ships heading for Madras appeared over the horizon. As the daylight faded three lights were hoisted on the flagstaff of the fort to guide them in. At eight o'clock that night they came to anchor in the roadstead. They carried the missing 600 men of Draper's Regiment from Bombay, escorted by a warship.

At two o'clock on the morning of 17 February 1759 Call recorded: 'The enemy fired pretty smartly with their musketry, but their shot flew high: fires appeared at the same time in their trenches and by morning we discovered the approaches were evacuated.' Lally and the French had gone, leaving fifty-two guns and fifty sick behind them. Lawrence distributed 50,000 rupees to the garrison as a reward. Losses had been heavy. Among the Europeans, out of 1,800 men 272 had been killed or died of disease, 196 wounded and 120 taken prisoner; nearly a third of the garrison had become casualties. The sepoys out of a strength of 2,000 lost 322 killed or wounded, but significantly 440 deserted.

Lally, smothering his anger and ignobly blaming the soldiers who had served him so gallantly, withdrew to Conjeeveram. Sea power had largely decided the battle for supremacy fought between the British and the French in the Carnatic. There can be little doubt that if it had been a French fleet that appeared off Madras in February 1759 Fort St George in due course would have surrendered. Lally therefore must be judged correct, lacking as he was in sea power, to attempt to storm Madras while the British fleet was absent, even though, in orthodox terms, he lacked the resources normally considered necessary. He came close to success; but now, as he and his men marched away, his last chance of expelling the British from India had vanished in the smoke of the stores burning in the trenches they had just deserted.

Chapter 14

The Conquest of the Northern Circars

In May 1758 Clive returned to Murshidabad from his expedition into Bihar. He had every reason to feel satisfied. Mir Jafar had surrendered the rents from the Districts of Nuddhea, Burdwan and Hooghly until his debt to the Company was paid off. In addition, without firing a shot he had established the Nawab's authority over the whole of his Viceroyalty, but in such a fashion that a number of his governors, and in particular Ram Narain of Bihar, owed their positions to the British and were fully aware that without the strong arm of Clive's soldiers their heads would roll. At the same time Mir Jafar now had few illusions about how long he would survive without backing from Calcutta. A Moghul prince might have imposed just such a solution; it was the great strength of this extraordinary man, Clive, that he seemed immersed in India's past history, knew almost instinctively how the Indian potentates thought and acted, and they for their part understood him, trusted his good faith and judgement, felt certain he would never indulge in the curious and inconsistent policies that, in their eyes, the European traders so frequently adopted.

Towards the end of the month he received a letter dated 22 May 1758 from Manningham, a senior member of the Calcutta Council, telling him about the long expected French descent on the Coromandel coast; he wrote, 'I need not intimate to you the critical state of the Company's affairs . . . I heartily wish for your assistance; you will have weight none else seem to have any'. Clive left three sepoy battalions at Cossimbazar and returned to Calcutta with two more to find the city gripped by a panic inflamed by garbled reports suggesting Pocock had been worsted by d'Aché. Governor Pigot wrote instructing him

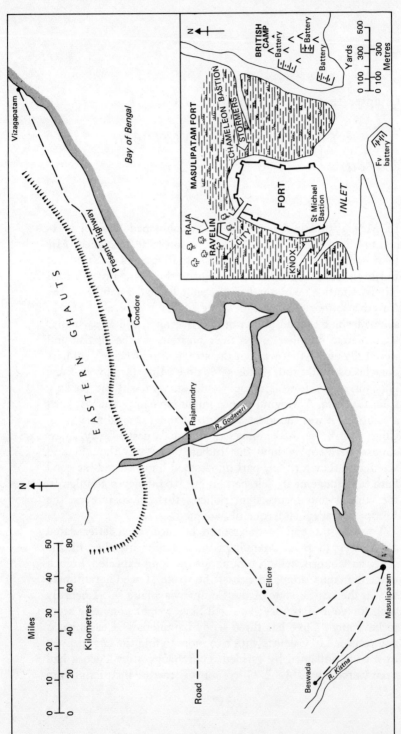

The Campaign in the Northern Circars

to return to Madras at once with every soldier that could be spared. But in the meantime a ship arrived at Calcutta carrying the inevitably out-of-date and often inappropriate instructions from the Directors in London. Drake was ordered home to offer a belated explanation for the fall of Calcutta two years ago, and the Directors named three councillors to take over his responsibilities; each was to govern the Presidency in turn for a period of four months. Clive's name had not been included, for the Directors mistakenly believed he had gone back to the Carnatic.

Such a method of government in time of war was patently absurd. Clive, with some initial misgivings and only after some fervent pleading by Drake and the other councillors, consented to disregard the Directors' instructions and assume the mantle of the governor himself. Now there could be no question of him returning to Madras. He expressed his views on the situation to Pigot in a letter dated 14 August 1758, remarkable for its prescience. He was confident that the naval squadron he knew so well would establish supremacy in the Bay of Bengal, that Lally, cut off from France and hamstrung for lack of money, would eventually be defeated, and that Pondicherry itself might fall.

He had learned from Bristow, an agent of the Company in Ingeram, that not only had Bussy left the Deccan, but that Ananda Raj, the Raja of Vizianagram, a state in the north of the Circars, had recaptured Vizagapatam and hoisted the Union Jack over the port. Ananda Raj had appealed in vain to Madras for help, and Bristow wondered if Calcutta was prepared to help the Raja parry the inevitable riposte from the French in Masulipatam. It was an alluring proposal. If the French were expelled from the Northern Circars not only would they lose their most lucrative possession in India, their influence at the court of the Viceroy of the Deccan, which had caused the Company so much anxiety in the past, would be ended; further a British expedition to the Circars would tie down French troops, rob them of any revenue from the provinces, and distract Salabat Jang from furnishing Lally with any help in the Carnatic.

On the other hand Clive possessed only about 1,000 European soldiers in Bengal with which to defend Calcutta and its outstations, and maintain the uncertain equipoise of British influence in Bengal, a province with a population perhaps three times that of England and Wales. If British sea power failed and Lally struck at Bengal, with his existing resources Clive would be hard put to survive; to deplete those resources seemed an act of lunacy, a view unanimously and vociferously endorsed by the members of the Council.

Yet there were some arguments on the other side. Clive knew that Nizam Ali, the younger brother of Salabat Jang, hated the French and nourished a secret ambition to overthrow the Viceroy. Clive, with the unerring judgement and foresight that belonged to him alone, weighed the issues and concluded that Pocock would prevent a French descent on Calcutta, Nizam Ali would paralyse Salabat Jang, and that his name, backed by the efficient sepoy army he was in the process of creating, would be sufficient to preserve order in Bengal, or repel an invasion from outside. He had, however, to convince a timorous Council, who almost daily expected to see the sails of d'Aché's ships coming up the Hooghly. He suavely explained to them that they could not ignore the cry for help from the Coromandel coast; if they sent an expedition to the Northern Circars, they would be honouring their obligations, but at the same time could retain control of their men and recall them if a crisis occurred in Bengal. Such was his dominance over them that, despite the gravest misgivings, the Councillors consented.

In part Clive owed his ability to seize this opportunity to the skill with which he had created, out of almost nothing, an effective sepoy army to remedy his deficiency in European soldiers. In the Carnatic European sergeants were frequently posted to command sepoy companies, and it was not unknown for a fort to be garrisoned by perhaps two such companies under a European sergeant-major. Clive had seen how well the sepoys could fight if properly officered and led. If they were to be something more than irregular bands of mercenaries, however, they needed to be organised in battalions commanded by officers who knew something of their men and had a proper standing in the army.

In Bengal there were numerous roving bands of Muslim mercenaries who took service in the armies of the princes and great nobles; their discipline was poor, their pay irregular and

their lives precarious. Such men welcomed the organised life
and regular pay of the Company's service. Clive recruited them
into battalions, consisting of ten companies each with a subedar
in command, three jemadars, five havildars (sergeants), one
carrying the company colour, four naiks (corporals), one trumpeter, two tom-tom men and seventy sepoys. Each company
had a stand of colours of the same colour as the facings of the
men within the centre, the subedar's device; to distinguish
them the grenadiers had a union flag in the top left-hand corner
of their colour. In each battalion there were an Indian commandant and adjutant, but command operationally and for
training was exercised by a British captain with under him a
lieutenant and an ensign to act as field officers, a sergeant-major
and an unspecified number of sergeants. These were all
seconded from the European battalion for a tour of duty.*

The battalions were uniformed and wore red jackets. When
Clive raised new battalions he drafted in a nucleus of officers
and NCOs from those already in being. The retention of a
complete Indian officer hierarchy – the subedars and the
jemadars – ensured that unless the British officers were exceptionally stupid – as regrettably some were, but these could be
dealt with by their superiors – the customs of their soldiers
were observed and their particular characteristics exploited to
the best advantage. It was on these sepoy battalions that Clive
was largely going to depend when the expedition to the Northern
Circars set out. In October 1757 the experienced and reliable
James Killpatrick died of a fever. Eyre Coote, probably to
Clive's relief, elected to return to England with the 39th Foot,
and Clive needed a senior officer for his troops. In the Carnatic
he had struck up a friendship with Major Francis Forde of the
39th, an Irishman and the second son of Matthew Forde of
Seaford, County Down, a member of the Irish Parliament.
Clive sensed some quality in him despite the reverse he suffered

* Capt. Williams, *The Bengal Native Infantry*. Broome asserts that
Clive inaugurated this organisation before Plassey in 1757, but Wilson
in his *History of the Madras Army* contradicts this view. However,
it is clear from the operations in the Northern Circars that if Clive did
not introduce this organisation before Plassey he must have brought it
in soon afterwards. Such was his genius that his basic organisation,
so far as the Indian element of a battalion was concerned, endured
almost unchanged up until the end of the Second World War.

at Nellore, and when the 39th sailed for England persuaded him to exchange into the Company's army and come to Bengal as a Lieutenant-Colonel. There was the customary haggle over money, Forde demanded £5,000 for his loss of prospects on leaving the regular army; the Council thought he overvalued his services, but eventually Clive paid him £2,500 out of his own purse and the Council made up the difference.

When he became Governor, Clive made Forde Commander-in-Chief in Bengal; now he appointed him to command the expedition to Vizagapatam, consisting of 470 Europeans, 1,900 sepoys, six field guns, six 24-pounder cannon, four 18-pounder cannon, a howitzer and an 8-inch mortar.

Adverse winds delayed Forde at the mouth of the Hooghly, but on 12 October 1758 the wind blew fair and on 20 October he disembarked at Vizagapatam. Ananda Raj lay encamped some twenty miles distant. De Conflans, the French commander in the Northern Circars who had been preparing in a leisurely fashion to recapture Vizagapatam, was at Rajamundry on the Godaveri River, about 120 miles to the south. On hearing of Forde's arrival, he halted there. Rajamundry commanded the main crossing of the Godaveri and its possession was vital either for an advance on Masulipatam or Vizagapatam.

On 3 November Forde with Ananda Raj started towards the French, but the advance was soon halted; Ananda Raj betrayed a certain reluctance to defray the costs of the expedition and progress was delayed until he could be persuaded to show a less frugal turn of mind. Andrews, a Company official who knew Ananda Raj, disembarked at Vizagapatam on 21 November to re-open the British factory. Thanks to his diplomacy the Raja agreed to pay 50,000 rupees a month towards the expenses of the army and 6,000 rupees as a field allowance to the British officers. The financial details having been satisfactorily settled, the advance was resumed.

On 3 December 1758 Forde and the Raja encountered the French strongly entrenched in a position across the high road by the village of Galapul, about forty miles the Vizagapatam side of Rajamundry. De Conflans had with him 500 French infantry, a large number of guns for which he had an inadequate number of poorly trained gunners, some 500 irregular horse and 6,000 Indian foot, some of whom were sepoys and some the retainers of local chieftains who had thrown in their lot with the French. Forde's army was supplemented by Ananda Raj's troops consisting of 500 extremely irregular horse and 5,000 infantry mainly armed with pikes and bows and arrows.

On 6 December Forde camped within four miles of the French; he thought their position too strong to attack frontally and resolved to march round it and menace their communications. By a coincidence, the same day de Conflans mustered sufficient energy to organise an attack himself. The British duly marched out at four o'clock in the morning on 7 December 1758, but Ananda Raj's men, most of them fast asleep, refused to stir. Forde left without them. De Conflans, leaving his camp at one o'clock in the morning, woke them up in a most compelling manner. They streamed away after the British with the French in hot pursuit, fancying they had won an easy victory.

Receiving a message imploring help, Forde halted by the village of Condore and allowed the fugitives to catch up with him. The French checked at the sight of the British and hastily formed line with their French battalion in the centre and the Indian troops on either flank. Forde assumed a similar formation with his Bengal Europeans in the centre and his sepoy battalions ranged on their right and left. Ananda Raj's men had found a large, dry, embanked pond behind the British line and from this safe haven watched the progress of events with interest.

The French infantry, the ardour of the pursuit still on them, rapidly closed on the British, in their impetuosity leaving their guns behind them. By chance the Bengal Europeans had formed behind a large field of corn that shielded them from the front. The British sepoys were wearing their red uniform; the French, mistaking those on Forde's left for his European infantry, veered across to engage them. Forde, realising their mistake, ordered the sepoys to conceal their company flags, for the Bengal Europeans, after the fashion of the British army, only carried two for the whole battalion.

As the French approached the sepoys delivered a somewhat ragged volley, then broke and fled with several French platoons chasing after them. Forde coolly wheeled round the Bengal Europeans from behind the cornfield, deploying two guns on their flanks. At short range a devastating volley accompanied by a shower of grape mowed down the French infantry. This sudden and appalling fire from a flank was too much for them; they turned and ran back towards their camp with the British close behind. The broken sepoys at once rallied to come forward with their British comrades. On the right the British sepoys under Captain Ranfurly Knox received the French sepoys with steady blasts of fire, and these, seeing the French battalion rushing away from the battlefield in a confused mob, hastened to join them. Near the French camp Forde halted his men and carefully reformed his by now disordered line, then the British drove forward. The French, not yet recovered from their panic, after a token resistance made off, leaving all but four of their guns and all their baggage behind them.

Their losses were estimated at about 200 French soldiers killed, wounded or captured. The British had forty-four Europeans killed or wounded and a hundred sepoys. Forde rested his Europeans in the French camp, but ordered Knox with the 1st Battalion the Bengal Sepoys, known as the '*Lal Paltan*', to pursue the French. Next day he reinforced Knox with two more sepoy battalions; with these Knox captured Rajamundry fort and harassed the French rearguard as it was struggling across the Godaveri, compelling them to abandon the four guns they had saved from the battle. The sepoy battalions were proving their worth. De Conflans himself had left the battlefield at some speed. Forde wrote to Clive, 'he is determined not to be taken prisoner unless by a greyhound'.

By now Forde's money was exhausted and Ananda Raj, possibly fearing further inroads on his purse, prudently disappeared. In the Carnatic Madras was under siege and no Indian merchant was prepared to extend credit to anyone so clearly doomed as the British. Infuriated almost past bearing, Forde remained as helplessly static as a pillar of salt while the French re-organised about Masulipatam. It was not until 28 January 1759, after Andrews had prevailed on the reluctant Raja to supply some more money, that the advance could be recommenced. But when on 6 February Forde reached Ellore, forty miles north of Masulipatam, he found himself once more destitute of all supplies; he had to pause while he frantically scoured the country for provisions. De Conflans, already granted a respite of two months, had plenty of time to organise his defences. He formed what he called his army of observation under du Rocher, consisting of 200 Europeans and 2,000 sepoys. He gave du Rocher strict injunctions to avoid battle but to harass the British lines of communication as they advanced. He himself with 500 Europeans and 2,000 more sepoys waited for Forde near Masulipatam; Salabat Jang with his brother Masalabat Jang was assembling an army of 15,000 cavalry and 20,000 infantry to go to the assistance of the French. As de Conflans sat with his army by the French port; he resembled a succulent piece of cheese, luring Forde into a well baited trap.

Forde, aware that owing to the delays his situation was fast becoming dangerous, nevertheless on 3 March pressed on to Masulipatam. On 6 March 1759 he came in sight of Masulipatam fort, situated in the middle of a gloomy swamp with its far side by the muddy water of an inlet from the sea. As he looked at it from the landward side he could see, issuing from the right-hand corner of the fort nearest him, an arrow-straight causeway, about 2,000 yards long, crossing the swamp away to his right to disappear over a low ridge beyond which lay the town of Masulipatam. To his left, or east, some 500 yards from the fortifications, a shallow creek about seventy-five yards wide ran inland. Beyond its far bank some low, dreary sandhills at least provided reasonably firm ground and here Forde pitched his camp; the creek would give good protection against a sudden sally by the garrison.

The fort itself was built in the form of a rectangle, the long sides running inland; halfway down their length they were a little bent in the direction of the creek. The short seashore side was about 400 yards, the long sides about 700. It was surrounded by a waterfilled ditch fed at either end from the inlet and consequently the level of the water fluctuated with the tide. The fortifications, although modernised by the French, were still rudimentary. Mud ramparts faced with brick connected a number of small, poorly constructed bastions; the ramparts were unprotected by ravelins and the ditch had no glacis; there was nothing to prevent an assailant descending into it and wading across; on its near bank a wooden palisade had been erected. There was one outwork, incorrectly called 'The Ravelin'; it was in reality a redoubt situated about 150 yards along the causeway to protect the main gateway. About a hundred guns were mounted on the bastions.

De Conflans, with his 500 Europeans and 2,000 sepoys numerically superior to his adversary, declined to fight a battle; he preferred to sit comfortably housed and sheltered behind his walls, and wait for Forde to realise the futility of his enterprise and retire. One minor point he overlooked. The Company's ship *Hardwick* and two small sloops had taken station off the fort, and whatever happened to Forde's communications inland those by sea would remain intact.

Forde's army had shrunk to 350 Europeans and 1,500 sepoys. With these and Ananda Raj's happy rabble he settled down among his sandhills and began solemnly to construct three batteries. He sited one on the seashore close to the bank of the creek and one, similarly placed, about 500 yards inland; both were designed to mount two 24-pounder cannon and two 18-pounder, but in addition in the seashore battery he placed three mortars. With these two batteries he proposed to blast the eastern face of the fort. In the centre, between his two heavy batteries and rather further from the creek, he traced a third to mount two 12-pounder guns which could protect his camp and sweep the flanks of the two advanced batteries.

The French, astounded by the temerity of these proceedings, constructed a four gun battery the far side of the inlet to take the seashore battery in the flank at a range of 700 yards. It was an injudicious move; it caused the British little annoyance and, since the British controlled the waters of the inlet, a strong guard had to be placed in the battery to guard against the possibility of a British sea-borne attack, thereby diminishing the number of men available for the defence of the fort. However, de Conflans found it difficult to take a siege by such a ridiculously inadequate force at all seriously. He merely waited comfortably enough for the inevitable British withdrawal.

While Forde was erecting his batteries, du Rocher with his army of observation had been active. He captured Rajamundry, cutting off the British land communications with Vizagapatam, and narrowly missed seizing a consignment of treasure destined for Forde to enable him to pay out his troops. The treasure was hastily backloaded to a place of safety. It was, however, the last straw for Forde's European troops. Their camp depressed them, the knowledge that they were engaged in the ridiculous task of besieging an enemy superior to them in strength depressed them still more, and when they learned their pay was missing their cup was full. On 19 March 1759 they fell in with their arms and announced that they intended to march away. Forde eventually persuaded them to fall out and to send him two representatives. To the two he frankly explained the situation and promised that although the Company's regulations allowed only half the loot of the fort to be distributed as prize money, he would recommend that in view of the special circumstances the Company waived the right to its half. Surprisingly enough this satisfied the two representatives and the men returned to their labours not sullenly but with alacrity; Forde must have possessed a certain magnetism, but it may also have occurred to them that there was nowhere to march to; the alternatives for most of them were to enter Masulipatam either as conquerors or prisoners.

On 25 March the batteries were completed and opened fire, apparently unaffected by the fire from the forty guns emplaced on the eastern face of the fort. But by 27 March, as de Conflans had anticipated, the situation of the British appeared desperate. Salabat Jang with his army of 35,000 men was reported at Beswada on the River Kistna, a bare forty miles away. The Viceroy summoned Ananda Raj as his vassal to repair to his camp immediately. The wretched Raja, for some time a prey to the keenest anxiety, now probably wished he had never left Vizianagram. That night he departed. Orme drily observed of him, 'notwithstanding the dilatoriness of his former movements he on this occasion covered 16 miles before daybreak'. Forde sent messengers after him to point out that if he continued on his way he would certainly fall into the unsympathetic hands either of Salabat Jang or du Rocher. If he remained, there was still the chance that Masulipatam would fall and his troubles be over. The Raja returned.

Forde refused to allow circumstance to overmaster him. He instructed Johnstone, an official of the Company accompanying him to represent the political authority, to visit Salabat Jang and assure him the British quarrel was exclusively with the French and that they had no intention of entering or in any way molesting his realm. Meanwhile he continued his bombardment.

It was impossible to trench forward towards the fort in the standard fashion as the ground was too marshy, and his entrenching parties, separated from his camp by the creek, would be at the mercy of a sally. The French fire continued to be ineffective and the bastions on the eastern face began to crumble as a result of the British bombardment. The French, however, industriously repaired during the night the damage of the day.

On 5 April heavy rain flooded the batteries and the swamp. On the evening of 6 April the news came that du Rocher had effected a junction with Salabat Jang and that both were marching on Masulipatam. Early on the morning of 7 April Forde's gunner approached him with a mournful countenance to tell him there was only two days' ammunition remaining with the guns; he added that if it was all fired that day he could certainly blow in the face of two of the bastions, but that the French would probably repair them that night.

The only choice open to Forde appeared to be to embark as many of his men as he could and sail away. Yet this was a solution that he refused to contemplate; better to fail gloriously than to return like a dog with his tail between his legs. The French throughout had been curiously apathetic. They seemed to think that a British assault was inconceivable. Forde came to the apparently reckless resolution to assault that night. The guns roared on while he laid his plans. At midnight the ebb tide would reduce the water level in the ditch to three feet; moreover Captain Martin Yorke, who as an ensign of the 39th had distinguished himself with Clive during the fighting round Calcutta, had discovered that the marsh the far side of the fort was only knee deep. There were four bastions on the east side of the fort and the gunner was now confident that he could batter all of them sufficiently to enable a storming party to clamber up them. By attacking only one, a measure of surprise would be obtained.

Forde now proposed to launch his main attack on the Chameleon Bastion, the furthest inland on the eastern face. To mislead the French as to his point of attack, he planned two diversions, one on the Ravelin outside the main gate by Ananda Raj and his men, and one against the St Michael Bastion on the seashore the far side of the fort by Captain Knox and 700 sepoys. For the main attack he pressed into service every fit European, including thirty volunteers from the *Hardwick*; the gunners were to leave their guns after firing their last round and join the infantry. By this means he mustered a total of 340 Europeans which he divided into two divisions of 170 each. The first division under Captain Callender was to lead the assault onto the Chameleon Bastion and, having obtained a footing on the ramparts, was to turn right-handed and clear them to the shore; Captain Yorke would follow with the second and turn left-handed with a similar task. The remaining sepoys were divided into two divisions as well, each 350 strong. One under Captain Maclean was to support Callender, while the other would remain under the direct control of Forde and act as a reserve. A detachment of the Raja's men would be responsible for protecting the camp.

At ten o'clock that night in tense silence the troops fell in while the moon sank slowly down behind the dark horizon. Knox with his sepoys, having furthest to go, moved off first; the main attack was not to go in until firing announced he had begun his diversion on the St Michael Bastion. Then the Raja's army disappeared into the darkness. The first division waited, but their commander, Captain Callender, was nowhere to be found; eventually Captain Fisher took over, the officers reshuffled their commands and the division slipped away quietly towards the fort.

As they neared their objective firing broke out the far side of the fort while by the Ravelin an extraordinary clamour accompanied by unearthly yells announced that the Raja's men were about their task. Fisher's soldiers struggled across the boggy ground undetected, but when they came to tear down the palisade in front of the breach, the French defenders, suddenly alerted, poured in a heavy fire. Yorke deployed his division to engage the left of the breach while Maclean did the same on the right with his sepoys. Fisher's division then rushed up the slope with an impetuosity there was no withstanding; the top of the breach was unfortified and the defenders fled. Fisher turned right-handed, Yorke followed up to turn left and a party of sepoys garrisoned the captured Chameleon Bastion.

Yorke thrust forward through the darkness and captured two more bastions with the bayonet, dropping off garrisons for them as he went. De Conflans woke horribly to a nightmare situation. The night had erupted in flame, and the crash of musketry echoed from every direction. No one could tell him what was happening. Away on the eastern face the bellowing volleys seemed to be rolling steadily towards the sea. He hastily sent off some sepoys to check the advance in this quarter, and fell in his grenadiers in the square beside his headquarters behind the St Michael Bastion, which seemed to be under heavy attack.

Yorke discerned the sepoys heading along a street towards the ramparts; he called down to them to surrender and they at once threw down their arms. He plunged with his men into the street and pushed on towards the last bastion by the shore. Then disaster nearly overtook him. Someone saw something burning by a house and raised a shout of a mine. His men, their nerves already strained to breaking point by the advance through the darkness against an unseen foe, panicked and ran back to the breach. Yorke stood on top of it with pistol levelled and threatened to shoot the first man to descend the breach. His officers backed him up with drawn swords. About thirty men, who had known him in the 39th before they joined the Company's service, rallied to him. He led them back to the last redoubt. This overhung them black and silent; then suddenly the blackness was rent by a storm of grapeshot. Yorke fell wounded through both thighs, and half his men fell with him. But now Forde himself was present; there was no panic; the garrisons in the captured bastions stood firm, and the survivors of Yorke's party carried back their wounded commander.

On the right, Fisher with his division methodically cleared the bastions, Maclean's sepoys garrisoning them as he went forward. When he came to the one overlooking the causeway he shut the gate, cutting off the French garrison in the Ravelin where the Raja's army was continuing its pantomime with unabated zeal. As Fisher progressed towards the St Michael Bastion and almost all the fortifications were in the hands of the British, de Conflans surrendered; the action had lasted little more than an hour; at one o'clock on the morning of 8 April, Palm Sunday, Masulipatam passed into the possession of Forde. Orme observed of this singular victory, 'the improbability of the attempt was the principal cause of its success'. One more cause must be assigned; although the disciplined valour of the Bengal Europeans laid the foundation, the Bengal sepoy battalions gave them sure support, while the 2,000 sepoys under de Conflans might as well have been in Pondicherry for all the good they did the French. Forde wrote to Madras, 'My 1,500 sepoys behaved very well. . . . They mounted the ramparts with the Europeans and behaved with great humanity after they got in. Captain Callender is among the slain as is Mooden Beg my commander of sepoys.'

The absence of Callender was never fully explained. He had been extremely depressed for several days before the assault. His servant reported that he was in his tent when the firing started, but that after the first shots he rushed out. He suddenly appeared in front of Fisher's division and was killed by nearly the last shot of the battle. Forde remarked in a letter to Clive, 'I think it was lucky for him that he was killed, for he must certainly have been broke if not worse'.

Forde had acted only just in time. On 15 April Moracin, with ships carrying 300 French reinforcements from the Carnatic, appeared off the port, but seeing British colours flying over it sailed on to the north. 500 French surrendered of whom 400 were soldiers. Forde lost eighty-eight Europeans and 130 sepoys killed and wounded. As a feat of arms his attack has few parallels. Once again boldness and surprise proved more important than numbers. Salabat Jang, only fifteen miles away when he heard the astounding news of the surrender, at once halted. He toyed with the idea of attempting to recover the fort, then learned that his brother Nizam Ali had advanced on Aurangabad to reform the government, as he phrased it. It was imperative he returned to his capital. On 14 May 1759 he signed a treaty with Forde ceding Masulipatam to the British and guaranteeing to expel every Frenchman between the Ganges and the Kistna within fifteen days.

Shortly after his victory the news reached Forde that the Directors had appointed Coote, his junior in the 39th, to take over command in Bengal. Clive urged him to remain, pledging he would do all in his power to have the appointment reversed, a promise that played a large part in the breach that was to open between Clive and Sulivan, the chairman of the Directors. Forde stayed in Masulipatam until October, then resigned the Company's service and went to Calcutta to take ship to England.

The importance of his campaign in the Northern Circars can scarcely be exaggerated; it deprived Lally of valuable men and resources at a critical period, it destroyed France's richest possession in India and nullified the finest achievement of Dupleix.

Chapter 15

The Campaign in the Carnatic, 1759–60, and the Battle of Wandewash

When he arrived in England in 1758, Eyre Coote enjoyed a certain celebrity. He was the regular soldier on whose advice Plassey had been fought and won, and in 1758 people in England had much to deplore, little to rejoice over. He struck up a friendship with Lawrence Sulivan, the newly elected chairman of the East India Company, a very useful friend for the sixth son of a not particularly wealthy Irish baronet from Limerick. Sulivan, for his part, liked the tall, sinewy, forceful soldier, then about thirty-two years old, with his long-nosed face that sparkled with energy and confidence. Coote knew Indian warfare, had distinguished himself in battle, was a regular soldier but one happy to return to the East; when the Government agreed to raise another infantry battalion to help preserve the Company's swelling dominions and enormous financial interests in Bengal, Coote, so it seemed to the Directors, was the very man to command it.

On 13 January 1759 Lord Barrington on behalf of His Majesty George II wrote to Coote instructing him to raise a battalion of foot, consisting of nine companies each of four sergeants, four corporals, two drummers and a hundred effective private soldiers; the grenadiers, to mark their standing, were allowed two fifers in addition. The battalion was numbered the 84th Foot. On 6 April 1759 Coote sailed with his regiment from Spithead, bound for Bengal; on arrival he was to assume the appointment of Commander-in-Chief in the Presidency.

Sulivan wrote to Clive jubilantly to inform him of his coup and point out that having a regular officer as Commander-in-Chief would ensure that the Company had a spokesman who would carry weight with the military hierarchy in London. Clive received the letter with cold fury. It was intolerable that his nomination for Commander-in-Chief should be reversed in London, particularly after Forde had vindicated his judgement in so conspicuous a fashion; but, of course, the Directors at that time knew nothing about the events in the Northern Circars. To make matters worse, Forde was superseded by an officer who, except for an abortive pursuit of Law, had never exercised an independent command in the field and was, moreover, one Clive cordially disliked. While trying to have the appointment reversed, he arranged with Pigot that, at least initially, Coote should go to Madras, and as a substitute accepted Major John Caillaud with 200 of the Madras Europeans. Vansittart of the Madras Council wrote caustically, if inaccurately, that Caillaud with his men would be worth more than Coote with his whole regiment. As with so many of Clive's projects, what happened to suit him personally was also long-sighted strategically.

After Lally retreated from Madras to Conjeeveram the war in the Carnatic languished. Both sides were exhausted by the prolonged strain of the siege and the fearful struggles that had seen the French entrenched actually on the glacis of Fort St George, generally regarded as a situation spelling the doom of the defenders. In March Lawrence took an army of 1,100 Europeans, 2,700 sepoys and ten guns towards Conjeeveram. He found the French too strongly posted to attack and, leaving his troops in the neighbourhood of the town, he himself returned to Madras to consult with Pigot. However, the strain of the past few months had taken its toll; he fell seriously ill, resigned the service on grounds of ill-health and sailed home to England. Draper, also suffering from ill-health, followed his example. Lally stalked off to Pondicherry, leaving the idle de Soupire in charge of his army. Brereton assumed command of the British. Pocock with his fleet came up from Bombay and cruised off the coast, keeping a wary eye open for d'Aché, who for his part showed little inclination to leave his pleasant anchorage in Mauritius.

The fighting had reached something of an impasse. Brereton was too weak to engage the French in a pitched battle and de Soupire saw no reason to tax his energies by attempting

anything so arduous. Brereton, however, was ambitious to make
his mark and had no desire to remain inactive. The French still
held the pagoda in Conjeeveram; he thrust to the south against
Wandewash drawing de Soupire in that direction, then doubled
back and on 18 April 1759, stormed the pagoda. In June he
snatched Kauveripauk, about nine miles from Arcot. But that
marked the limit of his achievements; de Soupire put in a
languid appearance and, leaving a garrison at' Kauveripauk,
Brereton returned to Conjeeveram. After this brief spurt of
activity the war stagnated.

At sea d'Aché with eleven ships of the line at last sailed for
Pondicherry. Pocock intercepted him with nine, not far from
that port. The two fleets clashed on 10 September 1759 and
in a hard fought action both suffered severely. Once again
the masts and spars of Pocock's ships were badly damaged,
crippling his ability to manoeuvre. D'Aché landed 400
sailors and marines and treasure worth four lakhs, then on
1 October, unwilling to risk another general engagement, made
off to Mauritius. On 17 October, to avoid the monsoon gales,
Pocock left Madras for Bombay. On 27 October Coote landed
with the main body of his regiment.

As the fleets left the Bay of Bengal the war flared up on land.
Early in September, 300 men of the 84th had disembarked at
Madras. With his strength thus increased and with the knowledge that Coote himself would soon supersede him, Brereton
resolved on one more play for military distinction. He went
towards Wandewash, planning on this occasion to attack the
fort. De Soupire learned of his intentions, reinforced his troops
in the town and laid an ambush. When in the early hours of
1 October 1759 Brereton stormed into the town he met with a
blast of fire that scythed his men down. He pulled back with
the loss of 200 Europeans. Lally, satisfied that after such a
defeat the British could be disregarded, removed Crillon and
900 Europeans from the central Carnatic and sent them to
Sriringham Island to re-establish French authority in the
district and collect some much needed revenue.

As soon as Coote came ashore, the Council ventilated their
fears that Lally meditated another attempt on Trichinopoly.
They suggested that since the number of French troops in the
area round Arcot must be severely depleted, he should begin

active operations in that region and at least compel Lally to recall Crillon. Coote neede no urging. On 20 November 1759 he joined Brereton at Conjeeveram and took over command. On 21 November he convened a council of war consisting of his three field officers to plan the strategy to be pursued. It was agreed that, with the French about Arcot so weakened, a sudden lunge against Wandewash was undoubtedly feasible.

Coote took some of his troops towards Arcot to mislead de Soupire, while Brereton marched on Wandewash. Brereton captured the town on 26 November 1759 and Coote with the main body of the army came up on the 29th. The Governor of the fort, feeling only a tepid loyalty towards the French and seeing little advantage in having his valuable property destroyed offered to ransom the fort if he was kept on as fort commander. Before he could complete his negotiations, unhappily for him, the French garrison of sixty-eight Europeans and 500 sepoys surrendered the fort themselves on 30 November.

Now Coote found that the path of a commander could be thorny. He again convened a council of war to determine his next move. His field officers, astonishingly, queried his right to call it and after some acrimonious discussion nothing useful was decided; perhaps they felt that their commander was trying to unload some of his responsibilities on them to spread the blame if anything went wrong. Coote did not try to convene another. Then someone, never identified, spread a rumour that Coote had accepted a present of 20,000 rupees from the Governor of the fort to allow him to retain his post. This was carried to the pitch where Brereton, who plainly resented his supersession, organised a formal petition, signed by all the senior officers, requesting that the money should be distributed pro rata through the army, and that the Commander-in-Chief should not try to keep it all to himself. Coote found it necessary to issue a document declaring on his honour that no such transaction took place. Brereton, still dissatisfied, drafted another petition, but finding himself this time supported only by the officers of his own regiment, let the matter drop. Coote, however, thought he had better make the situation unequivocally clear, and sent the Governor down to Madras under escort.

Having settled this unpleasant affair, he began operations

against his official enemy. The French were still too weak to oppose him in the field. He turned on his tracks to besiege Karangooly fort about twenty miles to the east. The fort, four miles south of the Palar river, would secure his communications with Madras. The French garrison resisted stubbornly, and to avoid delay and useless casualties, Coote let them depart with the 'Honours of War'. The Europeans marched out on 10 December 1759 with drums beating, colours flying, each man carrying his personal weapon with two rounds of ammunition for it, and six days rations to consume on the road to Pondicherry. The sepoys Coote disarmed and told to go home. He now held a useful trio of strongpoints along the Palar river, with Conjeeveram and Chingleput to the north of it, and Karangooly providing a bridgehead to the south if he had to succour his garrison at Wandewash. He had cut one of the main arteries from Pondicherry to Arcot and needed only to capture Chittapet on the Gingee–Arcot road to seal off the capital almost entirely from the French.

Lally, by splitting his forces, had blundered badly. He recalled Crillon and went himself to restore the situation about Arcot. Bussy without much success had been searching for allies. Morari Rao now sent his army under Yunus Khan to the neighbourhood of Arcot to auction his support to the highest bidder. After the fall of Karangooly the weather had turned wet and windy, and Coote quartered his army in billets at Kauveripauk while negotiations with the Mahrattas proceeded. The British offered bills of exchange, the French hard cash. Yunus Khan distrusted credit and joined Lally with 3,000 horsemen and an equal number of foot soldiers whose function was to guard loot rather than act on the battlefield as infantry.

Coote recognised that the situation had changed dramatically for the worse. Reports from Calcutta disclosed that a critical situation had developed with the Dutch; it was not the moment to risk a reverse in the Carnatic, as the Council informed him. Meanwhile Mahratta cavalry began to infest the road to Madras attacking his convoys. Then Lally swooped down on Conjeeveram. Now it was Coote who was in danger of becoming isolated. He hurried to Conjeeveram himself, arriving on 13 January 1760 to find Lally had disappeared southwards in the direction of Wandewash. The Frenchman had merely raided the town without making any attempt to molest the British garrison in the Pagoda, then, leaving Bussy with some troops to watch over Coote, had gone to retake Wandewash fort.

Next day a letter came from Captain Sherlock commanding the fort to announce Lally's arrival. Coote moved cautiously southeast to Karangooly, then swung west and a little north to reach Uttaramarur about thirteen miles northeast of Wandewash. Here, with his communications with Madras safeguarded by Conjeeveram and Chingleput, he was reasonably safe from the depredations of the Mahrattas and poised to react to any move by the French. On 17 January 1760 the news greeted him that Lally had taken Wandewash town without difficulty and was about to besiege the fort. He wrote to Sherlock to tell him he would relieve him 'when necessary'.

Now he had a vital decision to take; was he justified in risking a battle against a foe who equalled him in infantry and was markedly superior in cavalry? On 20 January Sherlock informed him he was closely invested. Next morning Coote took all his cavalry and rode towards Wandewash to find out what was happening. As he rode forward a messenger handed him a message from Sherlock telling him that the walls of the fort had been breached and that an assault must be expected next day. If Sherlock was to be rescued there was not a moment to spare. He sent an orderly galloping towards his camp with instructions to his brigade major that all the heavy baggage was to be stored in Karangooly and that the army was to march at three o'clock that afternoon to Tarimboorg, where he would meet it in the evening.

At seven o'clock that night Coote issued his orders at Tarimboorg, a little village about seven miles northeast from Wandewash. It cannot now be identified with certainty; it might be Thukavadi. His orders ran:

'The army is to march off tomorrow morning at 6 o'clock by the left upon the Taps beating. . . . All cavalry and five companies of sepoys to form the van of the army, except 200 black horse who together with three companies of sepoys are to cover the baggage in the rear. . . . The first line to consist of Colonel Draper's Regiment [The 79th commanded by Brereton] on the right, Colonel Coote's on the left and the Company's in the centre. . . . The second line to consist of the grenadiers of Colonel Draper's, Colonel Coote's and the Company's with one piece of cannon on each flank, who are to form 200 paces in the rear of the first line; an eight inch howitz to be between the two lines. . . . When the line forms the cavalry will have orders to form about fifty paces in rear of the second line. At the same time the five companies of sepoys that supported the cavalry are to form on the right of Colonel Draper's Regiment and five companies in the rear of the line of march to form on the left of Colonel Coote's Regiment. . . . The whole army as well European as black are to have a green branch of the Tamarisk tree fixed in their hats or turbans, likewise on the tops of their colours to distinguish them from the enemy.'

The orders are of interest not only for their lucidity but for the careful way in which Coote balanced his army. He used his sepoys and cavalry initially as a screen with which to mask his intentions; behind came his main striking force, his three European battalions; but from them he extracted their choicest men, their grenadier companies, to form a compact powerful reserve which he could throw into the battle at the moment of decision.

And so on 22 January 1760 was to be fought the battle that went far to decide finally whether Britain or France would prevail in India. By a curious paradox both armies were commanded by Irishmen, one from the Anglo-Norman Ascendancy the other from the old native aristocracy. Coote had with him 1,640 European infantry, made up of his two regular battalions and the Madras Europeans, with which to confront the Lorraine Regiment, the Lally Regiment and the French Company's Battalion of India which, together with 200 marines, totalled about 1,700 men. Coote, however, had only about eighty European troopers, mostly foreign, under a Swiss, de Vasserot, who had come out as a junior officer with one of the Swiss infantry companies, 1,250 locally recruited irregular horse, 2,100 sepoys and fifteen guns with which to oppose 200 French cavalry, 2,000 Mahratta horse, 2,000 sepoys and twenty guns.* Being inferior in cavalry and as he had little faith

* Estimates of the relative strengths are even more contradictory than usual. Colonel Malleson in his book *History of the French in India,* in

in his irregulars, Coote considered he must take every possible precaution against an attack by enemy horsemen.

As at six o'clock they marched out in the bracing early morning sunshine, Coote noted with satisfaction that his men pressed forward eager for the fray. He himself could not have been unconscious that the next few hours might bring death or disgrace. No doubt he was filled with an iron determination to succeed, but it was no light matter to fight a French army superior to his own, even if the superiority was only slight. Whatever his feelings, he rode forward with the impassive confidence of the true leader.

At about seven o'clock, riding with the vanguard, he entered a flat open plain stretching away to the west and chequered here and there by groves of tamarind, palm and banyan trees and tiny mudwalled villages each with its embanked pond or tank outside. About three miles in front of him he could see the vague outlines of Wandewash fort and the tree shaded houses of the little town; to his right, about three miles across the green plain, was a high solitary stony hill about one and a half miles north of the fort, beyond it a rocky ridge stretched away to the west. To his left front the plain extended into the distance flat and level, and about three miles from him and about two to the left or south of the fort he could see an entrenchment and the tents of Lally's camp near a series of tanks with embanked sides, rising a few feet above the level of the plain.

Then ahead sporadic firing broke out. De Vasserot and his cavalry had bumped into some French mounted patrols. He rode up to de Vasserot, ordered him to halt and form his line,

which he quotes from Lally's memoirs, gives the figures for the French as 1,350 European infantry, about 200 of whom were sailors, 150 cavalry, about 1,800 sepoys, and 2,000 Mahratta cavalry all but sixty of whom were away foraging. Lally's figures are, of course, suspect, and from his own account, it is clear that Coote saw a large number of Mahratta horsemen on the field of battle. Wilson gives a total of 2,500 Europeans and 9,000 natives for the French. His figure for native troops is inflated. In none of the figures quoted is any allowance made for gunners and train who must have numbered well over 120 on either side, taking into account the number of guns deployed. It seems safe to assume that in infantry the two sides were about equal, but that the French had an advantage in cavalry. In the description of the battle Coote's own account in the main has been followed so far as it is consistent with the map he drew.

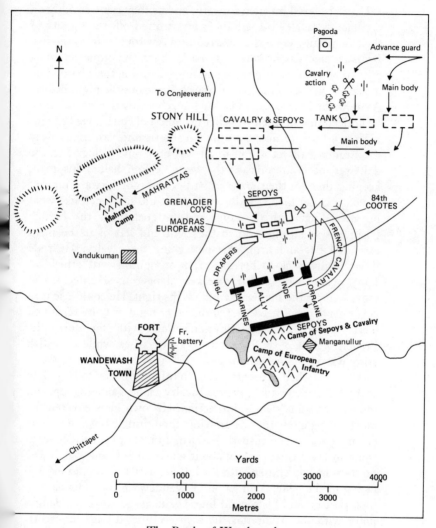

The Battle of Wandewash

then drew up the five companies of sepoys and two guns of the
vanguard beside them. Bands of Mahratta horsemen came
riding up, checked at the sight of the steady line and turned
back a few hundred yards to where their main body was taking
station on the left of about 200 French light cavalry.

Coote ordered his men forward, and as they came steadily on the enemy cavalry turned about and trotted off, the dignity of their departure somewhat marred by a few rounds from the two British guns. Coote now rode back about three-quarters of a mile to where he could see his infantry forming their battle line in accordance with the instructions he gave out the night before. As he walked his horse down the line, checking the dispositions, he noticed that his men were in the highest of spirits. He brought his army forward about a mile. In their camp two miles away the French had yet to fall-in. It was now nine o'clock and the day was becoming pleasantly warm. Coote halted his men, keeping them in their order of battle, and rode forward himself to take a closer look at Lally's camp. He did not much like what he saw. What with the tanks and entrenchments the French position was strong, and to the right and left of it the plain extended flat and firm, excellent going for cavalry. He rode thoughtfully back to his troops; a straightforward attack on Lally's camp would clearly be very dangerous. He decided to move over to the high stony hill on his right. He could use it to cover his flanks if need be. On the other hand, if Lally remained inert he could reopen communications with the fort; the French would never dare attack its breaches while a British army was in the neighbourhood.

As he marched across the French infantry began to form line of battle outside their camp, cavalry came galloping up and the French guns swung into action. His own guns covered the move, firing a few rounds, moving, then firing a few more. The enemy cavalry skirmished forward, but showed no desire to come to close quarters. By about ten o'clock Coote was in the position he had chosen with the hill to his right rear and his line facing in the general direction of Wandewash fort. His cavalry took post behind his second line. His baggage, always a danger point with the Mahrattas, he securely tucked with its escort, three sepoy companies and 200 irregular cavalry, in a small village behind him.

Some time after eleven o'clock the Mahrattas disappeared; they probably went off to eat their morning meal in their camp several miles distant from that of the French. Yunus Khan probably disliked his arrogant French ally and Lally viewed all Indians and almost everyone else with contempt.

The Frenchman had drawn up his European infantry in a single line with on the right the Lorraine Regiment, in the centre the Battalion of India, next to it the Lally Regiment, and on the extreme left his marines with some 400 sepoys. The remainder of his Indian infantry he held back in a second line. At about the time that the Mahrattas went off the French line advanced three-quarters of a mile to a position where their left flank rested on a tank with sides about twelve feet high. Their right swung a little to the left to face the direction of the British. The guns of both sides engaged in a long-range duel.

The Mahrattas had vanished; they had displayed no great enthusiasm for combat. About midday Coote decided to take the plunge. He deployed his sepoys in the rear with his cavalry to guard against a Mahratta attack and ordered his men to advance. The French, equally eager for the fray, came forward to meet him. The red line and the grey-white one slowly approached each other, the guns dropping in and out of action as they went and the cannonade steadily increasing in intensity. Then from the French right a column of about 200 French horsemen trotted out; Lally led them himself for their commander had declined to charge at this stage of the battle. They swung in a great arc round the British left. Coote faced round some companies of sepoys, two guns and his cavalry to oppose them. As the enemy drew near, the irregular horse lost their nerve, turned their horses' heads and bolted from the battlefield. The gunners and the sepoys, however, stood firm; before their fire the French hesitated; at once de Vasserot with his eighty stalwart troopers and a few of the more courageous irregular horse crashed into them. The French cavalry galloped back towards their camp in wild disorder. Lally, through his impatience, had thrown away his chief advantage and sacrificed his cavalry to little purpose.

During this time the opposing lines of infantry continued to close. Then the French, galled by the well-aimed grape of the British artillery, surged forward. On their right the Lorraine Regiment charged in column, shouting they would break the 84th. The 84th coolly awaited them, but the impetus of the French charge nearly carried them through the British line and a deadly combat at close quarters ensued. In the centre the European battalions of both Companies clashed, exchanging volley for volley without either gaining an advantage; but on their left disaster overtook the French. A lucky British shot hit an ammunition wagon; it blew up, injuring a number of men standing nearby, and throwing the marines and the left of Lally into confusion. Coote saw a gap appear; he ordered Brereton with the 79th to thrust through it and envelop the French left. Bussy commanded here. He led up a company of the Lally Regiment, rallied some of the marines, and lined them all along the bank of the tank on the left; from here they shot into the flank of the 79th as that regiment wheeled round to enclose the left flank of the French.

It was the crisis of the battle. Coote brought forward the grenadier company of the 79th from the second line and two guns. The guns flamed grape, the grenadiers plunged fiercely forward. The Frenchmen refused to stand before them; Bussy had his horse shot under him and was captured; the French left collapsed. Coote now brought up his two remaining grenadier companies to plug the gap widening between the 79th and the Madras Europeans as the 79th thrust ever deeper round the left of the French. The Lally Regiment recoiled on the centre, disordering its ranks; the gunners under close range fire abandoned their guns. For a few minutes the densely packed and confused mass of Frenchmen in the centre stood firm. Lally ordered his second line of Indian infantry to advance; they declined to enter the fiery cauldron in front of them. Then shot at from front, flank and rear French resistance suddenly ceased; the grey-white mass dissolved into knots of fugitives running madly towards their camp. The French cavalry, by now rallied, interposed between the French infantry and their pursuers, and saved them from complete destruction. But Lally could only watch helplessly as his broken regiments streamed away to the southwest. By two o'clock the battle was over. The Mahrattas, who by now must have finished their leisurely meal, saw no good reason to intervene.

The British buried some 200 French dead on the battlefield and captured 240, most of whom were wounded; altogether the French lost about 600 men, the British 180 Europeans, including Brereton mortally wounded, and seventy Indian soldiers; the 84th suffered most severely with eighty-three casualties. It has sometimes been claimed that Wandewash was fought exclusively by the British and French; the casualty figures clearly refute this contention; Coote used his sepoys with a skill that contributed to his victory whereas Lally was incapable of understanding how to employ or enthuse his Indian soldiers.

The French army was shattered and could retain little confidence in a general who charged prematurely with his cavalry and then, at the critical moment of the battle, found himself with no reliable reserves. Coote did not launch an immediate and ruthless pursuit; his men were exhausted, the French still superior in cavalry, and the intentions of the Mahrattas far from certain. He resumed the systematic subjugation of the central Carnatic, which had been interrupted when Lally arrived at Arcot in December. He considered that a premature move against Pondicherry might cost him all he had won.

First he struck at Chittapet, fifteen miles to the southwest, which commanded the pass where the second great road to Arcot from the south emerged from the Gingee hills. The French rested and reorganised there the night after Wandewash, before retreating to their near impregnable fortress of Gingee. He took it on 28 January. Fifty French soldiers of the garrison, and seventy-three more, wounded after the battle, fell into his hands. With the twin gates of Wandewash and Chittapet locked and barred against French interference from the direction of Pondicherry, Coote marched on Arcot. On 9 February 1760 the French garrison there, 250 strong, surrendered.

Now Coote paused to rest his men and repair his equipment. Pigot from Madras wrote him an irate letter, demanding to know why he was not 'at the back of Pondicherry'. Coote acidly replied that between 21 January and 21 February his army had marched 200 miles, won a general engagement and captured three places; he assured the Council, 'it is beyond my capacity to know how to act better'. Pigot's letter was intolerable, but Coote seldom remained on good terms with his superiors; it cannot always have been their fault. More usefully, Pigot wrote peremptorily to Yunus Khan, ordering him out of the Carnatic. The Mahrattas, no great supporters of lost causes, complied.

Chapter 16

The Second Siege of Pondicherry

Coote was in the tradition of a long line of British generals. He was deliberate in his actions, carefully planning each step in advance, never underestimating his opponent or hurrying his decisions. Such generals may seem ponderous and over-cautious, but they are often very hard to beat. He somewhat overestimated the strength Lally could deploy to defend Pondicherry, telling Pigot that it was between three and four thousand men. But he knew that every able-bodied Frenchman would shoulder a musket in the defence of his city; such men, lacking training and the ability to manoeuvre, might be of little account on a battlefield, but behind the ramparts of a fort they could be as formidable as fully trained soldiers.

Coote rested and reorganised his men at Arcot, then embarked on a systematic campaign to eliminate the French possessions outside Pondicherry and to isolate that stronghold. He did not intend to repeat Governor Saunders' error and become embroiled with Gingee. Admiral Cornish with six sail cruised off the coast; he decided to approach Pondicherry along the coast where the navy could safeguard his communications. His first objective therefore was the French-held port of Alamparva, sixty-two miles south of Madras. As a preliminary he had to take Perumakhal* about twenty miles inland. The fort was perched on an inaccessible hill; nevertheless on 5 March it surrendered; the sepoys mounted the main assault and suffered 113 casualties. Coote entered in his journal, 'the good behaviour of the sepoys was more remarkable than anything I could conceive. I have ordered a gold medal for Bulwan Singh a commander of sepoys who led the attack'. Captain Robert

* Called Permacoil in contemporary accounts.

Barker, commanding the artillery, also distinguished himself
by hoisting a gun under the very ramparts of the fort. Alamparva surrendered on 12 March and Coote turned southwards
towards Pondicherry some thirty miles away.

However, at Perumakhal he had been wounded in the knee
and the wound festered. He returned to Madras for treatment
and to discuss the next moves. To his annoyance he discovered
that, without letting him know, Governor Pigot had been
planning with the Admiral a descent on the French-held port
of Karikal which so often in the past had served as a gateway to
Tanjore and Trichinopoly. The scheme, however, had obvious
merit. Cornish was prepared to land 300 marines and only
required a land forces commander, an engineer and a few
pioneers. Coote appointed Major the Hon George Monson,
late of HM Footguards but now of the 84th, to command;
John Call was lent to supervise the engineer arrangements and
Captain Barker the artillery; some support from Trichinopoly
was also arranged. From his army Coote had only to provide
some fifty pioneers to dig the trenches and help erect the
batteries. Monson disembarked four miles north of the port on
28 March 1760 to be joined by 100 Europeans and 300
sepoys from Trichinopoly. The garrison, of 200 French and
200 sepoys under Renault, onetime Governor of Chandernagore,
surrendered on 5 April after a less than stubborn resistance.
Monson then marched north towards Pondicherry capturing
on the way French garrisons at Chillambrum and Verdachelum,
accumulating thereby sixty more prisoners. He rejoined Coote
on 3 May, whereupon the Admiral promptly demanded back
his marines.

Coote returned to his army early in April. He felt the need
for caution. He considered the French were still too strong for
him to risk a direct attack on Pondicherry. He therefore planned
to capture the towns on the main roads leading from the French
stronghold and to garrison them, using in the main his sepoys;
thus he would gradually throttle the French while keeping his
European troops intact and concentrated to counter any move
that Lally might make. First he took Valdavur, about eleven
miles out of Pondicherry on the Arcot road. Lally did nothing.
Then he despatched one of his sepoy commandants, Asaf Beg,
to hook round Pondicherry and capture Tiruvadi about twenty-

five miles to the southwest of it. Asaf Beg took Tiruvadi unopposed and on his own initiative carried on to take Cuddalore sixteen miles to the south of Pondicherry. The fleet landed some sailors to help him.

Since Wandewash, Lally seemed to have retired into some dream world of his own. After the battle he made no effort to reorganise his army to hinder Coote in his somewhat ponderous operations, or to withdraw his scattered garrisons, which could have more than replaced his losses; he watched Coote capture them one by one apparently with complete indifference. But now he broke out of his trance and raided Cuddalore on a number of occasions, but, except on one when he took prisoner a number of sick sailors, with little effect.

Coote methodically pursued his plan. To the north and south of Pondicherry he had, as it were, shaped the shoulders of a wide-bottomed bottle enclosing Lally, with the fleet cruising off the coast as the base. Now he had to cork it by cutting the routes leading inland to the west. This would be the decisive move and must provoke a violent reaction from the French, unless Lally had lost all interest in defending himself. Before starting he reconnoitred with great care all the ground about Pondicherry.

The fortress, like that of Madras, fronted the sea with a small river, the Ariancopang, running inland just to the south of its fortifications. The southern boundary of the port ran for some 2,000 yards inland along the north bank of the river. From here the boundary hedge, a formidable obstacle of thorn bushes, started; it ran initially northwest then curved round Pondicherry in the shape of a flattened semicircle some six miles in circumference to finish on the seashore about three miles to the north of the river mouth. It was pierced by roads in five places, each entrance being guarded by a redoubt.

The most southerly, the Ariancopang redoubt, guarded the exit of the coast road to the south; it was situated near the southern edge of the hedge about half a mile from where the road crossed the river. The far side of the crossing the French had constructed the Ariancopang fort that had proved so fatal to Admiral Boscawen when he attacked Pondicherry in 1748. Inland to the west two important roads pierced the hedge, the southerly one leading to Villanore and the northerly to Valdavur;

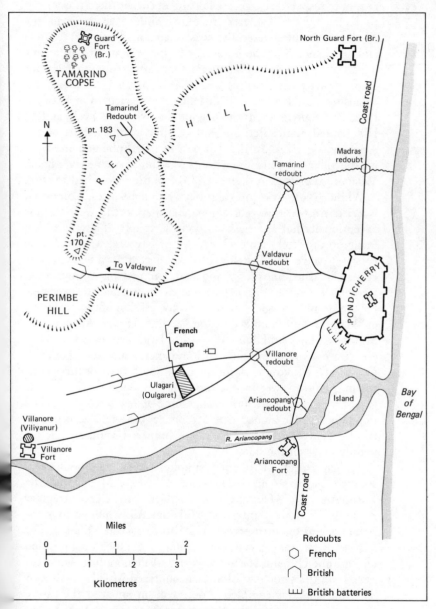

The Siege of Pondicherry

the two exits were guarded by the Villanore and Valdavur redoubts respectively. In the northwest corner there was an exit protected by the Tamarisk redoubt, while near the coast the Madras redoubt covered the coast road's northern exit. A mile and a half north of the boundary hedge and about half a mile inland rose a series of sandhills that, after running west for about four miles, swung southwards parallel to the coast, enclosing Pondicherry at a distance that varied from between three and four miles; these heights, known collectively as Red Hill, ended at the Perimbé hill about two miles short of the Ariancopang river. In the gap between Perimbé and the river lay the village of Villanore with its fort almost on the river bank. Villanore represented the neck of the bottle Coote had to cork.

While Coote was making his reconnaissances, somewhat worried by the sick rate among his men – the weather was exceptionally hot and he had 300 in hospital – Lally had been intriguing for help from Hyder Ali of Mysore, who had little reason to love the British. That soldier of fortune had succeeded in usurping power and had confined his young King, virtually a prisoner, in his palace at Seringapatam. In exchange for the promise of some money and the cession of the provinces of Madura and Tinnevelly, on 4 June Hyder Ali sent his brother-in-law, Mukdum Ali, with a large part of his army to escort a convoy of supplies to Pondicherry and to negotiate a firm treaty. Mukdum Ali followed the south bank of the Ariancopang, crossed over by the fort, and, although harried by the garrison at Cuddalore and losing some of his convoy, reached Pondicherry. He signed a treaty on 22 June and returned to the borders of Mysore, where he prepared another convoy, mainly meat on the hoof.

The prospect of further supplies reaching Pondicherry spurred Coote into action. He detached Major Moore with 180 Europeans, 30 Africans, 1,100 sepoys and 1,600 irregular horse to Tiruvadi to intercept Mukdum Ali, while he took the remainder of his men across Red Hill to assault Villanore.

Now events moved fast. On 17 June Coote took up a position on Perimbé Hill and started to besiege Villanore fort. Unfortunately, on the same day Moore encountered Mukdum Ali near Tiruvadi and was completely defeated, an omen of the future unnoticed at Madras at that time. Moore's Indian troops dispersed and he himself, with the loss of a quarter of his Europeans, took refuge behind the walls of Tiruvadi. Mukdum Ali, following his old route, came into Pondicherry by the Ariancopang fort with 300 head of cattle. Lally presumably kept his army poised to help in this valuable convoy, for he did not try to relieve Villanore fort until 20 June, only to find the garrison had surrendered a few hours before.

However, just as it looked as though Lally's fortunes were turning, events in Seringapatam robbed him of his ally. The Mahrattas made one of their periodical descents, demanding the payment of their chauth. The young King, seeing a chance of throwing off his chains while most of Hyder Ali's troops were in the Carnatic, told them he would be delighted to pay if they would rid him of his tyrant. The Mahrattas agreed and Hyder Ali's chief minister betrayed him. The ambitious soldier of fortune found himself in deadly peril. He hastily recalled Mukdum Ali and for the next few months fought like a cornered rat to survive. No more help could be expected from Mysore.

However, Lally's immediate problems over food had been solved. He now occupied a fortified camp outside the boundary hedge, extending northwards from the little village of Ulagari, which was about a mile and a half down the Villanore road; his camp faced Perimbé and the southern end of Red Hill. He occupied it with about 1,100 Europeans and Coote doubted his own ability to dislodge him. Instead he began to construct a series of redoubts across the eastern slopes of Perimbé and Red Hill, garrisoning them with his sepoys. But the cordon was too long to be effective. Lally slipped a force of 200 Europeans and two guns past it to go to Gingee and obtain more supplies. Preston, with 1,500 sepoys and the same number of irregular horse, kept watch on the road leading into the Gingee hills, but was unable to stop the French. Coote sent him reinforcements and Preston seized some heights overlooking the pass where the main road entered the hills, preventing the French from returning. However, the detachment further diminished the number of troops in front of Pondicherry.

Coote conferred with Admiral Stevens who had taken over command from Pocock earlier in the year and had come from Bombay, bringing the British fleet up to thirteen sail of the line. Coote was still dubious about his ability to attack Ulagari, and he tried to persuade Stevens to loan him some sailors. Then on 14 August drafts amounting to 600 men arrived for the 79th and 84th, and at the end of the month Stevens, not too anxious to remain off the coast during the monsoon, consented to lend him 400 marines; on 2 September Major Hector Monro disembarked with a wing of the 89th or Morris's Highlanders, the forerunners of the Highland regiments that were to render such notable service in India.

Now Coote planned to attack Ariancopang fort and Ulagari simultaneously. Lally, hearing of the British plan, realised that if the British split their forces in such a way it gave him his last chance of cutting the noose Coote was tightening round his neck; but unknown to him, Monson, designated to command the attack on Ariancopang fort, had objected and that part of the plan had been shelved.

Lally now proposed to anticipate Coote by a night attack. He planned to draw the British down towards Ulagari by attacking their redoubts blocking the road between Ulagari and Villanore, while a French force on the far or south bank of the Ariancopang stole up the river bank, crossed over near Villanore and attacked the British from behind. At the same time a strong attack was to be made on the most northerly of the British redoubts on Red Hill, the Tamarind redoubt; after capturing it, the attackers were to swing south, drive down the line of redoubts Coote had erected, taking them from flank and rear and finally turn southeast to complete the encirclement of Coote's troops near Ulagari. It was an extremely ingenious plan, but also an extremely complicated one to carry out at night. Success would depend on some precise timing. Lally was to fire two rockets near Ulagari as the signal for the attacks to begin.

At midnight on 3 September the French forces for the battle, totalling 1,100 European infantry, 100 European horse and 900 sepoys, moved off. They achieved complete surprise and captured and burnt one of the redoubts; but the attack on the Tamarind redoubt was beaten off and the project of clearing Red Hill from the north had to be abandoned. By Ulagari itself initially the plan worked well. Coote, perceiving his forward redoubts in danger, at once advanced with his reserve of Europeans. As the musketry volleys lit up the darkness the French waited impatiently for their encircling attack to materialise. Then, to Lally's horror, his outflanking column suddenly came into view behind his own front line. His plan in ruins he broke off the engagement, having suffered only a trifling thirty casualties. The officer commanding the out-flanking movement must have been able to see and hear the combat, and it must be supposed that his error was deliberate. Probably no one but Lally had any faith in his complicated plan. The British losses were a handful of sepoys. Lally's last throw had turned out a complete fiasco.*

Now occurred an extraordinary piece of interference by the military authorities in England. Just as Coote had superseded the unfortunate Forde so he himself was superseded by Monson. The ship carrying out Munro's men bore letters informing Coote and Monson that they had both been promoted Colonel, but the date for Monson's promotion antedated Coote's; Coote was instructed to return to Madras. Justly incensed, at first he proposed to take his regiment with him as a preliminary to going to Calcutta in accordance with his original instructions. Monson at once protested to the Council that this would ruin all that had been achieved at Pondicherry. Coote then con-sented to return by himself to Madras, leaving his regiment with Monson.

Monson now determined to end the siege at a single blow. He ordered Major Smith with the Madras Europeans to make a pre-dawn attack on the French positions round Ulagari, while with the 79th and 84th he himself drove through the Valdavur and Tamarind redoubts in the northwest of the boundary hedge, then followed round inside it to the south to cut Lally's troops at Ulagari off from the fortress.

On 10 September, in the darkness before dawn, the Madras Europeans smashed their way into Ulagari, captured nine field guns and stormed on to take the Villanore redoubt. Monson's men, however, in the darkness missed their way. Furious at the delay, Monson himself took the lead with his grenadier company, and the two regiments gallantly rushed the redoubts; but the fighting was heavy and Monson himself was shot through the leg. At this his troops, probably wisely, contented

---

* Malleson asserted that Lally suffered a sad blow of fate and that in the frontal attack the French never fought better. The casualty figures do not support this assertion.

themselves with consolidating their grip on the redoubts without attempting the ambitious encircling movement their commander had planned. British losses were not light, 117 men killed or wounded, but the boundary hedge had been breached and the French confined to the fortress. The engineers speedily reconstructed the redoubts to face inwards and the hedge now served to pen the French in, instead of protecting them.

When the news of Monson's wound reached Madras, Coote, after some persuasion, agreed to reassume command and arrived back on 20 September. After the loss of the Ariancopang redoubt the French evacuated the Ariancopang fort. Now the British could penetrate up to the French fortifications at will. However, with the rains about to break Coote thought it futile to attempt to build batteries and dig trenches. He maintained his grip on the redoubts in the boundary hedge, but moved the bulk of his army back to the healthier slopes of Red Hill, leaving starvation to do his work for him.

During the next two months little of note occurred. A French sally on 1 October resulted in their capturing a redoubt to the north; but after the death of his commander, a Danish officer, Subedar Coven Singh rallied his sepoys and recaptured the redoubt, inflicting fifty casualties on the French. In November John Call, now a major, came from Madras to supervise the construction of the approaches when Coote decided to begin them. On 14 December 1760 Coote had batteries constructed to bombard the fort both from the north and the south, rather with the aim of lowering the morale of the defenders than of breaching the walls.

Throughout the monsoon Stevens had kept some ships off Pondicherry to prevent any supplies reaching the French by sea. On Christmas Day he returned with the remainder of his fleet; a violent storm on 1 January 1761 wreaked havoc with his ships; two foundered, seven were dismasted and all the survivors driven out to sea. Lally wrote urgently to the French at Pulicat, imploring them to send him some rice by boat. Nothing, however, came of it before Admiral Stevens reimposed the blockade.

Now the end came quickly. Coote sited batteries against the southwest bastion of the fort and trenched forward to the ramparts. On 13 January 1761 they opened fire and by the evening of the 14th the bastion and the curtain wall near it had been reduced to a heap of rubble. On 15 January Lally, his garrison incapacitated through lack of food, asked for terms. Coote, addressing his letter to 'Charles Lally Esq', demanded what amounted to an unconditional surrender, and between eight and nine o'clock next morning he took possession.

With his habitual cantankerousness, Coote informed Pigot that he had captured Pondicherry for the Crown. He presumably knew nothing of the past history of Bombay, nor reflected whether the Crown would welcome his gift. Pigot resolved the issue deftly. He let Coote know that if he acted solely for the Crown he could be paid and supplied from England, and stopped all further money and supplies. Coote changed his mind.

Between 2,000 and 3,000 French surrendered of whom a little more than half were soldiers. Lally was parolled and returned to France. There he was imprisoned in the Bastille, tried for betraying his King and Company and condemned. He was executed in May 1766, an injustice as great as that of Admiral Byng's death before the firing squad on the quarterdeck of his flagship, and in India there were now no French generals to encourage.

The fortifications of Pondicherry were razed to the ground and the long contest in the Carnatic was at an end. The forts at Gingee surrendered on 5 April 1761. The British success must above all be attributed to the unspectacular but pervasive effect of sea power. The capture of Madras by the French in the previous war and their subsequent success at Fort St David occurred during the brief periods when they were supreme at sea. Had d'Aché been cruising off Madras when Lally besieged it, the issue might well have been different.

Malleson, and to a lesser extent Fortescue, attributed much of Lally's failure to the corrupt and inefficient officials of the *Compagnie des Indes* and the disloyalty of his subordinates. If this is so, he probably had no one to blame but himself. But it seems juster to attribute it to his vanity and arrogance, unsupported by any great capacity. He never planned a campaign in a comprehensive manner. After his setback at Madras, although his situation on land was by no means hopeless and time bound to be his enemy, he did nothing of importance for a period of ten months. In 1760, with the Mahrattas as his allies, he could have forced Coote to give battle at a disadvantage to free his communications or else retire to Madras. Instead he stumbled into a battle he did not desire over a siege of no great importance. After the battle of Wandewash he lapsed into apathy. Typically, he did not make his final effort to break the iron ring round Pondicherry until after Coote had received a numerous reinforcement and the French cause was hopeless.

Lally was brave, energetic and determined, but temperamental; he would lead his men personally into an assault; he possessed all the qualities of an excellent subaltern, but none of those of a general. Coote, calm, unhurried, patient, was in many ways the antithesis of his opponent. One other advantage he possessed. In the later stages of the conflict his sepoys were beginning to prove more effective on the battlefield and he knew how to handle them far better than his French opponent. The future pattern of Britain's Indian Army was evolving in Bengal under the aegis of Clive, but in the Madras Presidency parallel reforms were beginning to have their effect.

Chapter 17

The Rebellion in the South

In October 1758 Lawrence formed the Madras Europeans into two permanent battalions under Captains Polier and Caillaud. The numbers of the companies in a battalion seemed to vary according to its strength, but at full establishment a company consisted of a captain, a lieutenant, an ensign, six sergeants, six corporals and ninety-four private soldiers; the other ranks were divided into four divisions each under a sergeant responsible for the turnout and conduct of the men in his division.

At this time, all the officers of the regular army were senior to all the Company's officers of the same rank; hence every promotion to the rank of major in the Company's service was closely scrutinised by the captains in the regular regiments who frequently resented, extremely audibly, the promotion, as they thought, of some amateur soldier over their heads. Despite their opposition, in 1763 the Company authorised the formation of three European battalions, each 700 strong, to be commanded by majors; then in 1764 they converted the battalions into regiments, each with a colonel, a lieutenant-colonel and a major.

At the siege of Madras the Council noted that the conduct of the sepoys left much to be desired. In January 1759 Lawrence headed a committee with Councillors Pybus and Bourchier to examine the state of the sepoy army and to make recommendations. From time to time before, spasmodic attempts had been made to improve its quality. In November 1755 a formal pay code was introduced entitling a subedar to sixty rupees a month, a jemadar to sixteen, a havildar (sergeant) to ten, a naik (corporal) to eight and a sepoy to six. In 1757 a paymaster was appointed with the specific task of personally paying out the sepoys and seeing that every man had his due. In January 1756 the Council had directed that proper seniority rolls should be prepared and that, to prevent abuses, all vacancies for promotion to jemadar and subedar would be filled by the next senior, unless the Governor, the Deputy Governor or the Commander-in-Chief found good reason to order otherwise. The regulation in due course led to a somewhat elderly corps of Indian officers, but avoided the possibility of corruption and intrigue. The concept of promotion by right of seniority, or 'haq' as it was called, became a long and well-cherished tradition of the Indian army.

Just before the siege of Madras, it had become obvious that to throw together a mass of independent companies for an operation, and then to expect them to manoeuvre and co-operate with one another efficiently, was unduly optimistic. Two sepoy battalions under British subalterns had just been formed when Lally arrived in front of Fort St George, putting an end to all further reforms.

Lawrence's committee cannot have deliberated long, for he took the field early in March 1759 and returned to England in April. The new organisation recommended was, with minor variations, based on that of the European battalions. Seven sepoy battalions were to be authorised, each of nine companies including a picked grenadier company. Each company was to consist of a subedar as company commander, two jemadars as company officers, six havildars, six naiks, a trumpeter, two tom-tom men (drummers), two colourmen to carry the company colours – these were to be sepoys next for promotion to naik – a clerk and ninety-three sepoys. In headquarters there would be an Indian commandant who would, however, rank junior to any British officer, two interpreters and five armourers. There were to be two British subalterns to act as commanding officer and second-in-command, and three sergeant-majors distributed at a scale of one per three companies. Two captains were to be appointed 'Inspectors of Sepoys' with a special annual allowance of 2,000 rupees; one was to reside in Madras, the other be ready to take the field. The subalterns were to receive an allowance of 500 rupees per annum while serving with sepoys.

The battalions would be numbered from 1 to 7, the

first five wearing red jackets, with blue facings for the 1st battalion, yellow for the 2nd, green for the 3rd, black for the 4th and red for the 5th. The 6th battalion was to wear yellow jackets and the 7th green, both with red facings. Each company was to carry a flag to match its facings, with the subedar's symbol inscribed on it; the backgrounds for the flags of the 6th and 7th battalions were to be respectively red and yellow, and red and green striped diagonally. Each sepoy was to be docked six rupees per annum to pay for his clothing and to contribute one fanam a month to a provident fund for the families of men killed in action or disabled.

For disciplinary purposes sepoys were to be tried before regimental courts martial consisting of a subedar, two jemadars, two havildars, one naik, one colourman, all if possible from companies other than that of the accused. For a general court-martial the members should be four subedars, three jemadars, two havildars, two naiks, two colourmen and one private soldier, a remarkably democratic constitution. It is notable that the enforcement of discipline was made the exclusive province of the Indian ranks, and it seems clear that the British members of the battalion continued to be divorced from all responsibilities for administration.

Governor Pigot and the Council approved the recommendations, but the detailed orders for their implementing revealed a woeful lack of understanding. They directed that the number of Captains for the appointment of Inspector of Sepoys should be increased to three, that they should be carried supernumary to the establishment of the European battalions, and be officers next up for a European company; as a result, the most senior British officer serving with sepoys, perhaps with several battalions in his charge, would be junior to the most junior company commander of the Europeans. The arrangements for the subalterns serving with the sepoys were even worse. They were not to be carried on the European strength at all, but were to be called 'Ensigns of Sepoys'. Hence they would not be eligible to become 'Inspectors of Sepoys' nor to receive any form of promotion. It was proposed to award these dead-end posts to deserving sergeants in the Madras Europeans. This pedestrian organisation, devised after many long years of war in the Carnatic, throws up in stark relief the originality and clear-sightedness of Clive who, three years earlier, formulated an organisation which probably did as much as sea power to make Britain supreme in India. Biddulph, in his biography of Stringer Lawrence, dubbed him 'The father of the Indian Army'. The 'old gentleman' rendered sterling service to the Company and his country, but that claim can scarcely be allowed to go unchallenged.

The reforms were brought into effect in September 1759, but it is doubtful if any 'Ensigns of Sepoys' were ever appointed. When in 1762 an army had to be sent into Madura, the sepoy battalions at that time seem to have had no British officers serving with them, for Stringer Lawrence, back from England and now a major-general so that the commanders of regular battalions could not outrank him, posted in British subalterns to command them at the beginning of the campaign, and these subalterns grumbled unceasingly about the bitterness of their lot. It is therefore scarcely surprising that the European infantry bore the brunt of the fighting.

The campaigns in Madura had a lasting impact on British policy in India. In 1759, after the siege of Madras had ended, the Council presented Yusuf Khan, their Commandant of sepoys, with an amethyst ring to commemorate his faithful service. Now that Madras was safe, Yusuf Khan suggested that he should return to the southern provinces, where Mafuz Khan with his customary inefficiency was endeavouring to raise an insurrection. He offered to rent Madura and Tinnevelly from the Company for six years, at the rate of five lakhs of rupees for the first year and six for the remainder; he himself would pay all the expenses incurred in reimposing control. The offer looked like good business to the Council. So far it had not been able to recoup the expenses of the expeditions it had sent there. Without consulting Mohammed Ali, it agreed, but limited the appointment to one year only from 11 July 1759. Mohammed Ali, when he heard of the arrangement, protested bitterly but in vain.

Before leaving for Madura, Yusuf Khan distinguished himself at the capture of the Conjeeveram pagoda by Brereton. Muzaffar Beg, the commander of the French sepoys in the garrison, had been a subedar in the British service, but deserted to the French when Lally's star appeared to be in the ascendant.

He was captured, skulking behind a shrine. As Muzaffar Beg was led by him, Yusuf Khan drew his sword and with a single stroke nearly decapitated the unfortunate man, declaiming, 'these are the terms to be kept with traitors'. The statement came to have a sour irony over the next few years.

In April 1759 Brereton agreed to release Yusuf Khan and his men for the southern provinces. He first marched to Trichinopoly where he had an unhappy encounter with Mohammed Ali. An Indian writer described the scene picturesquely, if a little inaccurately:

'When his Highness the Lord of Wealth and Country was located at Trichinopoly and confined to bed owing to ill-health [and] was seated one day on his cot by himself with only one attendant, Mohammed Yusuf Khan, apparently with a view of enquiring into H H's health, accompanied with an imposing retinue, called on H H and observing the royal court void of guards and doorkeepers unsheathed his sword; but when that villain's eye fell on General Smith, he was overawed by the majestic appearance of that lion of the forest of war. He began to tremble and dropped the sword from his hand.'

Captain, as he then was, Joseph Smith, commanding at Trichinopoly, neglected to mention the incident in his reports to the Council, but undoubtedly a violent quarrel occurred and possibly he had to call the Commandant of sepoys to order. It is doubtful if Yusuf Khan, accustomed to absolute monarchs with unfettered power, ever understood his European masters. To his mind, as a reward for his devoted service, he had been appointed by the Company to be Nawab of the southern provinces in exchange for a specified tribute, in the same way that Nizam-ul-mulk, when Viceroy of the Deccan, appointed Anwar-ud-din Nawab of the Carnatic. He failed to comprehend the subtle nuances of the relationship between the titular ruler of the Carnatic and the Company, a failure that was to have tragic results.

After he arrived, Yusuf Khan with his usual energy set about reimposing order on the two southern provinces. Lally flirted with Mafuz Khan, hoping to embarrass the British, but could afford no troops. In December 1759 Yusuf Khan remitted two lakhs of rupees to Joseph Smith at Trichinopoly as an advance payment of rent, and on 28 January 1760 informed the Company that, except for the district of Vasudevellanur, the two provinces were pacified. In March he asked for the period of his rule to be extended for three years. The Company, desperately short of money during its ferocious struggle with the French, agreed to extend it but only for one year, leaving Mohammed Ali no option but to agree.

In June 1761 Pigot formally instructed Yusuf Khan to lower British colours and hoist those of the Nawab; at the same time he ordered that the rent should be sent direct to Mohammed Ali and not to the British at Trichinopoly. Yusuf Khan replied offering to pay rent to the Company for the next three years, nine lakhs for the first year and ten for the subsequent ones. Pigot urged Mohammed Ali to accept, but that Prince promptly demanded twelve lakhs a year. Yusuf Khan declined to consider so high a figure, and in the meantime continued to pay his rent to the British commander at Trichinopoly. A long wrangle ensued. Yusuf Khan refused point blank to pay any tribute to Mohammed Ali; for him such an action would be tantamount to acknowledging that Prince as his overlord.

This was the critical point. Pigot could have ordered Yusuf Khan to remit the rent to the Company and passed on to Mohammed Ali whatever he was due. But to Pigot, Yusuf Khan was the servant of the Company bound to carry out what orders he received; Madura and Tinnevelly belonged to Mohammed Ali and the Company only occupied the provinces as his agent. Yusuf Khan, undoubtedly become arrogant and overbearing after exercising unfettered command for several years, viewed the matter very differently. As the Nawab of the two provinces, for so he thought of himself, he expected to retain his post, probably until he died, so long as he met his obligations to his sovereign the Company. If he rendered tribute to Mohammed Ali he would become his vassal and his allegiance to the Company would be severed. Once he was in Mohammed Ali's power he knew that neither his fortune nor his life were likely to last long.

Robert Clive would have understood Yusuf Khan's motives and probably forced a compromise; it is doubtful if Pigot ever comprehended what was really at issue. When Yusuf Khan realised that the Company intended to deliver him, as he saw it, bound hand and foot to his enemy, there seemed to him no alternative to rebellion.

Pondicherry by now had fallen and a M. Maudave had come out from France, officially to look after the interests of the now numerous French prisoners of war; he resided at the neutral Dutch settlement of Negapatam. Maudave intended to harass the British in every way he could without too obviously violating the neutrality of his hosts; he began to exploit the rift that had opened between the Company and the Commandant of Sepoys. He instructed the bands of Frenchmen who had escaped captivity to take service with Yusuf Khan. A Chevalier Marchand – no one knew where that title came from and it was suspected that he had come out to India as the personal servant of Jaques Law – was appointed to command the European mercenaries.

Yusuf Khan contemplated the future with confidence; his firm but wise rule had endeared him to the population of the two provinces who had no wish to exchange his regime for the corrupt inefficiency of Mohammed Ali, and by the summer of 1762 it was estimated that he had accumulated armed forces amounting to 10,000 sepoys, 2,000 Muslim horse, 50–60 European horse and about 400 European infantry, including Africans and topasses.

During the summer strange stories about affairs in the southern provinces percolated through to Madras. In September 1762 Pigot invited Yusuf Khan to come to Madras, explain his actions and settle matters with Mohammed Ali. On 20 September 1762 the errant Commandant of Sepoys replied:

'I shall endeavour myself to come to Madras before your honour's departure to Europe in hopes to settle my affairs with the Nawab in a regular manner . . . and it is very hard after my taking so many troubles in this country, paying into the bargain, borrowing money for the credit for to get more honour . . . I shall lose my character.' Then followed a long enumeration of his past services. He ended, 'the first money I get shall be paid to the troops [for] their arrears and I shall proceed on my way to Madras. If I do not so, perhaps my troops may put some stop to my departure which will be very disagreeable for myself.

I most humbly beg Your Honour the favour to take all these causes in to Your Honour's most favourable consideration.'

But he never came. On 14 November 1762 the Raja of Travancore, a southern state on the west coast, informed the Council that he had been attacked by Yusuf Khan for refusing to join him against Mohammed Ali. It now appears that so far from Yusuf Khan attacking Travancore, Travancore had attacked him, and the letter was a blatant falsification of what occurred, designed to obtain for the Raja the support of the Company. It served its purpose. Their suspicions of Yusuf Khan confirmed the Company began to stock up Trichinopoly as the base for an expeditionary force. Events now assumed a momentum there was no reversing.

On 9 January 1763 Yusuf Khan lowered the British flag, burned it and hoisted the colours of France. On 13 January the Council resolved 'to reduce Yusuf Khan to obedience'. A force gathered under Major Achilles Preston at Trichinopoly. Stringer Lawrence, once again Commander-in-Chief at Madras, had no liking for rebels; he had not forgotten the Jacobite rebellion in his own country. He informed the Council, 'I will send Colonel Monson instructions to hang him up in the sight of the army'. A hard statement nevertheless from the commander who less than ten years before at Trichinopoly had virtually depended on the rebel for his existence.

However, matters hung fire. Hyder Ali had re-established himself in Mysore and had a number of French mercenaries at his disposal; an expedition had been sent to the Philippines, and Coote with his regiment had disappeared to Bengal. Then the news came that Britain and France had agreed to suspend hostilities. This compromised the position of Maudave and his French mercenaries or of any Frenchman aiding Yusuf Khan. It raised, however, awkward problems for the Company. The 79th, the regular battalion allotted to the Madras Presidency, was still in the Philippines; the 96th, which George Monson now commanded in Madras, had only been sent out to India as a war emergency measure and was therefore now due to return, a move of which Monson and his senior officers strongly approved.

Lawrence ordered Monson to deal with Yusuf Khan before going back to England. With considerable reluctance Monson and the 96th joined Preston at Trichinopoly on 20 August 1763 and on the 28th the column came in sight of Madura fortress which in the past had proved fatal to Cope and defied Caillaud for six long months. Monson had with him a strong force by Madras standards, about 1,200 Europeans including two troops of Europeans alternately called hussars or dragoons, 4,000 sepoys and 2,000 irregular Indian horse. Yusuf Khan, not prepared to face European infantry in a pitched battle, retired behind the walls of his city.

At the outset Monson suffered a reverse when his cavalry charged some 300 enemy horse. The Europeans galloped towards them in a wild mob, were deserted by the irregular cavalry, so they alleged, and were routed. It set the pattern for the siege; the season was late, Monson's health bad; the soldiers saw no reason why they should fight in a quarrel between two Indian princes, and no one prosecuted the siege with the slightest enthusiasm. Approaches were started from 1,500 yards away and progressed at a snail's pace. Early in November the trenches reached the lip of the ditch round Madura; for some extraordinary reason Monson was surprised to find it deep and twenty-eight feet wide; there must have been some at least who remembered its dimensions from Caillaud's lengthy siege. Now he concluded he could not mount an assault before the monsoon rain flooded the countryside. On 12 November he withdrew before the roads became impassable to his artillery. It was an inexcusable error to have under-rated the strength of the fortifications or the determination of its commander so gravely.

Yusuf Khan profited by the withdrawal to repair any damage and to build a ring of redoubts outside the city ramparts. He intrigued with the Raja of Tanjore and, more significantly, with Hyder Ali of Mysore. Hyder did not wish to risk his newly established regime by going to war with the Company, and equally he had not forgotten the drubbing Yusuf Khan had once administered to him. He had designs on Tinevelly and Madura and wished to prolong the war so that he could step in when both contestants were exhausted and take the two provinces for himself. Hence he encouraged Yusuf Khan not to treat with Mohammed Ali, while refraining from giving him any overt support.

The British were in some disarray. Monson and his senior officers firmly refused to have anything more to do with the Yusuf Khan affair and demanded passages back to England. Major Achilles Preston took over. To remedy what might be a catastrophic loss of European troops, the Council offered to any subaltern who would transfer to the Company's service with fifty soldiers the rank of captain. By this means some 400 soldiers of the 96th were induced to transfer. The sudden influx of captains into the Company's army that resulted excited enormous discontent among the Company's subaltern officers; in addition those posted to command sepoy battalions grumbled sourly that their allowances were insufficient. Preston wrote to Lawrence in Madras, 'they say (I believe you will allow with some justice, Sir) that the extraordinary pains and trouble which is required for the proper discipline of sepoys and the little credit to be got by them in comparison with Europeans makes it but fair and just that every officer in the infantry should take his tour'. He added significantly, 'But it is not every officer in the infantry (as you are very sensible Sir) that will do for the sepoys'. All the officers complained that their Batta or Field Allowance was insufficient. Fortunately Preston, a courageous leader and a kindly man, was liked and respected by all, and he managed to prevent the army falling to pieces.

In December 1763 Partap Singh of Tanjore died; he was succeeded by his son Tulsaji, reputedly an admirer of Yusuf Khan. The Council, aware that the state of the sepoy battalions left much to be desired, resolved to issue written commissions to all subedars and jemadars to increase their status, but it was another two years before the parchments were actually issued.

In January 1764 Preston took his far from happy army back to Madura. He wisely decided not to attempt a close siege, but to erect a cordon of strong points about the town and starve Yusuf Khan into submission. John Call organised, however, a siege train of eight 24-pounder and twelve 18-pounder cannon. Meanwhile Major Charles Campbell, at this time commanding at Vellore and senior to Preston, pointed out that since most of the Company's army was assembled round Madura he should command it. The Council reluctantly agreed to his request; he took over command in February 1764. Preston, true to his nature, accepted his supersession without a trace of acrimony.

On 16 February Call, writing to Madras, revealed the British army had shrunk to about 400 Europeans and 1,200 sepoys, and that the Kallans ceaselessly harried them.

However, by 9 March the investment of Madura was complete and Yusuf Khan cut off from all communication with the rest of his provinces. At this the loyalty of the Poligars to their chief, always uncertain, began to waver. The British, with Yusuf Khan and his main army safely confined in the fortress, set about reconquering his territories. On 16 March Preston took an expedition of 130 Europeans, a troop of hussars and some irregular horse to subdue the province of Tinnevelly in the south. He defeated Daud Khan, Yusuf Khan's governor, and brought most of it under the control of Mohammed Ali's administration. Leaving his small army to besiege Palamcotta, the principal fortress in the area, he himself returned to rejoin Campbell outside Madura on 20 April. Now Yusuf Khan's authority scarcely extended beyond the ring of redoubts surrounding his fortress.

On 8 April 1764 came the news that there had been a dangerous mutiny in the Bengal army and it was evident that Campbell would be more likely to lose troops than be reinforced. On 29 April he broke through the ring of redoubts, forcing Yusuf Khan to abandon five.

The relentless British pressure began to affect the mind of the old Commandant of Sepoys. Campbell wrote to Madras, 'he is grown crueller and crueller every day and cuts off people's heads with his own hand on the most trifling occasions. . . . He is jealous and suspicious of his officers and entirely supports his authority now by murder and bloodshed. . . . He seems quite deprived of his usual reason.'

By the end of May Yusuf Khan abandoned all his redoubts and Campbell began to construct batteries and dig approaches towards the northwest bastion of the fortress. On 7 June, 200 of the Bombay European regiment arrived. When on 11 June the breaching batteries opened fire, Yusuf Khan hung out a large yellow flag on the ramparts to signify he intended to fight to the death. By 21 June the breaching batteries, supplemented by two mines, had blown in some 500 yards of rampart and its debris, it was judged, would make a usable causeway across the ditch. Campbell himself felt certain of success, but a council of

war he convened insisted on a further bombardment. Finally
the storm was arranged for day-break on 26 June 1764. It was
to be made simultaneously by two columns, Preston commanding on the right, Major Wood on the left. No diversion
was planned. An account of the storm was given by 'A gentleman in the East Indies', as quoted by S. C. Hill:

'The storming party consisted of two troops of dragoons who
were dismounted, two companies of grenadiers and three
hundred battalion men. . . . Our people descended into the
ditch with great cheerfulness. In the middle they found an
obstacle they were not aware of, a deep narrow ditch into which
our men fell up to the very neck. Nevertheless they pushed on
through a heavy fire of grape and musketry. When they reached
the foot of the ditch and were forming to attack, they found
they had wet all their ammunition, not a single cartridge being
dry. The dragoons and grenadiers tried to force the breach
sword in hand, but were repulsed by the enemy's horsemen who
defended the gap with long pikes and behind them were the
sepoys.

'Our commanding officer, seeing they could not succeed,
ordered a retreat, in performing which we suffered much from
the enemy's grape, small arms, arrows and stones. Our loss on
this occasion was so considerable that it was not thought safe
to hazard another attack. Among the slain was the gallant Major
Achilles Preston at the age of thirty. He died justly lamented
by all who knew him; he was the darling of the army and an
ornament to the service. The reduction of the French garrisons
did not cost the Company half the blood that Yusuf Khan has
spilt them in the two sieges.'

Preston did not die immediately and at one time it seemed
as if he might recover, but he relapsed and died on 12 July.
Padre Schwartz, a Danish missionary, offered consolation to
the wounded; he wrote: 'oh war is a terrible punishment from
God. I went from one to the other, talked with them and
prayed with them, but at times I felt dumb for the misery was
too great.' And of a young Englishman, 'He was wounded in
the arm. . . . Mortification attacked the wound and his arm had
to be amputated. The surgeon asked him if he felt much pain,

to which he replied, "it is of no consequence, you also suffer while you perform the operation".' Schwartz offered him spiritual consolation. 'Splinters came out of his arm and consumption with several diseases brought him to his grave, but his soul we may believe, to the peace of the righteous.'

Yusuf Khan was jubilant over his victory and assumed the Company would now treat. He might have known his old employers better. Campbell adopted an ancient Roman siege tactic. He dug a ditch crowned with a fence or thorn hedge completely round Madura, a circuit of six miles. Now the rebel chieftain was isolated and doomed; even Hyder Ali wrote to Madras earnestly protesting his undying friendship. Through August and half way through September, a vice of steel slowly choked Madura. Yusuf Khan's men began to desert in ever-increasing numbers; that a large number still stayed faithful reveals the magnetic nature of his personality.

On 14 September he tried to negotiate a capitulation. Campbell refused to grant any terms. Yusuf Khan, so Marchand his French adviser related, fell into a lethargy of despair, punctuated by sudden wild outbursts of fury. During a fearful quarrel with the Frenchman he lashed him with a whip. Speechless with rage the Frenchman drew his sword, but was forcibly restrained by those around him. Marchand, furious at the insult, resolved to betray his master; but it must also have been obvious to him for some days that the misery in Madura could not be endured much longer. Using the European mercenaries, he organised a coup, seized Yusuf Khan and delivered him and the city to the British on 11 October 1764.

Campbell handed over the Commandant of Sepoys to the Nawab's officials. At five o'clock that same evening he was hanged from a large mango tree. It was recorded that the rope broke twice. Yusuf Khan, with the grim courage that never deserted him, removed the chain round his neck from which was suspended the gold medal given him by the Company which he habitually wore and suggested this might be the cause of the trouble. The third time the rope did not break. It was a tragic end to a man who had many characteristics of greatness and who for much of his life served the British so faithfully and well. He was long revered in Madura under the name of the Khan Sahib. His rebellion cost the Company a million pounds and the deaths of some thirty-six officers and 600 European soldiers.

About a hundred European mercenaries surrendered with the fortress of whom thirty-four were deserters from the Company's army. Campbell, as part of the conditions on which Marchand surrendered the city, granted them their lives. The Council at Madras, while remarking that it disapproved of his clemency, said that his terms must be honoured. Marchand's act of treachery caused a distrust of the French that possibly influenced Hyder Ali at a later date and did the French reputation much harm.

The rebellion had a far-reaching effect on Company policy. The Directors, with their customary wisdom after the event, wished to know how Madras could be so incredibly gullible as to appoint a man such as Yusuf Khan to a position of authority and then leave him unsupervised. The Council admitted their folly. In consequence, for the next 150 years all senior political and military positions in the British administration remained barred to Indians.

In June 1762 the British Declaration of War on Spain was received and read out, and in August, Draper, his health fully recovered, sailed with his regiment and a battalion of Madras sepoys in a squadron under Admiral Cornish to attack the Philippines. Manilla was stormed on 6 October 1762 and the Philippines delivered to the British. However, the countryside remained loyal to the Spanish and in practice British authority did not extend outside the bounds of the city. When the Seven Years' War ended Manilla was handed back to Spain.

The expedition was chiefly notable for a quarrel between the Governor, the General and the Admiral over how the plunder should be divided, and as the first occasion that Britain used Indian troops outside India. On this occasion the sepoys were mainly Muslims or low caste Hindus and the passage across the sea caused no problems over caste, such as subsequently arose in Bengal. For a very short period there was to be peace in the Carnatic.

Chapter 18

Bombay; The Consolidation of British Power in Bengal; The Battle of Buxar

During the years after Clive's expedition to Gheria, the Bombay army furnished invaluable contingents both of artillery and infantry to support the Madras and Calcutta Presidencies. Without the reinforcements from Bombay, Fort St David might well have fallen to Dupleix and Clive could scarcely have hoped to capture Chandernagore. But with the Mahrattas on their doorstep and the fate of the Portuguese fresh in their minds, the Council eschewed major adventures on the mainland. At the outbreak of the Seven Years' War their garrison consisted of three companies of Royal Artillery, totalling about 220 men, 285 men of the Company's artillery and a European battalion of about 800, perhaps half of whom were Topasses; in addition there were about 2,000 miscellaneous peons.

At this time the Presidency had outstations at Anjengo, Tellicherry, Surat and Broach. Although after the capture of Gheria the gravest threat to the Company's shipping had been removed, sporadic attacks by pirates still occurred and a number of minor expeditions had to be organised to keep their depredations within bounds. The Sidis who manned the old Moghul Navy, their employment long ended, settled along the west coast wherever they could find a port or city to fleece. In their home port, Surat, they seized the Castle and not only levied the *Tanka*, one third of the port's revenues, originally granted to them to meet the costs of their ships, but imposed taxes of their own. In 1756, Mussooti, a leading Sidi, died and the port fell into a state of anarchy with various notables competing violently for power. Leading Indian merchants petitioned Mr Ellis, chief of the British factory, to take over the government. The Council at Bombay feared one of the contenders for power might call in the Dutch, then behaving oddly in Bengal, or the French, or worst of all, the Mahrattas, who would certainly complete the ruin of the port. In February 1759 Admiral Pocock with two ships, *Sunderland* and *Newcastle*, bombarded the city and landed Captain Maitland RA with 800 Europeans and 1,500 sepoys. The town was taken after some fighting and on 4 March the Sidis surrendered the Castle. The British installed a garrison in the Castle and drew up an agreement with the chief citizens and the Mahrattas. The British now took a third of the Tanka, the Mahrattas a third, and a third went to the Circar, or Imperial Government.

After Pondicherry fell, Hector Munro, with his regiment, the 89th, and some 700 sepoys, sailed round Cape Comorin in February 1761 and secured the capitulation of the French settlement at Mahé. As Mahé was on the west coast, Munro came under the command of Bombay. Britain now dominated the western coastline of India, but the Bombay Council was careful to avoid extending its influence inland and risking a clash with the Mahrattas.

During the whole of this period Bombay gave the British an unspectacular but decided advantage over the French, most of whose reinforcements had to endure all the hazards and delays of the long ocean voyage from Europe. In 1759 Major Frazer, the Garrison Commander, recommended the establishment of proper sepoy battalions on the model of Clive's famous *Lal Paltan*, or Red Battalion, that had served Forde so well in the Northern Circars. Thus it was Bengal that furnished the model for the sepoy army that was eventually to spread British power over the whole of India. Clive initially forged the weapon; the years 1760–65 were to see it tempered.

In 1759, while Forde was away in the Northern Circars and Eyre Coote in the Carnatic was beginning his struggle with the French, Clive relied on his name and a handful of troops to maintain the British presence in Bengal. Late in 1758 Mir Jafar had been the victim of an attempted assassination by a group of disaffected nobles who tried to implicate Clive and the British. Clive scouted the idea as ridiculous, but some doubts may have lingered in the devious mind of Mir Jafar. He entered into an agreement with the Dutch, permitting them to increase

the number of men in their garrison, presumably in the hope
that they would counterbalance the formidable power of the
British. The Dutch, not unnaturally, resented British pre-
eminence both on the Hooghly and at the Court of the Nawab.
Seeing an overwhelming French force descending on the
Carnatic, their hotheads, despite the misgivings of their
Governor Bisdom, who knew Clive and feared his ability,
thought the moment had come to cut the British off from
Murshidabad and replace them as the foremost European nation
trading in Bengal.

During the spring and summer of 1759, while the Dutch
were assembling an expeditionary force in the Spice Islands,
Ali Gohar, the Shah-Zada or heir apparent to the Emperor, in
open rebellion against his father in the customary Moghul
fashion, sought the assistance of Suja-ud-daula, the Nawab of
Oudh, whose extensive dominions in the east bordered on
Bihar. The Shah-Zada, looking for a sound base from which
to launch an attempt on the Empire, considered that the
distraught viceroyalty of Bengal under the incompetent rule
of Mir Jafar might well answer his purpose. He persuaded
Suja-ud-daula to help him by lavish offers of rewards if the
enterprise succeeded.

The two were joined by Mohammed Kuli, a cousin of Suja,
who ruled the small state of Allahabad. The three Princes proceeded to invade Bihar, still governed by the Ram Narain who
had treated Coote in such a cavalier fashion. After some thought,
and some extremely tortuous negotiations, Ram Narain decided
to remain loyal to Mir Jafar. Suja-ud-daula suddenly disappeared to annex Allahabad from his unsuspecting cousin and
Mohammed Kuli, furiously trying to punish his treachery, was
himself killed. Meanwhile Clive had pushed up the river to
Murshidabad with 400 Europeans and 2,000 raw sepoys. He
managed to stiffen Mir Jafar into resisting the invader, the
Nawab had contemplated buying him off, and with the miscellaneous riff-raff that represented Mir Jafar's army pressed on
to relieve Patna. On his approach, the Shah-Zada, deserted by
both his allies, hastily retreated into Oudh. His army, perceiving
little hope of ever receiving any pay from their commander,
deserted and the Shah-Zada became little more than a penniless
fugitive. After this episode it was obvious to Mir Jafar that

Clive had never contemplated any form of treachery, but now he was committed to the Dutch against an ally he feared as much as he admired. When confronted by a dilemma Mir Jafar had a simple and well-tried solution; he did nothing. He conveyed some veiled warnings to the Dutch that he might object if they increased the size of their garrison in Chinsura, but the Dutch appear to have interpreted these warnings as nothing more than a praiseworthy attempt to disguise his intentions from the British.

In October 1759 six Dutch ships, crammed with troops, about half of whom were Malays, put into the mouth of the Hooghly. Clive was utterly determined to prevent them reaching Chinsura, but his situation was decidedly delicate. Britain and Holland were ostensibly friendly powers, and the British had no right to deny the navigation of the Hooghly to any but the French. He refused them passage, however, on the pretext that Mir Jafar had forbidden European troops to go up the river and that as the Nawab's ally he was bound to carry out his wishes, a piece of hypocrisy which, not surprisingly, infuriated the Dutch. Nevertheless, it gave them pause.

Mir Jafar himself prevaricated uneasily and procrastinated. Against the Dutch force in the Hooghly that numbered some 700 Europeans and 700 Malays, Clive could muster only about 240 Europeans and 800 sepoys; but Forde was back at Calcutta and he had at least a tried and trusted commander at his service. He considered it vital to prevent the Dutch at the mouth of the river joining forces with their garrison at Chinsura, and resolutely declared that in accordance with his obligations to the Nawab he would fire on their ships if they attempted to sail upstream. For nearly a month the Dutch hung about the mouth of the Hooghly while their Council at Chinsura vainly tried to negotiate their passage with Clive. Finally, exasperated beyond bearing, on 16 November, very foolishly, they sacked British property at Fulta. Now that he could claim that the Dutch had started hostilities, Clive acted fast and decisively.

He ordered Forde to advance towards Chinsura and ensure that the garrison there did not link up with their compatriots near Fulta. Mir Jafar, seeing that he must make a choice, came down on the side of the British and closed all the Dutch establishments in Bengal. The Dutch troops in the Hooghly disembarked and marched up the river. On 25 November 1759, by the little village of Bedarra, Forde with his men, reinforced by some fifty troopers raised from volunteers in Calcutta and 150 of the Nawab's horse, took up a position commanding the road to Chinsura. The Dutch, with about 700 Europeans, by the standards of oriental warfare held a commanding superiority but they had brought no artillery, or cavalry to scout the way ahead. When they saw the British position they threw themselves at it headlong, stumbled on a nullah just before the British line and suffered a complete disaster. A few days previously three East Indiamen that Clive had turned into improvised warships had attacked and captured the six Dutch vessels in the Hooghly. The Dutch débâcle was complete; they accepted their responsibility for the attack, and undertook not to maintain more than 125 soldiers in Bengal nor to enlist any sepoys. The last European threat to British supremacy in Bengal was extinguished.

But for the next three years British power was in peril from attacks by the Shah-Zada, Suja-ud-daula of Oudh and disaffected nobles in Bengal itself. During this period the Company's Europeans rarely numbered as many as 1,500. It was the Bengal sepoy army, founded and organised by Clive, that enabled the British to survive. In 1757 when he raised the first properly uniformed sepoy battalions, he insisted that the battalion organisation should be adopted and that they should have a due complement of British officers and sergeants, a policy carefully observed by his successors. Hence, while the Bombay sepoy army was little more than a raw militia and in Madras the British officers viewed their sepoys with a near contempt that assured a contemptible performance, in Bengal the sepoy showed how well he could fight when led by men he understood and respected and who understood and respected him, and that his loyalty, if he was properly treated, never wavered. Hitherto he had been employed when the British fought as an ally of an Indian prince, and doubts had been expressed about his loyalty if called on to fight against a fellow countryman exclusively on behalf of the British.

Having rendered his last service to the Company, Forde departed shortly afterwards for Britain, finally settling down in Ireland. The cool and experienced Caillaud arrived in

November 1759 as his relief. At this time Ahmad Shah Abdalli, the King of Afghanistan, had penetrated into the heart of India. On 14 January 1761 he bloodily defeated the Mahrattas at the Battle of Panipat. The defeat dealt the Mahratta confederacy a lasting blow. Although they appeared to recover from their disaster with remarkable resilience, their unity, always fragile, had been finally shattered, and their chance to rule all India had vanished. As for the Afghan, his dearly purchased victory proved barren; in March 1761 he left India never to return, having accomplished nothing but the final ruin of the Moghul Empire.

While these great events impended, the Shah-Zada again tried to conquer the Bengal viceroyalty. But now he styled himself the Emperor Shah Allum, for Ghazi-ud-din, grandson of Nizam-ul-mulk and son of that Ghazi-ud-din who had been poisoned at Aurangabad, having kept the old Emperor Allumgyr captive, murdered him and proclaimed one of his sons Moghul with the title of Shah Jahan III. So contemptible a transaction excited nothing but ridicule, and on Shah Allum, as undeniably the rightful heir, descended some of the ancient majesty that he now represented.

In January 1760 Clive resigned as Governor to be replaced in due course by his friend Henry Vansittart from Madras. Before he left he took Caillaud with him to Murshidabad and introduced him to Mir Jafar. After Clive's departure Caillaud continued up the Ganges with 300 Europeans, two battalions of native infantry and about 15,000 horse and foot of the Nawab's army under his son Miran to safeguard Patna, 300 miles up the river.

Shah Allum as the man to be Emperor attracted much support. He promised the viziership of the Empire to Suja-ud-daula in exchange for his help and was joined by an old friend, Kamghar Khan, Governor of Tirhoot and a leader of the dissidents in Bihar, with between 5,000 and 6,000 horse. At Patna, Ram Narain assembled a large army to oppose the invaders who arrived near the city towards the end of January. Despite urgent appeals from Caillaud to await his arrival, Ram Narain gave battle and was defeated. A small British detachment serving with him lost all its officers and was almost cut to pieces, but a remarkable medical officer named Fullarton took command, held the survivors together and withdrew to Patna with Ram Narain. Their presence helped to prevent the city capitulating to the Shah-Zada.

On 19 February, before the Shah-Zada, never a man to hurry, had mounted a serious attack Caillaud arrived in the neighbourhood with his small army and Miran with Mir Jafar's. On 22 February he advanced towards his enemy, intending to camp that night in a position from which he could attack next day. Towards evening he came in sight of the Shah-Zada's men. He halted and occupied two villages with his sepoys, deploying his Europeans between them; Miran with his ill-disciplined mob he instructed to form a second line behind so that he would be shielded from any initial enemy attack. That worthy, however, decided to form his army to the right rear of the British line.

As night drew on Shah Allum suddenly launched a ferocious attack on the British; his troops met a rock-like resistance, but beyond the British right his cavalry charged home on Miran's men. In a letter to Eyre Coote, Caillaud related what happened.

'He for some time stood the shock well, but being wounded and turning his elephant – which in plain English is running away – the whole army in an instant were following his example. Luckily for him, however, I brought up a battalion of sepoys which was on our right with which I flanked that body of horse which made the attack. The first fire threw them into confusion, and that repeated fairly set them running. The Nabob's Dewan [Miran's] who was in the rear and not yet seized with panic came to support the runaways and thus ended the Battle of Seerpore with a loss of about 500 killed and wounded on both sides.'

A pursuit was impossible as Miran 'On account of two scratches from arrows which he was pleased to think were very dreadful wounds' refused to allow his cavalry to continue the action and Caillaud had none. So, as he drily observed, 'we set out for the dancing girls of Patna'.

Shah Allum, after what was nothing more than a minor repulse, now showed uncharacteristic boldness and vigour. He hooked round the British to the south and set off by jungle

tracks eastwards towards Murshidabad. Owing to his lack of
cavalry it was two or three days before Caillaud heard of his
move and started off in pursuit. The Shah-Zada approached
Murshidabad to find Mir Jafar standing in his way, and his
nerve failed him; while he dallied Caillaud appeared. Shah
Allum promptly turned round and headed back to Patna.
Caillaud ordered Knox, back from his triumphant activities in
the Northern Circars, to take 200 Europeans and his battalion
of sepoys and hasten back to Patna, now denuded of troops, by
forced marches. Knox covered 300 miles in an astonishing
thirteen days and just managed to lock the Shah-Zada out of
the city.

Caillaud followed with Miran at a more leisurely pace. Shah
Allum withdrew to the banks of the River Soan about twenty-
five miles west of Patna. Khadam Hussain, Governor of
Purnea, who hated Mir Jafar and Miran, now resolved to join
him. Knox moved to intercept. As soon as he saw the British
Khadam Hussain attacked. Caillaud related:

'a very warm action ensued. Captain Knox with 200 Europeans
and a battalion of sepoys, five pieces of cannon and about 300
horse maintained himself for six hours opposed to an army of
12,000 men with thirty pieces of cannon. He was totally
surrounded near the whole time, but . . . he at length compelled
them to quit the field with the loss of eight pieces of cannon,
three elephants and between two and three hundred men killed
on the spot.'

Khadam Hussain's army probably numbered considerably less
than Caillaud's estimate; there is a natural tendency to magnify
the numbers of the enemy, but Knox clearly fought a distinguished little action. When he came up Caillaud pursued the
defeated army vigorously. However, four days after the pursuit
began it was halted by a singular event. Towards midnight on
17 July Miran was resting in his tent while a flautist soothed his
anxieties with lullabies and a servant massaged his limbs, when
a flash of lightning struck the tent and incinerated all three.
The occasion could scarcely be called a tragedy as none
mourned Miran, but it would appear to the soldiers as an omen
of catastrophe. On the advice of his senior Indian officers,

Caillaud merely gave out that Miran was injured, and hastily
took the army back to Patna before admitting his death. He
remained there waiting for the monsoon to finish. Mir Kassim,
son-in-law of Mir Jafar, took over command of Miran's army.

In October the Council in Calcutta took a momentous step,
they deposed Mir Jafar on the grounds of maladministration
and replaced him by Mir Kassim. As a reward for the Company's support, Mir Kassim assigned to it the revenues of
Burdwan, Midnapore and Chittagong, in theory to pay for the
upkeep of British troops which the Company guaranteed to
hold for him on call. The Council members themselves received
some extremely handsome presents of money. Mir Jafar,
violently protesting, allowed himself to be pensioned off in
Calcutta.

The transaction violated the treaty concluded with Mir Jafar
and owing to the large sums of money received by members of
the Council bore an ugly taint of bribery; it dealt the authority
of the Nawab and his officials a damaging blow, one that the
more venal of the merchants in Calcutta were quick to exploit;
it led finally to a British catastrophe which in turn led to the
establishment of British power throughout Bengal. A number
of the Company's servants, including Caillaud initially but he
allowed himself to be over-persuaded, and Carnac, were utterly
opposed to the whole affair, and it excited the indignation of
Clive, at that time in England.

In December 1760 Caillaud was recalled to Madras to assume
command of the Company's armies in the Carnatic, and Major
John Carnac, a very close friend of Clive took over. Accounts
of the events of the next two years were undoubtedly influenced
by the *Seir Mutaquerin*, a delightful and wildly inaccurate
Indian contemporary account, and the life of Clive by Caraccioli. Caraccioli, whoever he may be – it was probably a
pseudonym for a syndicate – sought to vilify Clive and discredit
all his associates. A number of years later John Carnac
shouldered the blame for a disaster inflicted on a Bombay army
by the Mahrattas. Perhaps for these reasons some of the
aspersions cast on his conduct may well be ill-founded.

Early in 1761 Carnac wrote to Eyre Coote:

'at the time of my receiving charge the Shah-Zada was in

peaceable possession of a considerable portion of this province and was collecting revenue within fifteen coss [about thirty miles] of Patna. His followers were greatly increased by his having kept his ground so long and from a kind of veneration which people of all castes here have for him as the King's son. The Nabob's troops were almost outrageous on account of the immense arrears due to them.'

To stifle their murmurings Caillaud had promised them money which in due course Mir Jafar failed to pay. In January 1761 at the village of Suan, a few miles west of Patna, Carnac attacked the Shah-Zada's army and dispersed it. Jean Law with his handful of French had accompanied the heir-apparent; he surrendered to his British adversaries, who received with courtesy a man whose courage and persistency they had long admired. The Shah-Zada pleaded for terms. Carnac, well versed in such matters, invited him to the British camp at Gaya and received him with all the ceremonies and honours due to the Emperor. The gratified prince, now accepted by the British as the Emperor Shah Allum, decided to pitch his camp beside that of his new-found friends. He asked for British troops to help him march on Delhi, but although they toyed with the enticing idea, the Council, already over-extended militarily, refused to accept any further commitments. In view of the uncertain situation they raised two new sepoy battalions.

Mir Kassim, deeply suspicious of the growing intimacy between the Emperor and the British, hastened to Patna. His suspicions were not wholly unjustified. In a letter to the Directors in London the Calcutta Council remarked, 'The King [Shah Allum] had offered to confer on the Company the dewannee [diwani] of Bengal on condition of our being responsible for the Royal revenue, but we were sensible that our accepting this post would cause jealousy between us and the Nabob; we thought it more prudent to decline it.' Mir Kassim was uneasily conscious that what the Company had done to Mir Jafar it might do to him. To make matters worse, Carnac had been foremost in opposing the coup that deposed Mir Jafar and from the outset relations between the two were strained. Ram Narain, whom Mir Kassim had once laboured to supplant, did all he could to exacerbate the situation with considerable success.

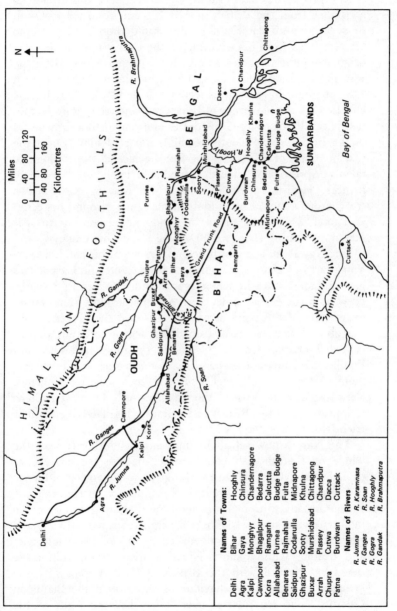

N

Miles
0 40 80 120
0 40 80 160
Kilometres

HIMALAYAN FOOTHILLS

R. Brahmaputra

B E N G A L

Chittagong

Chandpur

Dacca

SUNDARBANDS

Bay of Bengal

Khulna
Hooghly
Chandernagore
Chinsura Calcutta
Burdwan Budge Budge
Bedarra Fulta
Midnapore

R. Hooghly

Purnea
Rajmahal
Bhagalpur
Monghyr
Sooty Murshidabad
Oodanulla Plassey
Cutwa

Chupra
Patna
Bihar
Arrah Gaya
Ghazipur Buxar
Saidpur
Benares

R. Gandak

R. Gogra

R. Soan

OUDH

Grand Trunk Road

B I H A R

Ramgarh

Cuttack

Cawnpore
Kalpi Kora

R. Ganges

R. Jumna

Agra

Delhi

Names of Towns:

Delhi	Bihar	Hooghly
Agra	Gaya	Chinsura
Kalpi	Monghyr	Chandernagore
Cawnpore	Bhagalpur	Bedarra
Kora	Ramgarh	Calcutta
Allahabad	Purnea	Budge Budge
Benares	Rajmahal	Fulta
Saidpur	Codanulla	Midnapore
Ghazipur	Sooty	Khulna
Buxar	Murshidabad	Chittagong
Arrah	Plassey	Chandpur
Chupra	Cutwa	Dacca
Patna	Burdwan	Cuttack

Names of Rivers

R. Jumna R. Karamnasa
R. Ganges R. Soan
R. Gogra R. Hooghly
R. Gandak R. Brahmaputra

Oudh, Bihar and Bengal

In April 1761, Shah Allum, convinced he could obtain no assistance from the British or Mir Kassim, returned to Oudh to seek Suja-ud-daula's aid. The same month Eyre Coote arrived, fresh from his triumphs in the Carnatic, to assume his original appointment as Commander-in-Chief Bengal. After the way Ram Narain had treated him when he was chasing Jean Law, it might have been expected that he would cherish little affection for the Governor of Bihar; but since then Ram Narain had faithfully discharged his duties and remained a firm friend of the British. Eyre Coote steadily supported him against the machinations of Mir Kassim. But he lacked the diplomatic talents or prestige of Clive and failed to reconcile the two Indian princes. Hearing a rumour that Mir Kassim meditated a treacherous attack, Coote doubled his sentries round his camp at Patna, then burst pistol in hand and, according to Mir Kassim, shouting strings of 'Dammees' into his tents.

The Nawab lodged a bitter complaint about his conduct with Vansittart in Calcutta, alleging that both Coote and Carnac had joined Ram Narain in a plot against himself. Vansittart withdrew both the British officers from Patna, leaving Ram Narain to his fate. Mir Kassim at once imprisoned the Governor, on the ground that he had falsified his accounts, a not unprecedented charge. Coote, the conqueror of Wandewash and Pondicherry, was not prepared to stomach such cavalier treatment. After returning to Calcutta he took ship for England. Vansittart's action was, at the least, unwise. To most Indians it appeared that the British had callously betrayed one of their friends; they wondered who would be next.

The Nawab now set about imposing his authority over the whole of Bengal with considerable success. He moved his capital from Murshidabad to Monghyr, to lessen the influence of Calcutta, reduced and reorganised his army, recruiting some European adventurers as generals and arming some of his infantry with flintlock muskets, and reformed Mir Jafar's corrupt administration. Unmenaced by any of his neighbours and dealing with a short-sighted British administration he inevitably clashed with the British, a clash hastened by the arrogant and corrupt behaviour of the British merchants in Calcutta. The old quarrel over 'dustucks', the right of the British merchants to trade free of tax, flared up once again. In utter exasperation Mir Kassim in 1763 decreed that all merchants of whatever nationality might trade on the Hooghly free of all tolls and taxes. The British, furious at losing their privileged position, protested violently. Mill, in his not always glowing account of British activities in India, observed that the incident 'furnishes one of the most remarkable examples upon record of the power of interest to extinguish all sense of justice, and even of shame'.

As the dispute deepened the Council alerted its army, at that time widely dispersed among its possessions. Its Europeans consisted of one regular infantry battalion, Coote's 84th 400 strong, two troops of dragoons and one of hussars, the categories of cavalrymen in practice were indistinguishable, amounting in all to about a hundred effectives, the Bengal European Battalion of twelve companies each about sixty men strong, and two companies of artillery, giving a grand total of about 1,500 Europeans. In addition there were ten sepoy battalions plus some local companies raised to police specific areas, and two troops of irregular cavalry, known as the Moghul horse, numbering about 200 troopers; the Indian troops amounted to about 10,000 men. The European horse were composed of such infantrymen as showed some ability to remain seated on a charger and the Moghuls were recruited from bands of irregular Muslim horse that roamed the provinces ready to hire out their services. Both had been raised to remedy the difficulties Caillaud had experienced from having no cavalry actually under his command, and there is little to suggest that any of the British officers had anything more than the most rudimentary idea of cavalry tactics.

The largest field force was concentrated at Patna to watch the border with Oudh. It consisted of four European infantry companies, one artillery company and three sepoy battalions totalling about 300 Europeans and 2,500 sepoys. In the region round Calcutta was stationed the largest proportion of the Company's troops. The 84th garrisoned Fort William; between Fort William and Ghyretty, the cantonment that had grown up outside Chandernagore, were placed five companies of Europeans, a French ranger company recruited from French prisoners of war captured at Pondicherry, the cavalry, the second company of artillery and three battalions of sepoys, in all about

1,000 Europeans and 2,500 sepoys. To safeguard the western
districts now belonging to the Company, two sepoy battalions
were stationed at Burdwan, and three European companies,
two sepoy battalions, a troop of artillery and a detachment of
Moghul horse at Midnapore. In eastern Bengal, at that time
generally trouble-free, two sepoy battalions and some local
defence companies were distributed between Dacca, Chittagong
and Luckipore.

In a last effort to avert a complete break with the Nawab the
Council sent two envoys, Amyatt and Hay, to Monghyr to try
to negotiate a settlement. They arrived on 12 May 1763 to a
frigid reception. Matters dragged on until on 14 June 1763 Mir
Kassim demanded that the British garrison at Patna should be
withdrawn to Monghyr, and ordered one of his European
mercenary generals, Markar, to advance on the city with a large
body of men. Since the Company's troops at Patna were
stationed there ostensibly to defend his dominions, he can
scarcely be thought to have exceeded his rights. The Council
at Calcutta, however, looked on the request as nothing less than
an ultimatum. Orders were issued for the army to concentrate
at Gyretty. There were signs that Mir Kassim was thinking
better of forcing a clash – he released a British convoy of arms
he had been holding – when Ellis, the chief of the Company's
factory at Patna, took a hand. He was a stupid hot-tempered
man, appointed to the Council at the behest of a venal Director
despite the protests of Clive, at that time Governor. In the early
hours of the morning of 25 June, Ellis, hearing of Markar's
approach, launched an attack on Patna, the garrison of which
was still happily asleep. It could not be regarded as other than
a treacherous attack on an ally, however strained relations had
become, particularly in a century when the niceties of declaring
war were still observed.

The city fell without difficulty; then Ellis and his officers,
without bothering to secure the citadel, returned to have a
belated and no doubt in their opinion well-earned breakfast,
while their troops occupied themselves plundering the shops.
Two hours later Markar arrived, surprised the scattered British
troops and chased them back into the British factory which
he at once besieged. After four days, lacking provisions, Ellis
tried to break out and escape to Oudh. He was, however,

surrounded and all his Europeans either killed or captured; significantly a substantial number of his sepoys deserted and enlisted in Mir Kassim's army. When measured against what other tiny British forces subsequently accomplished it is clear that British unscrupulousness was only matched by British ineptitude.

The monsoon had broken, but immediate military action was essential. On 7 July, after officially declaring war on Mir Kassim, the Council extracted Mir Jafar from retirement in Calcutta and once more proclaimed him Nawab. On 5 July 1763 Major Adams of the 84th left Gyratty for Murshidabad with his own regiment, four companies of the Bengal Europeans, the European cavalry, the company of artillery with ten guns under Captain Jennings and three battalions of sepoys. The sepoy battalions at Burdwan and Midnapore under Captain Knox and the Moghul horse and the sepoy battalion from Chittagong were ordered to join him at Murshidabad. Before Adams could arrive, Mir Kassim's troops captured Murshidabad, killing or capturing a weak detachment in the city, and advanced to the neighbourhood of Plassey. But from now on things for Mir Kassim began to go awry. A battalion of sepoys under Lieutenant Glenn, escorting treasure and supplies from Burdwan, was attacked on the march by an enemy force estimated at about 17,000 cavalry, unaccompanied by infantry or guns. In a bloody encounter Glenn beat off all attacks and brought his convoy safely to Cutwa, where Adams was encamped.

His action set the pattern for the campaign. On 19 July Mir Kassim's general, Mohommed Taki Khan, attacked the advance-guard of the British near Cutwa and drove it back; a general engagement followed, but the troops so roughly handled by Glenn refused to join the battle. Mohammed Taki's men attacked with great spirit, but after their commander had been killed gallantly leading a charge, his army broke up and lost heavily in the subsequent pursuit. That night Adams camped his army within sight of Plassey grove. On 23 July he took Murshidabad and installed Mir Jafar once again as Nawab. Here Knox joined with his troops, bringing Adams' force up to 1,000 Europeans and 4,000 sepoys organised in seven battalions. Carnac served as second-in-command to Adams, in accordance with the accepted rule that all regular officers were senior to all Company's officers of the same rank.

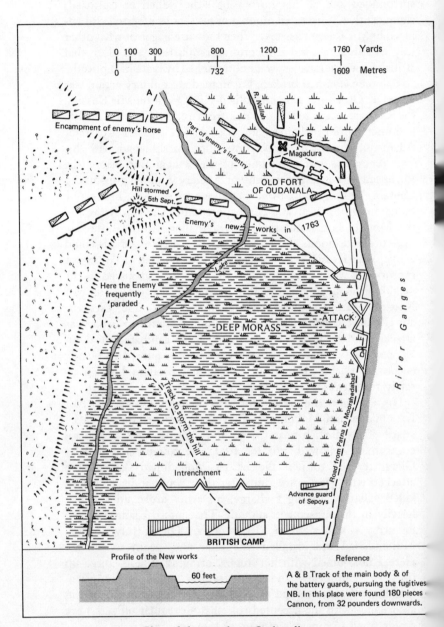

Plan of the attack on Oodanulla

At Sooty on 2 August 1763 Adams encountered a fresh army commanded by Markar and Sumroo – Sumroo was the Indian name given to a renegade Alsatian named Walter Reinhardt. Originally a member of one of the Swiss companies in the Carnatic, he was to distinguish himself for his cruelty among men not noticeably humane. In a hard-fought battle, despite the considerable superiority in numbers of Mir Kassim's army, the British gained the day, capturing seventeen enemy guns.

After a short pause of three days to reorganise, Adams continued his victorious advance up the Ganges. Mir Kassim directed his army to fight to the death to hold the narrow defile at Oodanulla on the road to Rajmahal, where the hills came down within a mile of the river. It numbered about 40,000 men, all his remaining strength. His generals constructed a strong redoubt on the hill overlooking the defile and an entrenchment from its lower slopes to the river. The ground in front of the entrenchment was a sea of mud steadily deepening under the incessant monsoon rains. Adams paused for a month in some perplexity, erecting batteries as though proposing to commence a regular siege; but the bog in front baffled him, until a deserter told him of a path across it which would enable him to reach the hill overlooking the defile. On 5 September Adams launched a night attack. A column stealthily crossed the morass, scaled the hill and overwhelmed the enemy entrenchments by a sudden fierce charge out of the darkness. As this attack went in another column crept up the river bank and penetrated the edge of the entrenchments by the river. In the black night the enemy troops fell into hopeless confusion, fired furiously on each other and finally gave way to panic: 15,000 were reputed to have perished, most through their own action. Broome observed, 'to the credit of the English no unnecessary slaughter was committed. After being assured of success, none fell by their hands save those in actual opposition.'

Now Mir Kassim was doomed. Filled with impotent fury, on 9 September he wrote to Adams: ' . . . If you are resolved on your own authority to proceed with this business, know for a certainty that I will cut off the heads of Mr Ellis and the rest of your chiefs and send them to you. . . .' Adams replied: '. . . if a hair of their head is touched you will have no title to mercy from the English . . . they will pursue you to the utmost extremity of the earth'. Ellis managed to deliver a message to Adams telling him that he and his fellow captives were reconciled to their fate and that he was on no account to allow considerations of their safety to interfere with his plans.

In October Adams took Monghyr and Mir Kassim issued orders for the slaughter of his captives. Only Sumroo was prepared to execute so barbaric an order; under his instructions all the British prisoners were butchered. Adams advanced on Patna, arriving near the city on 28 October 1763. But the citadel was strong and it was not until 6 November that after fierce fighting he succeeded in capturing it. Mir Kassim fled to Suja-ud-daula in Oudh. On 9 December Adams handed over command to Knox, now a major, for Carnac, the next senior, was on the western frontier investigating a rumoured Mahratta incursion; finding the rumour groundless he went on to Calcutta.

Their exertions during the peak of the monsoon had undermined the health both of Adams and Knox. Adams died in Calcutta, waiting for a ship, and Knox died shortly afterwards. Adams had fought a remarkable campaign against heavy odds during the worst weather of the year, and the troops that compelled the British garrison at Patna to capitulate were by no means contemptible.

Captain Jennings of the artillery, somewhat to his surprise, now found himself commanding the army and facing a very awkward and unpleasant situation. The war was over for the time being and the troops clamoured to be rewarded, a clamour Jennings had no means of satisfying. The 84th was en route back to England, although most of the men had transferred to the Company's service, and the Bengal Europeans had been reinforced by two companies of French ex-prisoners of war who were to prove a hotbed of disaffection. Alarming stories about the behaviour of their troops on the frontier began to filter back to Calcutta. The Council refused to allow the remnant of the 84th to embark and hastily borrowed some marines from warships in the harbour.

The stories were no more alarming than what actually occurred. On 30 January 1764 the Bengal Europeans refused to obey an order; their spokesman told Jennings they had been promised a donation when they had cleared Bihar of the enemy and now, two months later, nothing had been forthcoming; they proposed to carry out no more duties until they were paid. The men had much justice on their side, and their complaint was likely to be upheld by the sepoys. Jennings temporised, saying that he would write to Calcutta and that he had heard that some money was on the way. The men returned to duty.

Then at half-past nine on the morning of 11 February Jennings heard to his astonishment the assembly being beaten when no parade had been ordered. He hurried to the parade ground to find the European battalion fallen in with some field pieces, although most of the gunners, out of respect for their commander, refused to join the unauthorised parade. The sepoys showed signs of wanting to join in but their officers managed to dissuade them. A private soldier called Straw, when Jennings approached, called the men up to attention and announced that, since they had received no money, they intended to march to Patna. Nothing that Jennings could say could alter their determination; they marched off in good order towards Oudh, saying they intended to bring in their comrades on detachment guarding the Karamnasa river before going back to Patna.

Captain Martin, a Frenchman commanding the French companies, followed his men to try to persuade them to return to duty. They suggested that he should accompany them as their commander, and confessed that the story about going to Patna was a blind; their real intention was to go to Oudh where they were convinced they would soon make themselves masters of the country. This was appalling news. Jennings rushed off to the detachments on the Karamnassa river that marked the border and intercepted the marchers with two battalions of sepoys. Ensign Davis, with a frontier company, remarked to Jennings that he thought the men were fully determined to desert. Jennings replied: 'Oh, no. Englishmen desert? Never! A dram and a biscuit will send them all back again.' Jennings proved a true prophet so far as the English were concerned, most of whom, when they discovered what was really intended, returned to duty. The sepoys, nevertheless, categorically refused to stop the deserters and 600 out of the two battalions joined them with their arms. In the end, however, only about 150 Europeans, mostly French, and a hundred sepoys crossed the

Karamnassa and disappeared into Oudh, not to be seen again. Jennings managed to acquire two lakhs of rupees from a reluctant Mir Jafar, not unaccustomed to such situations, for he seldom paid his soldiers until they had mutinied; but although the worst consequences of the mutiny had been avoided, the failure to punish such flagrant indiscipline was bound to have far-reaching results. It seems incredible that a junior captain should have been expected to deal with such a situation; it is doubtful if Jennings felt any sorrow when in March he handed over command to Carnac.

Now a new and formidable enemy menaced Bihar. Mir Kassim had lavished his blandishments on Suja-ud-daula, who had become vizier to Shah Allum; he discharged his duties by keeping the unfortunate titular Emperor virtually a prisoner. In return for actual payments from the treasure Mir Kassim had brought out from Bengal with him and the promise of extravagant rewards once the enterprise succeeded, the Nawab of Oudh promised to restore him to power in Bengal.

Carnac observed the situation carefully. He was short of supplies and transport and unhappy about the discipline of his troops. The firebrands in Calcutta urged on him an immediate advance into Oudh, but he preferred to allow Suja-ud-daula to bring the war to him. While waiting for the Prince, he amalgamated his European cavalry into a single troop and enlarged his Moghul horse to 1,200; he declined to form them into a regular regiment on the grounds that he had no competent British cavalry officers and that the superior type of man recruited into the cavalry would never tolerate ignorant or incompetent officers.

When Suja-ud-daula advanced, Carnac fell back to entrenchments he had constructed outside Patna. On 3 May 1764 Suja attacked the lines, but was repulsed without difficulty. On 30 May, as the monsoon was about to break, he returned to Oudh. Carnac has been heavily censured for his inactivity, but the defensive attitude he took up may well have been justified at this time. In July he left the army. The Directors, ironically enough, had ordered him to be dismissed the service for his opposition to Vansittart over the coup that brought Mir Kassim to power, and the news had only just arrived in Calcutta.

He was replaced by Major Hector Munro who, in view of

the threatening developments in Bengal, had been sent from Bombay with the remnants of his old battalion the 89th, and the 90th, together totalling little more than a hundred men. In August he assumed the appointment of Commander-in-Chief and at once left to take command at Patna. He did not find the state of the army much to his liking and issued stringent orders on how matters were to be conducted. Possibly the presence of the regular troops and a company of marines was sufficient to ensure the discipline of the Europeans; perhaps they recognised a good commander when they met one, but there was no obvious trouble from them; the sepoys, however, used to going their own way in accordance with the particular prejudices of their commanding officers, deeply resented being regimented in this fashion. Munro brooked no opposition and insisted that his orders should be rigidly enforced.

On 8 September the 9th Sepoy Battalion mutinied; the sepoys locked up their British officers and sergeants without harming them, but marched off as a formed body with their arms. Captain Wemyss, commanding the marine company, at once pursued them with his company and a battalion of sepoys. He surprised them and forced them to surrender. Munro ordered that twenty-four of the ringleaders should be brought before a general court-martial made up of Indian officers drawn from two different sepoy battalions. The court-martial found all the accused guilty and sentenced them to death by being blown from the muzzles of guns. Munro ordered that the sentence should be executed at once. He paraded the two sepoy battalions with the company of marines, the grenadier company of the Europeans and the artillery, and ordered the first four of the captives to be fastened to the gun muzzles of four field guns. The grenadiers among the mutineers claimed that as they were entitled to the right of the line they should be executed first. They were tied to the gun muzzles; the order to fire was given and they were blown to pieces. A murmur of horror arose from the whole parade; the officers commanding the two sepoy battalions rode up and said their men would not tolerate any further executions. Munro was a humane man, but he knew that the lives of his soldiers and the fate of his army might depend in the near future on the standard of their training and discipline. He ordered the guns to be loaded with grape, swung them round towards the sepoys and crisply ordered them to ground their arms. Almost instinctively they obeyed the familiar word of command. Munro ordered them to stand clear, marched them to a flank and stationed the Europeans over their muskets. The executions continued, the men under şentence, so Broome recorded, 'marching boldly up to the instrument of their execution and awaiting the fatal signal with firm and unmoved countenances'.

Having enforced discipline, Munro now began to prepare for an advance into Oudh. On 13 October he marched out with 900 Europeans and eight battalions of sepoys, 700 of the Moghul horse and twenty-eight guns, leaving 300 European infantry and four battalions of sepoys for the defence of Bihar. His advance was harassed by Suja's cavalry, who scored a minor success against a careless vanguard, but generally the horsemen made off when the guns dropped into action.

In Oudh Shah Allum desired nothing more than to escape from his gaoler, while Mir Kassim had suffered the final disaster; he had exhausted all his money. Suja-ud-daula had no patience with a penniless ally. He confiscated all of Mir Kassim's treasure that he could discover and confined the Prince under an armed guard. Meanwhile he took up a strong position just to the east of Buxar, where the flat open plain would be particularly favourable for the operation of his strong force of cavalry. He waited with confidence for the British to approach.

At about nine o'clock on the morning of 22 October 1764 the leading British troops entered the plain dotted with copses of mango trees to see the buildings of Buxar looming up some three miles away on the banks of the Ganges. Suja-ud-daula's army, about 40,000 strong, was drawn up in order of battle outside their entrenched camp by the town. The British vanguard veered across to rest its right flank on the river, here about three-quarters of a mile wide, while the rest of the army formed up on its left. Suja's guns fired a few random shots at long range, then his whole army withdrew into camp.

Munro halted the advance; he stationed a sepoy battalion in a village about 1,000 yards in front and ordered the remainder of his army to pitch camp. In the afternoon he convened a council of war. It was agreed that the army should rest next day

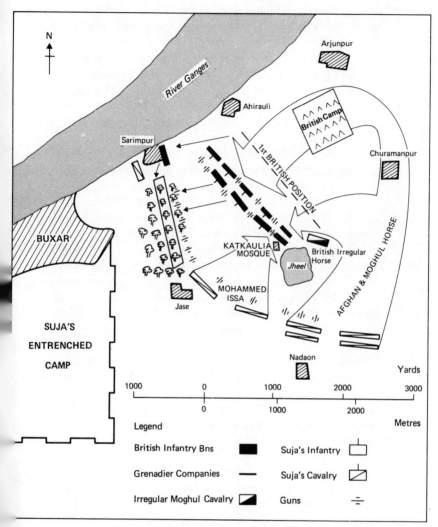

N

River Ganges

Arjunpur

Ahirauli

British Camp

Sarimpur

Churamanpur

1st BRITISH POSITION

BUXAR

KATKAULIA MOSQUE

British Irregular Horse

Jheel

AFGHAN & MOGHUL HORSE

MOHAMMED ISSA

Jase

SUJA'S
ENTRENCHED
CAMP

Nadaon

Yards

1000   0   1000   2000   3000

0   1000   2000

Metres

Legend

British Infantry Bns

Grenadier Companies

Irregular Moghul Cavalry

Suja's Infantry

Suja's Cavalry

Guns

The Battle of Buxar

and attack Suja's camp the day after. For security all the heavy
baggage was loaded in a convoy of boats that had accompanied
the army up the Ganges. In preparation for the attack Munro
issued detailed orders about the formation the army should
adopt. It was to form in two equal lines about 200 yards apart,

with a reserve stationed in between; the Moghul horse were to cover the exposed left flank which projected into the plain. The first line would be composed of four sepoy battalions, two on each flank with in the centre a composite European battalion consisting of all the regular troops, two companies of Bengal Europeans and a detachment from Bombay. The second line was to be formed in a similar manner, with two sepoy battalions on each flank and in the centre the rest of the Bengal Europeans, except for their two grenadier companies which he placed as a reserve fifty yards behind the centre ready to move to reinforce any sector that might be threatened. His twenty-eight guns were to be inserted in pairs and threes in the intervals between units. During their advance up the Ganges Munro had discussed his tactics with his officers. In view of Suja's immense superiority in cavalry he considered that the army must be prepared for an attack from any direction. In the event of an attack round a flank, the flank units of the first and second lines were to wheel inwards and lock together while the remainder of the second line faced about. The army would thus be able to form a long thin bayonet-fringed rectangle with the Moghul Cavalry positioned on the open flank away from the river.

Soon after sunrise on the morning of the 23rd, Munro, as he informed the Earl of Sandwich in the despatch he wrote to him on the 26th, rode out with some of his senior officers towards Buxar to have a good look at the ground and plan for the battle he proposed to fight next day. To his astonishment, as he approached the town he saw all Suja-ud-daula's host assembled and starting to come towards him. He hastened back to his camp and ordered his drummers to beat to arms – there was no time to pack any baggage or to strike the tents. In the clear, bracing, early morning sunshine the regiments formed up rapidly and in good order; Munro noted that his battle line was complete in twenty minutes.

About 1,000 yards forward from the left flank of the British was a mudwalled village; opposite their centre stood a large copse or minor wood still about 1,000 yards away, while on the right flank and rather closer lay a small cluster of mud daubed houses. Suja's army, stretching far beyond the British left, swarmed forward, occupying all three features, while all along the battle line, now curving round the outer flank of the British, teams of oxen and elephants laboriously dragged heavy guns into position. Then from perhaps nearly a hundred muzzles white smoke blossomed and round shot came winging towards the steady scarlet ranks; it was about nine o'clock in the morning. The lighter British guns lacked the range to reply. At first the Indian artillery fire was wild and badly aimed, then suddenly from the hamlet on the right the enemy gunners began to find the range. Munro judged it imperative to silence them. He ordered his right-hand sepoy battalion to advance and storm the hamlet. The battalion commander hesitated to plunge straight at the enemy guns. Lieutenant James Nicol, standing by Munro, ran over and shouted to the sepoys to advance; at once the battalion swept forward and rushed the houses with the bayonet. Munro reinforced it with a battalion from the second line.*

Now he ordered his whole line to close with the enemy so that the British guns could come into action. The ground in front of the British left was marshy; the line had to side-step to the right and the manoeuvre was slow and tedious; had Suja's guns been better served it would also have been very costly. But the line succeeded in reforming without undue loss and the British guns opened a fire as rapid and well-directed as their enemy's had been slow and ineffectual.

The battle flared up. In the plain far beyond the British left columns of cavalry could be seen wheeling and forming, then they came down in a head-long gallop. After a short sharp struggle the Moghul horse were routed. But already the flank battalions had wheeled inwards, the flank guns trained outwards and the reserve moved over to check any possibility of a break-through. As the massive wave of horsemen curled down a murderous hail of shot greeted them and it receded. Now 5,000 choice Afghan horse swept right round the scarlet rectangle and came thundering through the British camp behind. The camp guards withdrew while the second line of Munro's army faced about to meet this new challenge. With reckless gallantry the Afghans spurred their horses forward; on the

---

* Williams, in his account of the battle, places this incident later, but Munro's despatch, written three days after the event, must be accepted as best evidence.

British left flank some even burst through, only to be checked by the steady bayonets of the grenadiers behind.

Now everywhere Suja's cavalry hurtled down on the long slender British rectangle. The tiny British army appeared to be submerged under the swirling clouds of horsemen. To Suja and his generals watching on their elephants Munro and his men seemed surely doomed. They had already lost their tents, baggage and stores; at any moment the scarlet rectangle must be breached and the scarlet ranks dissolve and disappear beneath a whirling mass of sabres. Fifty-one years later a greater general than Suja on a more famous battlefield was to harbour a similar delusion.

But the British volleys continued to ring out with the measured certainty of drumbeats. The horsemen plunging furiously into the flame-fringed smoke were beginning to pull back, their ranks thinned and disordered. In the rear the Afghan horse early abandoned the deadly struggle for the more lucrative pursuit of plundering the British camp. In front, as failure piled on failure, the horsemen began to lose heart and their charges to stop short of the death-dealing muskets. Munro sensed the time had come to take the battle to his foe. In the large copse in front of the British centre Suja had deployed most of his infantry and a large proportion of his guns, and both were pouring a damaging fire on the British line. Munro now ordered the sepoy battalion that had taken the hamlet on the right flank to swing leftwards and take the copse from the right. The red line thrust steadily forward, then from in front gusts of musketry shattered its ranks while Suja's cavalry galloped down on its open right flank. The line shivered and broke; but some unsteadiness revealed itself in the copse. Munro told Major Pemble, the senior officer serving with the sepoys and the commander of the second line, to face it about again and prepare to support the first. Then he ordered forward the European infantry in the centre of his first line with two more sepoy battalions. As they strode forward Nicol's men rallied and went with them. The British attack with an irresistible momentum smashed through the copse and Suja's infantry ran back, abandoning twenty-seven guns to their enemy.

As the British right and centre charged forward, Mia Issa,

one of the most gallant of Suja's generals, with some 6,000 horse and foot tried desperately to break through the British left. Here the marshy ground that had initially delayed the British advance proved of advantage. It slowed down Issa's horsemen and before a wall of fiery steel they recoiled. In a final despairing charge Issa fell, a bolt of grapeshot lodged in his brain, and his men turned their horses and fled. It was now about noon and all Suja's charges had failed; everywhere his disheartened cavalry were pouring away from the battlefield, while on the right by the river the British had broken through his line. Munro rode along the British line waving his hat in the air and shouting congratulations to the men who had served him so well. He called for three cheers, then the whole British battle line thrust forward. The retreat became a rout. As the British plunged through Suja's camp and the ruined streets of Buxar, panic gripped their enemy. Beyond Buxar lay the wide, steep-sided Tora nullah, and here many perished in a wild scramble to escape.

Munro halted the pursuit by the nulla. For the next three days he remained in Buxar, burying the dead and caring for the wounded of both sides. His casualties amounted to seventy-nine Europeans, out of a present strength of about 850 and 735 out of 5,800 sepoys. For perhaps the first time the sepoys suffered proportionately a greater number of casualties than the Europeans. Munro estimated that 6,000 of Suja's men died; his army as a fighting force had largely ceased to exist. Sumroo, who had changed his allegiance after Suja incarcerated Mir Kassim, now meditated a further change of employment.

The battle, the first fought by a properly organised Bengal army, established Britain as one of the major military powers in India. The rank of the British officers present can only be a source of wonder. Here was an army, about 8,000 strong, commanded by a major, with three majors to command divisions of his battle line and captains as his unit commanders. Britain was fortunate in the quality of many of the young men she sent out to India.

The sepoy battalions organised by Clive had proved their worth and loyalty beyond challenge and the Bengal army, the backbone of British military power in India, had come of age. The joint stock company that but twenty years before was a suppliant at the court of the Moghuls and their viceroys, which had cringed before Siraj-ud-daula and been contemptuously spurned by the French, was soon to enjoy a pre-eminence unparalleled in the history of commerce and likely to remain forever unique.

Appendices

Appendix 1

Order of Battle of European Troops at the Siege of Madras – 14 December 1759 to 17 January 1760

Unit	Officers	Other ranks	Total
Troop Hussars	3	35	38
Royal Artillery	16	132	148
Company's Artillery	6	64	70
64th/79th Foot (Drapers)	16	195	211
Detachment Marines	2	100	102
1st Bn Madras Europeans	23	625	648
2nd Bn Madras Europeans	23n	575	598
Supernumaries	5	32	37
Totals	94	1,758	1,852

Casualties

	Killed or died	Wounded	Taken prisoner	Total
Officers	15	14	–	29
Other Ranks	257	182	122	561
	272	196	122	590

Note. These figures are taken from Love, *Vestiges of Old Madras.* Wilson gives somewhat lower figures but appears to have excluded officers. Returns in those days are no more likely to be accurate than they are at the present time.

Appendix 2

Return of the Strength of the Bengal Army (Company's Troops) – 14 February 1763 submitted by Major Carnac

THE EUROPEAN ESTABLISHMENT

	Officers						Staff						Other Ranks							
	Majors	Captains	Captain-lieutenants	Lieutenants	Lieutenant Fireworkers	Ensigns/Cornets	Adjutants	Quartermasters	Surgeons	Riding Masters	Volunteers	Sergeants	Farriers	Drums/Trumpets	Bombardiers	Gunners	Matrosses	Rank & File	Total All Ranks	Horses
Cavalry																				
C-in-C's Guard		2				1						2	1	3				28	35	46
Dragoons (two troops)				4		2	1	2		1	2	7		4				101	123	137
Hussars			1	1		1						3	1	1				33	39	50
Total Cavalry	1	2	1	5		4	1	2		1	2	12	1	8				162	197	233
Infantry																				
At the Presidency		5	1	8		7	1	1	2		6	30		20				242	324	
Patna		4		4		7	1	1	1		1	16		12				192	239	
Midnapore		3		2		4	1	1	1			8		5				107	132	
Total Infantry	1	12	1	14		18	3	3	4		7	54		37				541	695	
Artillery																				
At the Presidency		1	1	2	1	2	1				2	9		4	6	16	31	66	74	
Gyrettee			1			1						2		1	5	6	18	32	37	
Patna		1			4		1					6		2	4	10	38	60	66	
Midnapore												2			3	2	16	23	24	
Islamabad															2	3	6	11	11	
Total Artillery	1	2	2	2	5	4	2	1			2	19		7	20	37	109	192	212	
Grand Total Europeans	1	16	3	21	5	26	6	6	4	1	11	85	1	52	20	37	109	895	1,104	

THE INDIAN ESTABLISHMENT

	British					Indian						
	Captains	Lieutenants	Ensigns	Adjutants	Sergeants	Subedars	Jemadars	Total Officers	Havildars/Dafadars	Drums & Trumpers	R & F	Total All Ranks
Infantry												
At the Presidency	1	1	1		4	11	27	38	64	36	1,016	1,090
Gyrettee	1	1	1		3	9	27	36	64	36	1,008	1,082
Patna	3	3	2		11	25	73	98	170	94	2,630	2,822
Burdwan				1	2	8	24	32	57	32	905	969
Midnapore	1	1	1		5	12	36	48	85	48	1,360	1,456
Islamabad	1	1	1		2	8	22	30	57	32	624	686
The Expedition to Meckly		1	1		4	9	25	34	54	32	905	971
Luckipore		2	2		1	1	3	4	7	4	113	121
Dacca					1	1	3	4	7	4	113	121
Malda							1	1	3		56	57
Cossimbazar					1	1	3	4	7	4	113	121
Total	7	10	9	1	34	85	244	329	565	322	8,843	9,494
Cavalry: Moghul Horse												
At Ghyrettee						1	3	4	6		93	103
Minapore						1	3	4	6		93	103
Total						2	6	8	12		186	206

Notes to Appendix 2 on page 324.

Notes

1. The Total of British Officers by Ranks:

Majors	1
Captains	23
Captain Lieutenants	3
Lieutenants	31
Ensigns	35
Lieutenant Fireworkers	5
Adjutants	6
Quartermasters	4
Riding Master	1
Total	109
Volunteers	11

2. Officers were listed on a common seniority roll, and at this time served either with British or European troops as vacancies occurred.

3. The establishment was remarkable with only one field officer for an army of over 10,000 men. The single major commanded the Bengal European Battalion and any sepoys serving with them. In practice, one or two captains seem to have been appointed field officers on the authority of the Governor; they probably drew the pay of captains. At this time, Stringer Lawrence in Madras, as the senior soldier in the Company's army, had been granted the rank of Major-General while serving in the East Indies.

4. In addition to the Company's troops there was a battalion of the regular army in Bengal, Coote's regiment, the 84th. Major Adams, officiating after Coote's departure, became automatically Commander-in-Chief.

5. By 1764 there were eighteen Indian sepoy battalions; in April for the first time they were allotted numbers; previously they had been named after the commanding officer of the moment. The numbers in 1764 were as the table on facing page (they were all renumbered by General Clavering in 1775).

Regimental number	Old name
1	Captain Giles Stibbert
2	Captain Mclean
3	Captain Hugh Grant
4	Captain Campbell
5	Captain Trevannion
6	Captain Trevannion
7	Captain Brown
8	Captain William Smith
9	Captain Galliez – mutinied before Buxar
10	Captain Ironside
11	Captain James Morgan
12	Captain James White
13	Captain Swinton
14	Captain Hampton
15	Captain Stable – frequently called 'the Matthews', raised in Calcutta, 1757
16	Captain Scotland
17	Captain Goddard
18	Captain Dow

Appendix 3

Order of Battle of the British Army at Buxar

(Extract from Major Hector Munro's copy of the Gazette)

British Troops

Unit	Officers	Other ranks	Total	Remarks
H.M. 84th Foot	1	33	34	
H.M. 89th Foot	9	81	90	commanded by a major
H.M. 90th Foot	4	41	45	including a surgeon
H.M. Marines	4	64	68	
Bengal Eur. Bn.	35	421	456	commanded by a major
Bombay Det	7	165	172	commanded by a major
Eur. Cavalry	3	45	48	
Eur. Artillery	18	152	170	
Totals	81	1,002	1,083	

Indian Troops

Cavalry – The Moghul Irregular Horse

Subedars	2
Jemadars	24
Daffadars	58
Privates	919 (troopers)
Total	1,003

Infantry – 8 Sepoy Battalions

British Officers	25 (including one major)
British Sergeants	36
Subedars	82
Jemadars	276
Other Ranks	5,297
Total All Ranks	5,716

Sepoy Battalions present at the Battle (extracted from Williams),
1st (on the right of the line), 3rd, 6th, 8th, 10th, 11th, 14th, 15th.

Summary

British Officers	106
British Other Ranks	1,038
Total	1,144
Indian Officers	384
Indian Other Ranks	6,273
Total All Ranks	7,801

In addition to the total of 7,801 infantry and cavalry shown, there would have been a number of gun lascars and train probably amounting to some 400 men who would normally be classed as combatants in a European army. There would also have been a large number of followers and bullock drivers, etc., present, probably amounting to the same number as the combatant troops. Munro probably had about 20,000 men under his command.

Appendix 4

Glossary of Anglo-Indian Terms

Arzi, araz   A petition or request.

Aumildar   A collector of taxes, manager, minor nobleman (Mahrattas).

Aurang   A goods depot or group of warehouses.

Badshah, padshah   Emperor.

Bakshi   Paymaster-General, hence also Commander-in-Chief.

Balaghaut   Highlands, particularly Tableland of Deccan.

Bunder   Customs House.

Buxerrie   Indian soldier armed with a matchlock (Bengal).

Chauth   Right to a quarter of the revenue of a state. Initially conceded by Emperor to the Mahrattas for the states of Southern India.

Chettie   Hindu Banker (S. India).

Choakey   Police station, customs or toll house, military patrol post.

Chop   Imperial or royal seal.

Choquedar   A sentry; later, a night watchman.

Choultry   (S. India) large shed with only three walls; rest house.

Coffree   An African, generally an African soldier.

Cos, Coss   Measure of distance, variable, generally about two miles.

Cossid   A courier or running messenger.

Crore   100 Lakhs = 10 million. One crore of rupees = £1 million approx.

Cutwal, cutwall	A magistrate or chief of police.
Dalaway	Commander-in-Chief (S. India).
Dandi	A boatman, used chiefly on Ganges.
Dewan, diwan	Head financial minister responsible for transmitting taxes to the Imperial treasury.
Dhobi	Washerman.
Dhooli	Covered litter.
Droog	Fortified rock.
Dubash	Interpreter, clerk, steward of a house.
Durbar	A court, also the executive government of a state.
Dustuck	A pass or permit.
Factor	Originally the chief of a factory or trading centre, latterly the third grade of Company civil servant.
Fanam	Silver, or debased gold coin varying from 36 to 42 to the Pagoda, worth from 2d to $2\frac{1}{2}$d, depending on where minted.
Faujdar, phousdar	A military commander of a fort or a district.
Gauda	Village headman (S. India).
Gentoo	A Hindu.
Ghaut, ghat	A landing place; a mountain pass. In Deccan applied to mountain ranges themselves.
Gomasta	An agent.
Griffin	A newcomer to India.
Gunge	A wholesale market, chiefly for grain.
Jemadar, jemidar	Commander of a body of troops; in the Company's Indian Army, the commander of an infantry platoon.
Killadar	Commander of a fort.
Koatey, koti	A lock-up.
Lakh	100,000, especially of rupees = £10,000 approx.

Mansubdar	High-ranking Moghul noble, generally of so many horse.
Maund	A measure of weight: 76 lb (Bengal) to 37 lb (Surat).
Mohur	A gold coin varying in worth from 10 to 14 rupees; eventually stabilised at 16 rupees in nineteenth century.
Moor, moorman	An Indian Muslim.
Musnud	Large cushion used by Indian princes as a throne.
Mussoola	A surf boat used at Madras.
Naib	Deputy to the ruler, governor.
Naik	Leader, headman. In the Company's army equivalent to corporal.
Nawab	Ruler of a Muslim province or viceroyalty; subsequently debased to the ruler of a large tract of land.
Omra	A noble or high official at the Imperial court.
Pagoda	A Hindu temple. Also a coin in use at Madras, value 36 to 42 Fanams or $3\frac{1}{2}$ rupees = 7s 6d.
Palankin	A covered litter.
Pattamar	Runner, courier, a lateen rigged packet boat.
Payen Ghaut	Lowlands, literally 'below the passes'.
Peon	A foot-soldier, often armed only with a sword and buckler.
Pergannah	A sub-division of a district.
Perwanna	A grant or letter under the royal seal.
Peshcash	Tribute or present.
Petta	A suburb outside the walls of a fort.
Poligar	A minor feudal chief (S. India).
Pollum	A district ruled by a poligar.
Puttum	Town office.
Raja	Hindu king; later debased to include great noble.

Ramzan Ramadan	Ninth month in the Muslim calendar; to be passed fasting.
Riot, ryot	A peasant or small farmer.
Rupee	Silver coin, the main currency in India. Fineness and value fluctuated according to where minted. Sicca rupees or new rupees were worth about 2s 3d or 2s 4d.
Sahib	Honorific title, extended to all Britons.
Sahukar	Hindu banker.
Sanad, sunnud	A patent or deed.
Seerpaw	A ceremonial dress given by a prince as a mark of favour.
Shroff	Moneychanger, banker.
Sipahi, sepoy	Soldier; in Company's army an infantryman.
Suba, Soubah	A large province or viceroyalty.
Subahdar	Ruler of a large province, viceroy.
Subedar	Company commander or equivalent in Company's army.
Tank	Artificial pond, normally with embanked sides.
Tappy	Post (letters), post office.
Topass	Indian Christian claiming Portuguese descent.
Vakil	Lawyer, advocate, diplomatic representative.
Wazir	Chief minister in a Muslim state.
Writer	Most junior grade of covenanted civil servant of the Company.
Zakhmi Puttee	Pension for war wounds (Mysore).
Zemindar	A man responsible for collecting the Imperial revenue including some for himself, from a given area of land; the post became hereditary and hence he was in some ways the equivalent of the English squire in the eighteenth century.

Bibliography

MANUSCRIPTS
Clive Papers; India Office Library.
Fort St David Factory Records; India Office Library.
Fort St George Diary and Consultation Book; India Office Library.
Home and Miscellaneous Series, Calcutta; India Office Library.
Orme Manuscripts; India Office Library.
Powis Papers; National Library of Wales.
Sutton Court Collection; India Office Library.
Verelst MSS; India Office Library.

PRINTED RECORDS (India Office Library)
Country Correspondence, Madras; Edited by A. G. Cardew, Madras, 1908.
Fort William, India House Correspondence, Vol. 2, 1752–59; Edited by H. N. Sinha (1957); Vol. 3, 1760–63, edited by R. R. Sethi (1968); Vol. 4, 1764–66, edited by C. S. Sriniraachain (1962).
Madras Almanack; Printed by the Boys of Charity, Madras, at 2 pagodas each copy.
Military Consultations, Madras; Edited by C. M. Schmidt, Madras, 1910.

BOOKS

ANON, *Complete History of the War in Hindustan 1749–61*, 1761.
ATKINSON, C. T., *The Dorsetshire Regiment*, 1947.
BEVERIDGE, HENRY A., *A Comprehensive History of India*, Vols 1 & 2, 1871.
BIDDULPH, COL. J., *Stringer Lawrence, Father of the Indian Army*, 1901.
BROOME, CAPT. A., *History of the Rise of the Bengal Army*, Vol. 1, 1850.
CADELL, SIR PATRICK, *History of the Bombay Army*, 1938.
CAILLAUD, COL. J., Letters in the *Journal of the RUSI*, Vol. LVIII, 1914.
CAMBRIDGE, R. O., *Account of the Wars between the English and French, 1750–61*, 1761.
Cambridge History of India, Vols 4 & 5, 1937.
CARACCIOLI, CHARLES, *Life of Robert Lord Clive, Baron Plassey*, Vols 2 & 3, c. 1770.
CATTO, W. E., *The Calcutta Light Horse*, 1957.
CORNEILLE, MAJOR J., *Journal of my Service in India 1754–57*, edited with an introduction by Michael Edwardes, 1966.
DALTON, C., *Memoir of Captain Dalton, H.E.I.C.*, 1885.

DAVIES, A. M., *Clive of Plassey*, 1939.
DODWELL, H., *Dupleix and Clive, the Beginning of Empire*, 1967.
  Madras Despatches 1744–55, 1930.
EDWARDES, M., *The Battle of Plassey*, 1963.
  History of India, 1961.
FORDE, COL. L., *Lord Clive's Right-hand Man*, 1910.
FORREST, SIR G., *The Life of Lord Clive*, Vols 1 & 2, 1918.
FORTESCUE, SIR J., *History of the British Army*, Vols 2 & 3, 1899, 1902.
GHULAM HUSSAIN, *Seir Mutaquerin*, Translated from the Persian by
  Haji Mustapha, 1789,
GLEIG, REV. G. R., *The Life of Robert, First Lord Clive*, 1861.
GRANT DUFF, JAMES, *History of the Mahrattas*, 1826.
HICKEY, WILLIAM, *Memoirs of William Hickey*, 3rd Ed., 1919.
HILL, S. C., *Bengal 1756–57*, 3 vols, 1905.
  Yusuf Khan, the Rebel Commandant, 1914.
IVES, SURGEON E., *A Voyage from England to India 1755–57*, 1753.
KINCAID AND PARASNIS, *A History of the Mahratta People*, Vols 1 & 2,
  1922.
LOVE, H. DAVISON, *Vestiges of Old Madras*, Vols 1 & 2, 1913.
MCCANCE, CAPT. S., *History of the Royal Munster Fusiliers*, Vol. 1, 1927.
MACAULAY, LORD, *Historical Essays*, 1908 edn.
MAINWARING, MAJOR A., *Crown and Company, The Historical Record of
  the Second Battalion The Royal Dublin Fusiliers*, 1911.
MALABARI, P. B. M., *Bombay in the Making*, 1910.
MALCOLM, SIR J., *Life of Lord Clive*, 3 Vols, 1836.
MALLESON, COL. G. B., *Rulers of India – Dupleix*, 1890.
  History of the French in India, 1893.
MILLER, SGT. J., Diary of James Miller. Extract from the *Journal of
  The Society for Army Historical Research*, 1924, Vol. III.
MILL, J., *History of India*, Vol. 3, 1817.
MINNEY, R. J., *Clive*, 1931.
OLDHAM, C. E. A. W., *The Battle of Buxar*, 1926.
ORME, ROBERT A., *A History of British Transactions in Hindustan*, Vols
  1 & 2, 1803.
OWEN, SIDNEY J., *The Fall of the Mughal Empire*, 1912.
POOLE, STANLEY LANE, *Rulers of India – Aurangzebe*, 1893.
RAM GOPAL, *How the British Occupied Bengal*, 1964.
SARKAR, SIR JADUNATH, *The Fall of the Moghul Empire*, Vol. 2, 1934.
SCRAFTON, LUKE, *Reflections on the Govt., etc. of Industan with a Short
  History of Bengal*, 1763.
SPEAR, PERCIVAL, *India, A Modern History*, 1963.
STRACHEY, HENRY, *A Narrative of the Mutiny of the Officers of the
  Bengal Army in the year 1766*, 1773.
WATSON, STEVEN, *The Reign of George III, 1760–1815*, 1960.
WILKS, LT.-COL. MARK, *History of Mysore*, 1930.
WILLIAMS, CAPT. J., *The Bengal Native Infantry*, 1817.
WILSON, BECKLES, *Ledger and Sword*, 1903.
WILSON, SIR CHARLES, *Clive*, 1902.

WILSON, G. R., *Records of the Old Fort William*, 1906.

WILSON, LT.-COL. J., *History of the Madras Army*, Vol. I, 1882.

WOODRUFF, PHILIP, *The Men who Ruled India – the Founders*, 1953.

WYLLY, H. C., *Life of Lieutenant-General Eyre Coote*, 1922.
  Neill's Blue Caps: the Royal Dublin Fusiliers, 1924.

YULE, H. AND BURNELL, A. C., Hobson Jobson: *A Glossary of Anglo-Indian Colloquial Words and Phrases*, 1968.

Index